An Illustrated History

of the

STRATFORD ON AVON
to
CHELTENHAM

Railway

Labour of Love

Audie Baker

ACKNOWLEDGEMENTS

Over the years all authors have had the evergreen chestnut of thanking everyone who has assisted in the everyday help that is essential in the writing of a book. My thanks therefore go out to the following; H Burrows, H Carter, H Coldicott, T David, I Dixon, A Hale, A Henshaw,S Jacobs, B Kedward, J W Kinchin, T W H Lane, B Leek, S Marshall, P Mathews, B Nicholls, I Pardoe, F Phillips, F M Salmon, L Seabright, M Shorland, H Silvester, T Sims, C M Smith, Dr W Smith, E A Tredwell, M P Walker, S Webb, A Wilks, C J Wilkes, Mrs R Wynniatt and A York. A mention also of J Perry and the late K Hopkins whose encouragement was greatly appreciated when the going got tough. Thanks also to Mr B Scott (The Racing Post) whose special assistance with regards to the Scott's of Buckland proved invaluable.

To the staffs of the Public Record Office Kew and the County Record Offices of Worcester, Oxford, Warwick and Gloucester I extend my gratitude, likewise to the Evesham Almonry Museum, the Brunel University Uxbridge and the Shakespeare Birthplace Trust. Specialist information was supplied by Mr Ayto c/o Henry Pooley & Son Ltd. and Mr R Hunt c/o R M Douglas Holdings. Thanks also to the Press Office of the Gloucestershire Constabulary for allowing me to look at certain registers with regards to the area. Technical assistance from D Piddington and G Stone is acknowledged.

To the Signalling Record Society (SRS) I extend a hearty thanks and in particular to M Christensen, J P Morris, M R L Instone, and G H Tilt. I would strongly recommend to any budding authors of railway histories that they contact the SRS for help lest any errors are made in their work. For the kind loan of photographs I would like to place on record an appreciation to P Abbott, D Bath, 'Dick' Blenkinsop, P Campion, P W Durham, G England, T Guest, L C Jacks, A T Locke, Mrs K Parker, W Potter, R S Potts, M Shorland, G H Tilt, J Wood and T Petchey of the Winchcombe Railway Museum whose doors are always open every afternoon throughout the year.

And to the late C N Clemens whose kindness and enthusiasm will I hope be reflected in this work.

For those students who seek more information with regards to working time tables then Rail 921 and 937 should be consulted at the Public Record Office Kew, and likewise if more detailed plans of locations are required then Rail 274/39 and 104 should be consulted.

And lastly I would like to place on record my thanks to Peter Abbott JP BSc CEng FBCS for his help and assistance in taking this work to his heart and making it presentable for public consumption.

DEDICATION

To my Wife Helen

AUTHORS NOTE

I have endeavoured to make this history as accurate as possible but would be pleased to receive any corrections. I am aware that there must be many stories of which I have no knowledge but which are worth recounting, and I would be very pleased to receive details of these. Similarly, I would be extremely grateful for the loan of photographs taken along or in association with the line.

A Baker

Contents

©1994 IRWELL PRESS, A Baker and P Abbott
ISBN 1-871608-62-7
Published by
IRWELL PRESS
15 Lovers Lane, Grasscroft, Oldham OL4 4DP.
Typeset in Baskerville by Peter Abbott
Printed by Amadeus Press, Huddersfield.

The Stratford on Avon to Cheltenham Railway

(Gloucestershire Warwickshire Railway*)

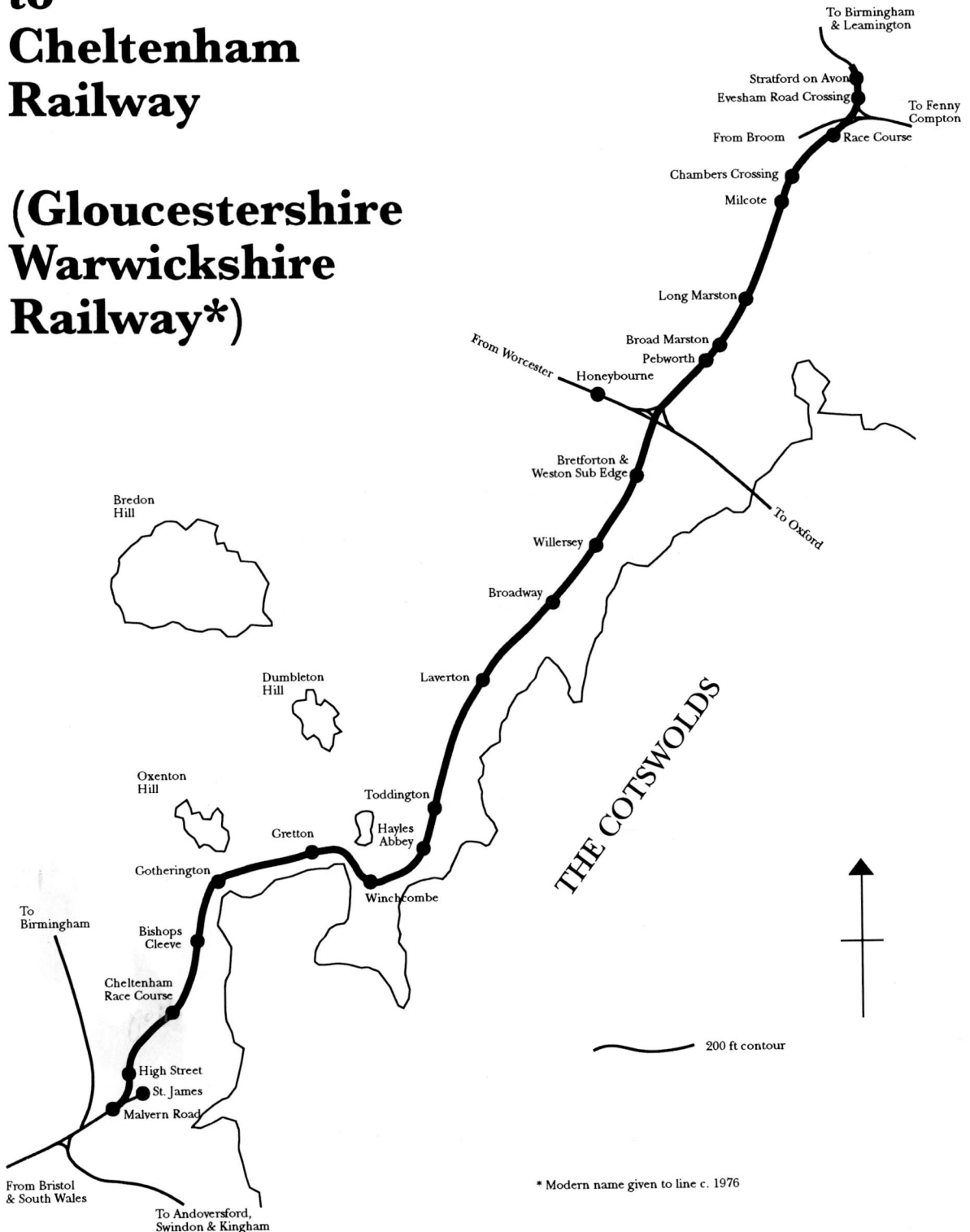

To Birmingham & Leamington

Stratford on Avon

Evesham Road Crossing

To Fenny Compton

From Broom

Race Course

Chambers Crossing

Milcote

Long Marston

Broad Marston

Pebworth

From Worcester

Honeybourne

Bretforton & Weston Sub Edge

To Oxford

Willersey

Broadway

Laverton

THE COTSWOLDS

Bredon Hill

Dumbleton Hill

Oxenton Hill

Toddington

Gretton

Hayles Abbey

Winchcombe

Gotherington

To Birmingham

Bishops Cleeve

Cheltenham Race Course

High Street

St. James

Malvern Road

From Bristol & South Wales

To Andoversford, Swindon & Kingham

↑

200 ft contour

* Modern name given to line c. 1976

1

Introduction

At a very early age I was aware of how lucky I was to be born in the Vale of Evesham. I was also aware of being overlooked by the Cotswold escarpment always giving a dominant perspective. My village of Bretforton had hardly altered since enclosure and there was still a harping back to the old days with Squire Ashwin, the Lord of the Manor. Market gardening and the many characters from that period fill my youthful memories. With my family (mothers side) having been in the village since 1810, I naturally felt an affinity with the area.

However my most fondest memories and earliest recollections were with my local railway. It was from our house, that I could see the line and that my mother would take me in the afternoons to see the local train. Always arriving at Weston Sub Edge Station to see the ex 2.30 pm from St. James, Cheltenham arriving at the station at 3.23 pm, it then trundled on to Honeybourne where it terminated at 3.30 pm. All these times I learnt later but even recently my mother recalled this train known to us all as 'The Coffeepot' and its time at Weston Sub Edge, a gap of some 35 years. This was the highlight of my day and if really lucky we would see a freight train clanking its way through the cutting going towards Broadway while feeding the donkey in the adjacent field.

It was at about this time that my father acquired his first van. We often went to Stratford on most Saturdays and would cross over Honeybourne bridge, what a complex system of rails it seemed to a youth. He would tell me of the wonderful community spirit that existed in this lovely village which was naturally very much railway influenced. If they did not have anyone immediately 'on the railway' they had a relative or friends.

As a direct consequence of the line being built many local people were employed upon the railway. It was in June 1905 that one such 'Local' entered the service of the Great Western Railway as a cleaner in the shed at Honeybourne. Mr Charles Jelfs was one of lifes rare 'gentlemen' and a great assest to the railway. After 46 years service he retired as a driver being greatly respected for his manner and engine prowess both of which he was well renowned for along the line. As a youth and living around 'the corner' he would often tell me about the days past and how locomotives were not 'pooled' but kept by individual drivers and firemen. His locomotive was always up to the mark and is well remembered to this day.

Over the years the line became more of an important part of my life, from observation and conversation. To seeing it effect an area such as ours was nothing short of magic, one day there employing a large number of people the next not. Had it just have been kept intact who knows what would have happened perhaps we could all have got the produce etc. back onto the rails and left the roads for the people.

With everything being axed literally, (the hedgerows of my youth where have they gone?) and with the Dutch Elm disease that followed resulting in a major change to the landscape. Then when it was time to pull the plug on the Stratford to Cheltenham railway line at least three other people felt the same as I, and that something had to be attempted to at least try and retain a little of that past. From very humble beginnings it is so nice to see so many smiling faces now at Toddington. I can see the efforts of ordinary people from everyday life, seeking to provide pleasure for all.

It was inevitable on reflection that this account would come to be written for you my reader. Living for a long time along the line and talking with many of its employees, I hope that you can sense the pride that lies within these pages of ordinary folk from a rural background.

So let us travel back in time to the birth of the railways...............

Gloucester & Cheltenham Area c. 1847

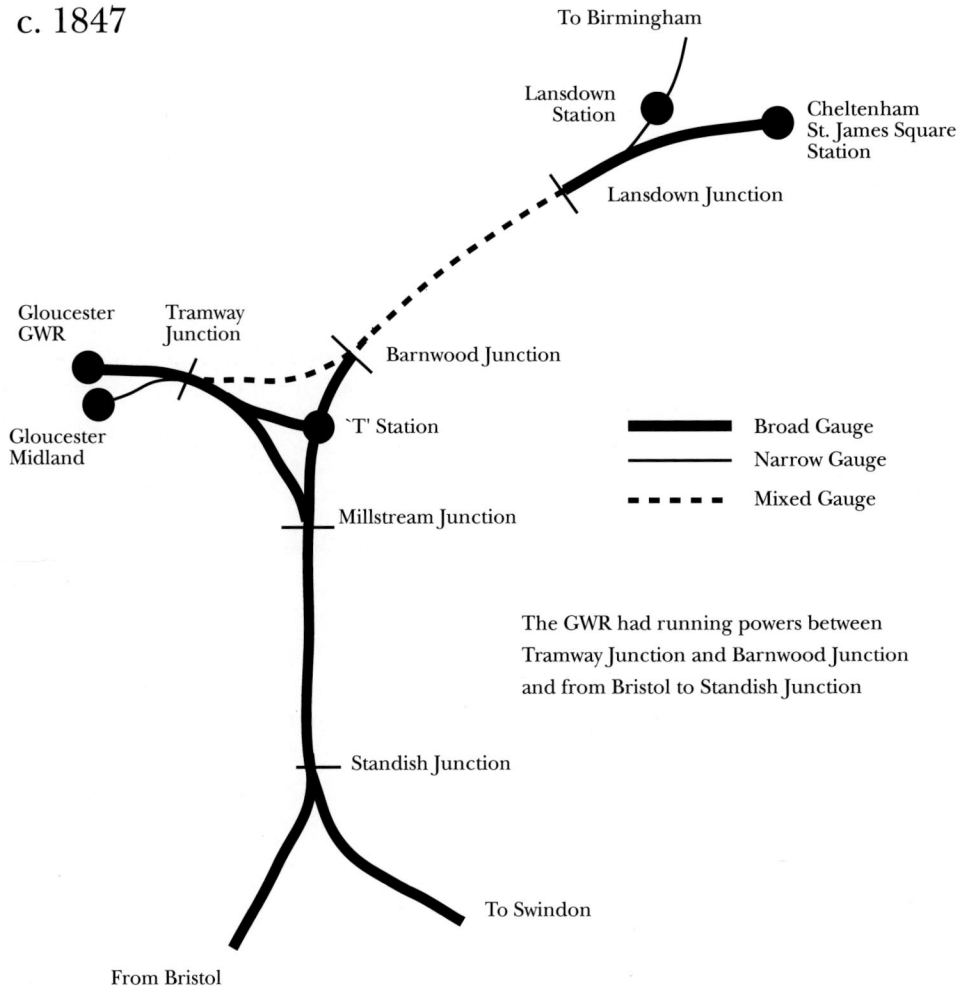

To Birmingham

Lansdown Station

Cheltenham St. James Square Station

Lansdown Junction

Gloucester GWR

Tramway Junction

Barnwood Junction

Gloucester Midland

`T' Station

— Broad Gauge

— Narrow Gauge

--- Mixed Gauge

Millstream Junction

The GWR had running powers between Tramway Junction and Barnwood Junction and from Bristol to Standish Junction

Standish Junction

To Swindon

From Bristol

2

From Humble Beginnings

With the onslaught of the Industrial Revolution, the latter half of the 18th Century placed a great emphasis on the transportation of raw materials. The Midlands soon became a centre for the Revolution, with manufacturers requiring delivery of these raw materials and as wide market as possible in which to sell their produce.

Before railways arrived on the scene, the Midlands were 'blessed' with very poor roads. These were mainly 'Turnpikes' dating from the early 1720s. By extracting a toll on road users, money could be put back into the maintenance of roads, but generally the Turnpikes were to result in a general restriction on trade.

The use of waterways had long been established for the transporting of goods. To the south west lay the River Severn, this at one time being navigable all the way from Gloucester up to Welshpool (a distance of 128 miles). To the south east ran the River Avon which ran from a junction with the River Severn at Tewkesbury up to Stratford on Avon, this section of the Avon becoming navigable as early as 1639. From Stratford a 25$\frac{1}{2}$ mile canal was brought into use in 1816 reaching to Kings Norton near Birmingham. With the opening further to the south of the Gloucester & Berkeley canal (1827) the merchants of Birmingham seized upon the opportunity of exporting their merchandise via the port of Gloucester.

However with the embryonic railways being proposed in the early 1830s, the canals were to have a short-lived time as the merchants soon gave their backing to the Birmingham & Gloucester Railway, a 45 mile line authorized in 1836. This would save 3 days passage over the Worcester & Birmingham canal and then on down the Severn to Gloucester.

The Birmingham & Gloucester Railway was originally planned as a most direct route missing out many towns on the way, notably; Bromsgrove, Droitwich, Worcester, Tewkesbury and Cheltenham. Only after much protest from the latter were the plans amended to take the line on to its present course to a station at Lansdown. The Birmingham & Gloucester Railway looked at the problem of getting around the Lickey Hills but in the end they decided on the most direct route, that of going straight up them on a gradient of 1 in 37.

The easiest piece of engineering was from Cheltenham to Bromsgrove and this section opened on 24th June 1840. Cheltenham to Gloucester followed on 4th November 1840 with the 17th August 1841 seeing the line finally open into the Curzon Street terminus in Birmingham.

At the same time as the authorization of the Birmingham & Gloucester Railway, the Cheltenham & Great Western Union Railway was also being given the Royal Assent. The latter proposed a line between Cheltenham and Swindon, down the Stroud Valley via Gloucester. Both these railway companies agreed to joint purchase of the land between Cheltenham and Gloucester, between which towns there already was a tramroad of 9 miles in length. This was then the Gloucester and Cheltenham Railway (having received the title from its Act of 1809). Both companies (the B&G and C&GWU) were to build their own stations in Gloucester and Cheltenham. The C&GWU became amalgamated with the Great Western Railway in 1844.

The mixed gauge line from Gloucester (Tramway Junction) to (Lansdown Junction) Cheltenham along with the 1 mile 6 chain broad gauge 'branch' from Lansdown Junction to St. James Square station was opened on 23rd October 1847. Between Tramway Junction and Lansdown Junction the broad gauge third rail of the C&GWU, had been added to that of the 'narrow' standard gauge system of the B&G. Thus the trains were able to travel to London from the popular Spa town some 120$\frac{1}{4}$ miles away running via Swindon and onto the main Bristol to London line.

Over 25/6/7th May 1872 the 7 ft 0$\frac{1}{4}$ in broad gauge of the Cheltenham to Swindon route was converted to the 4 ft 8$\frac{1}{2}$ in 'narrow' standard gauge.

3

Lines to Stratford

To the north of Cheltenham a tramway had been opened (5th September 1826) between Moreton in Marsh and Stratford on Avon, this being part of an elaborate plan to develop a route from the coal mining area of Coventry to London. The 'narrow' gauge of the Stratford & Moreton Tramway ran for a distance of 16 miles. When the Oxford, Worcester and Wolverhampton Railway came into being it set about the renting of the tramway, which it succeeded in doing and from then on proceeded to wind it down! Thus with the opening of the OWW's own line to Stratford, the tramway almost became redundant overnight!

When the OWW had its second Act passed in 1846, two branch lines were authorized off the main line; one to Witney, the second to Stratford on Avon. This latter branch was projected from the Parish of Weston Sub Edge at a point where the B4632 (formerly A46) passes underneath the present Oxford to Worcester line, near to the village of Mickleton.

Isambard Kingdom Brunel, the then engineer of the OWW proposed that the line pass through Norton Estate, then owned by the Earl of Harrowby. The line from Long Marston onwards taking the eventual course. The distance for this original projected branch was 8 miles 6 furlongs. With all the difficulties that the OWW experienced within that company, the branch did not materialize in this form. Nine years later in 1854 the branch was modified during proceedings in Parliament, making the junction in the Parish of Church Honeybourne. Simultaneously the time allowed for construction was extended by five years, though the OWW found that in 1858 they needed another extension to this time, being awarded a further three years.

Meanwhile in August 1857, the Stratford Upon Avon Railway Co. had obtained approval for a branch line from Hatton (on the Birmingham to Oxford line) to Stratford. All was not lost yet in the battle to be the first to get to Stratford, for the OWW objected most strongly, managing to get the line built to mixed gauge. With the passing of this Act the OWW had its hands forced; it had to get things moving. John Fowler was now the engineer for the company with E V Ponsonby appointed the resident engineer for the construction of the branch to Stratford on Avon. They set about the building of the line in February 1859, starting from Honeybourne, using the company's own men. The line was single track throughout to standard gauge, with stations at Long Marston and Milcote (or as it was known Milcote, Weston and Welford) both these places having level crossings.

The whole line was built within six months. Construction was straightforward with the two main bridges being built, one 30 ft span over the River Stour and the largest structure on the line, the bridge over the River Avon. Situated about 1¹/2 miles south of Stratford, this viaduct had 8 flood arches each being 25 ft span and 2 centre arches over the river each of 50 ft span. This work was carried out by Messrs Clunes, Vulcan Works, Worcester. The contract for the other bridges at Honeybourne, Pebworth and Long Marston were set to Mr Horton of Brierley Hill. At Honeybourne about ¹/2 mile after the branch line left the main line, a cutting of some 42 ft in depth had to be blasted out, it also being nearly ¹/2 mile in length.

Sufficient land was reported to be purchased for the laying of a second line when the traffic warranted it, but this did not come about until 1907, when the Honeybourne to Stratford line was being developed into a main line route. At the end of May work on the bridge over the River Avon was well in hand. A ceremonial stone was laid with various current coins being placed underneath it, by Charles Lucy Esq. of Stratford and Directors of the OWW Co. A small celebration then followed at which Lucy made a speech, in which he expressed the wish that the bridge might one day prove to be a portion of a successful line, and that its foundations might never give way. He was correct on both accounts, the railway did succeed in becoming an important route and the foundations of the bridge still stand some 135 years on, even despite the widening in 1907. On 21st June 1859 a vast quantity of woodwork arrived from Worcester, thus Stratford's first station was delivered to the terminus site in Lady(e) Meadow near the Evesham Road – being served by Sanctuary (Sancta) Lane (now Sanctus Road) some ¹/2 mile from the centre of the town. The following day saw some 200 men set about the station construction in earnest.

OXFORD, WORCESTER & WOLVERHAMPTON RAILWAY
(Second Act 1846)
Branch to Stratford on Avon

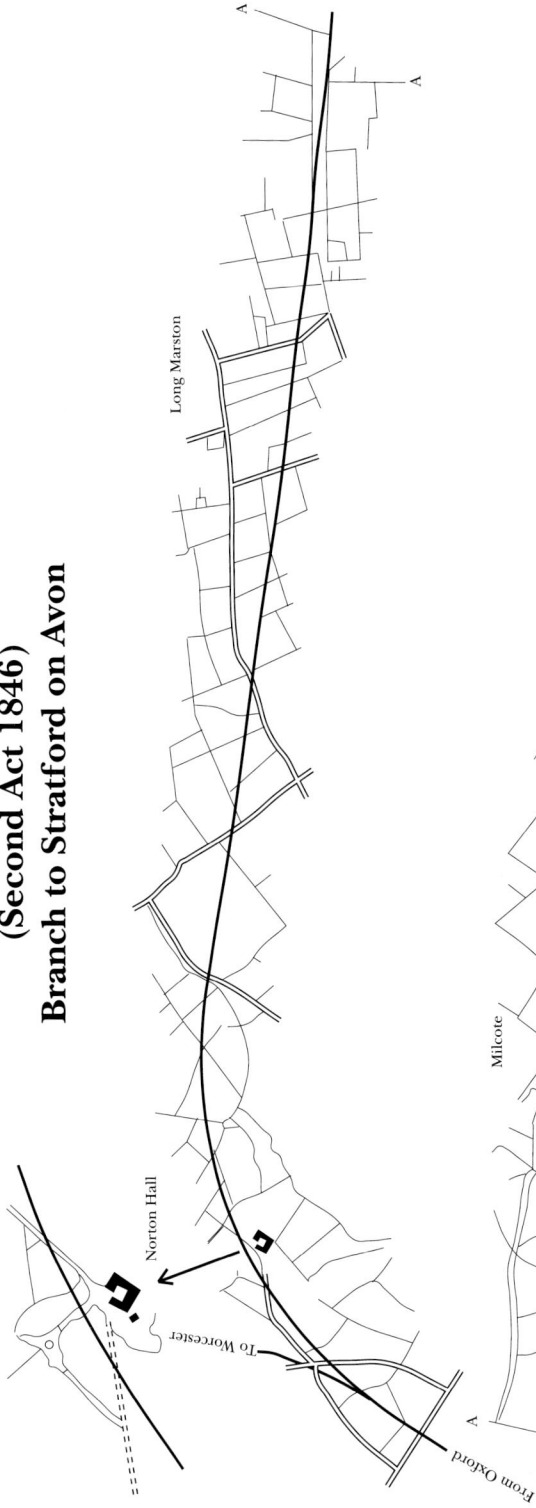

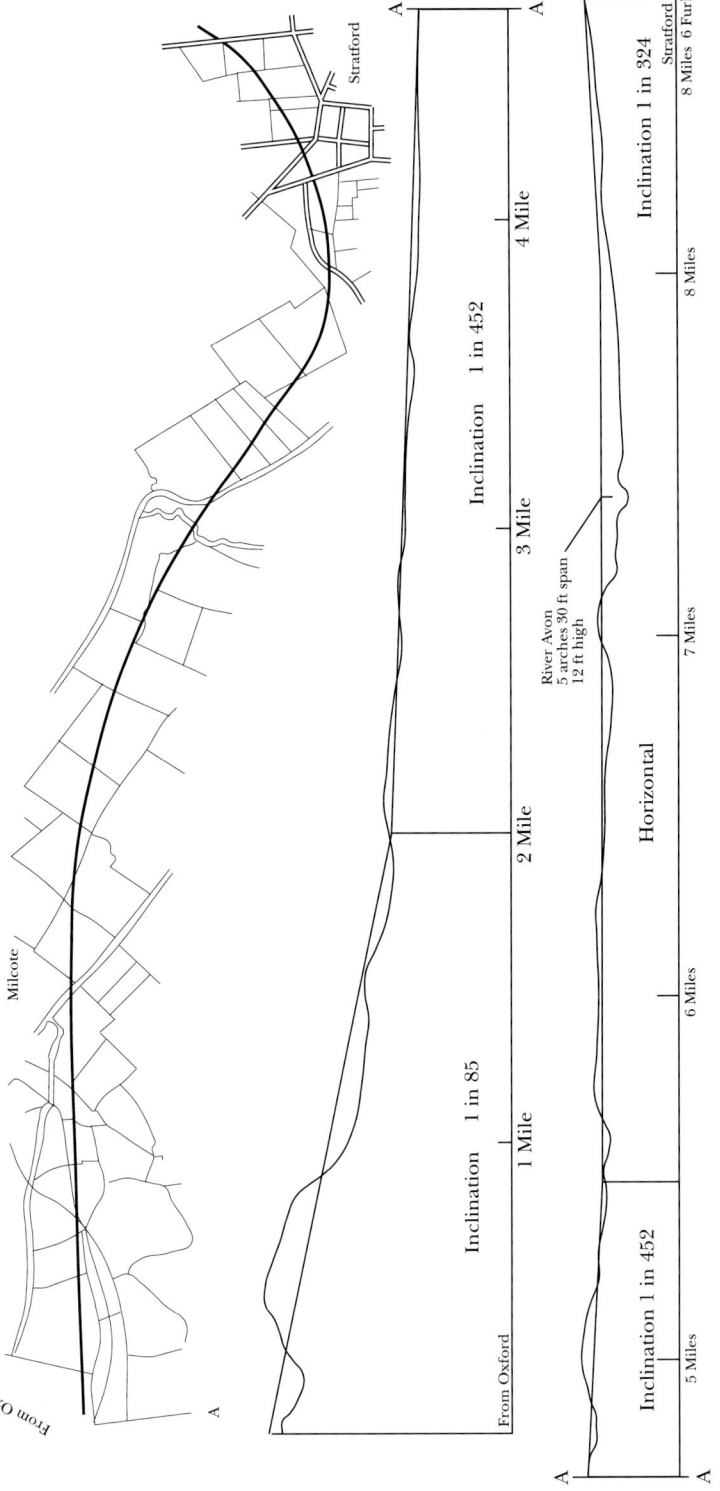

Norton Hall

To Worcester

From Oxford

Long Marston

A

A

Milcote

Stratford

A

A

From Oxford

Inclination 1 in 452

1 Mile

Inclination 1 in 85

2 Mile

Inclination 1 in 452

3 Mile

River Avon
5 arches 30 ft span
12 ft high

4 Mile

A

A

5 Miles

Inclination 1 in 452

Horizontal

6 Miles

7 Miles

8 Miles

Inclination 1 in 324

8 Miles 6 Furlongs

Stratford

A

A

With all the activity in the area the townsfolk of Stratford would flock daily to witness the progress being made.

All was well in hand. On 8th July 1859, Captain G Ross the Government Inspector, surveyed the line. He passed it fit for public traffic and the OWW announced that a special train packed with dignitaries would leave Worcester at 1.00 pm, Monday 11th July, the next day seeing the line open to the public.

The train consisted of 22 carriages being drawn by two locomotives; namely No. 51 *Will Shakspere* a 2-2-2 built by E B Wilson in 1856 and No. 52 *Ben Jonson* a 2-2-2T built by R Stephenson & Co. in 1859, both engines were decorated with flowers, evergreens and flags. At Honeybourne the train halted for some time, awaiting the arrival of Mr Fenton, the Chairman, by another train from Wolverhampton. The party eventually arrived at Stratford at 2.45 pm. All the buildings were decorated for the occasion and the whole population of Stratford (it would appear) turned up for the event. A tented pavilion (some 36 yards long, capable of seating 500-600 people) had been built to seat the guests. A dancing platform and large tent for the ladies made up the picture. For the preparation of the food the engine shed had been converted into a kitchen. A good time was had by all with the train returning to Worcester around 9.00 pm, arriving shortly before 11.00 pm.

The first timetable dated 12th July 1859 provided the following service;

						Sundays	
Stratford	7.25	9.20	12.45	4.00	7.50	8.45	5.30
Milcote & Weston	—	9.27	12.52	4.07	7.57	8.52	5.37
Long Marston	—	9.35	1.00	4.15	8.05	9.00	5.45
Honeybourne	7.48	9.43	1.10	4.23	8.13	9.08	5.55
Honeybourne	8.05	11.20	1.20	6.20	9.40	11.40	6.30
Long Marston	8.15	11.30	1.30	6.30	—	11.50	6.40
Milcote & Weston	8.22	11.38	1.37	6.37	—	11.57	6.47
Stratford	8.30	11.45	1.45	6.45	10.00	12.05	6.55

The total cost for the construction of the branch, some 8 miles 35 chains in length was £46,000. The branch line differed in construction to that of the main line, which used bridge rail on longitudinal sleepers, in using narrow gauge rail on conventionally laid sleepers.The 75 lb per yard rail was secured by 'jaw' chairs, an early forerunner of the conventional rail chair of today. The branch was worked by one engine in steam, the engine being allocated to Stratford. Honeybourne

had an engine shed since the opening of the main line in 1853.

The line from Hatton eventually arrived in Stratford, terminating in the Birmingham Road. The contractors for the line, Messrs Branson & Gwyther, started upon the construction of the 9 1/4 mile branch on 8th February 1859. The total cost for this mixed gauged line being £90,000. Intermediate stations were provided at Claverdon, Bearley and Wilmcote.

Unlike the OWW branch from Honeybourne, there was no official opening ceremony, but a special train conveyed 20 carriages of dignitaries on 8th October 1860 from Warwick and Birmingham (joining at Hatton) to Stratford. The 9th October saw the commencement of the public timetable. The Stratford Upon Avon Railway did not possess any locomotives of its own so it came to an agreement with the Great Western Railway; that the GWR would work the branch. Broad gauge locomotives did enter Stratford (Birmingham Road) station but they were few and far between, becoming extremely rare sights when the latter station closed to passengers from 1st January 1863. The facility of running broad gauge trains was eventually done away with, being converted to narrow gauge on 1st April 1869. The actual spare rail was taken away some time later.

To give some idea of the fare structure at that time (8/1861) the West Midland Railway made the following scale of charges for a single from Stratford to:-

	1st Class	2nd Class	3rd Class	Parliamentary
Milcote	6d	4d	3d	2 1/2 d
Long Marston	1s	9d	6d	5d
Honeybourne	2s	1s 6d	1s	8 1/2 d

The OWW (Honeybourne branch) was not built to its full extent. Although it stopped at Sancta Lane, the OWW retained the power to construct its line through to the canal near to the Birmingham Road, and it also had the power to connect with the SOA Railway from Hatton. Work on this extension was soon undertaken and within six weeks of the commencement, both lines were joined. The contract for the work went to Messrs McNea & Holroyd. The chief engineer for the company being Mr E B Wilson. Even on the construction of a short connection such as this men were injured, complacency being the common enemy of the navvy. More than once, men were pinned/crushed between contractors wagons. This short connecting line was inspected by Colonel Yolland on 22nd July 1861 and opened to the public two days later. From the 1st August through trains started running between Leamington and Malvern. Within the first fortnight many excursions were run especially to Malvern. On one of these occasions several passengers missed the return train and then had to walk from Worcester (some 30 miles!)

Initially three level crossings existed on the connecting line. Although work had commenced on the building of a bridge over the line in Alcester Road later known as Glebe bridge, it was not completed until mid October 1861. Debate then raged about the wisdom of level crossings at Sancta Lane and Evesham Road. The former did get a bridge (1864) but after much discussion, Evesham Road remained a level crossing.

Both terminal stations had short lives in passenger use, although the one in the Birmingham Road lived on (but only for goods) until closure in 1963. A new joint station (off the Alcester Road) was constructed to the north of Glebe Bridge in a field known as 'The Stile Ground'.

When it was opened on 1st January 1863, the original OWW and SOAR stations closed, although the SOAR station in the Birmingham Road continued to be used for excursion traffic.

This new station soon gained a bad reputation, for it was considered a mere 'Shed' with a single narrow platform. It was constructed on a sharp curve, which apparently caused much alarm in itself, for (according to one report) on approaching, trains could not be seen until they were only ten yards from the station. So outraged by the insult were the people of Stratford that some would travel to Warwick to catch a train or meet a friend there, than be subjected going through the 'Shed'.

After much debate Stratford got a replacement for the 'Shed', although it did not have to come a great distance. In 1865 the SOAR station in the Birmingham Road was dismantled and re-erected at the Alcester Road site by Mr Ballard of Leamington.

The OWW became the West Midland Railway on 1st July 1860, and this latter company was amalgamated with the Great Western Railway on 1st August 1863.

The East & West Junction Railway arrived in Stratford from Kineton on 1st July 1873 forming a junction at the old Sancta Lane terminus and for a short time it used the GWR station in the Alcester Road until its own station was finished.

The Stratford Upon Avon Railway Co. lasted a little longer than that of the West Midland before being amalgamated, on 1st July 1883 it was taken into the Great Western Railway's system.

Peter Abbott

One of the first locomotives to use the line from Honeybourne in this early period on a regular basis was the Beyer Peacock built 2-4-0 side tank No. 68 (OWW No.) which later became No. 225 under GWR ownership. She was built in 1861 and withdrawn in September 1883.

PROPOSED LINES

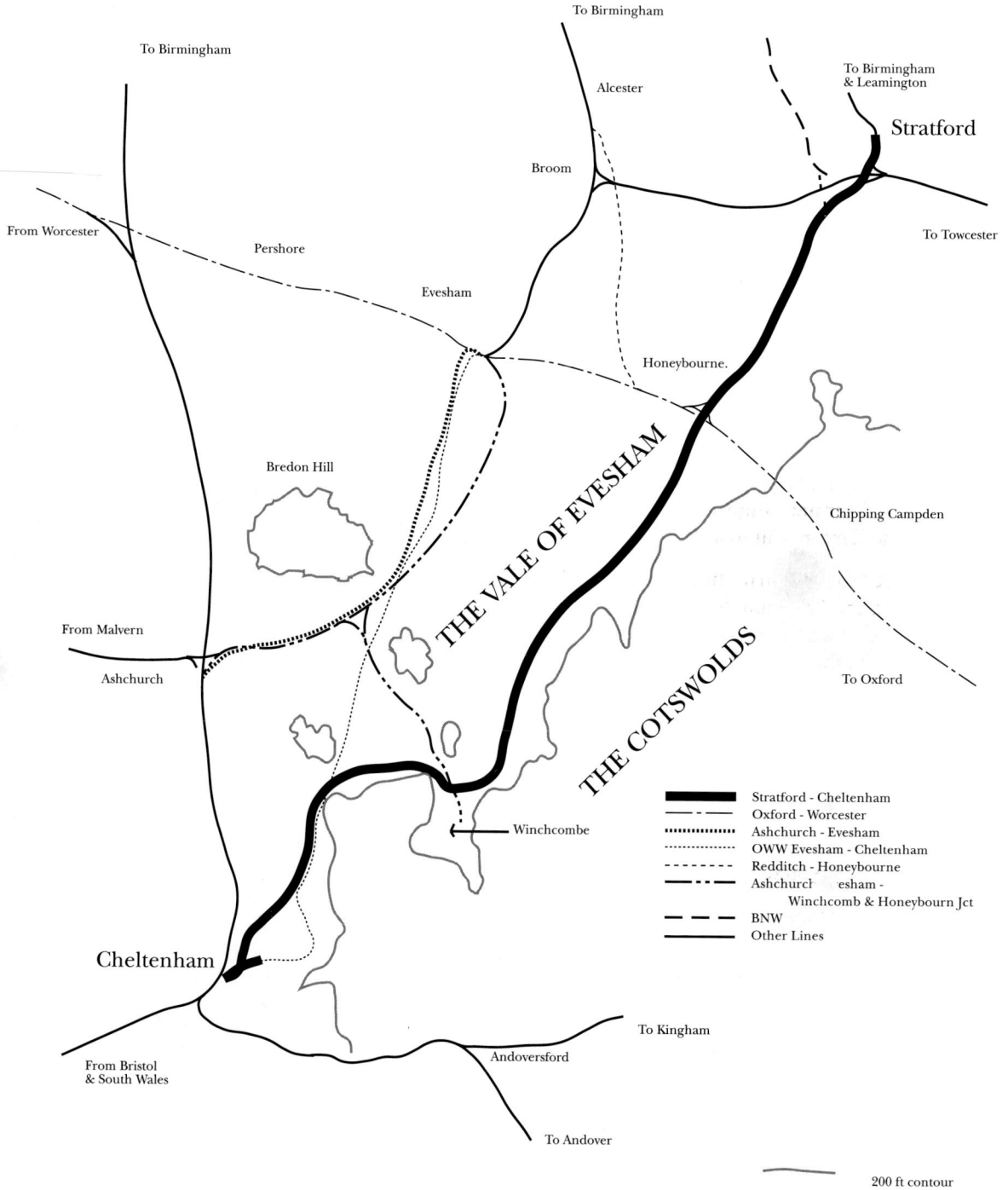

To Birmingham

To Birmingham

Alcester

To Birmingham
& Leamington

Stratford

Broom

From Worcester

To Towcester

Pershore

Evesham

Honeybourne.

THE VALE OF EVESHAM

Bredon Hill

Chipping Campden

From Malvern

THE COTSWOLDS

To Oxford

Ashchurch

Winchcombe

	Stratford - Cheltenham
	Oxford - Worcester
	Ashchurch - Evesham
	OWW Evesham - Cheltenham
	Redditch - Honeybourne
	Ashchurch esham - Winchcomb & Honeybourn Jct
	BNW
	Other Lines

Cheltenham

To Kingham

From Bristol
& South Wales

Andoversford

To Andover

200 ft contour

4

Proposed Routes and Forgotten Failures

1. The Oxford, Worcester & Wolverhampton Railway extensions and amendment Bill 1846.

   This line was planned by the OWW engineer I K Brunel, to run a distance of 15 miles 3¹/₂ chains. Running north to south it left Evesham near the eventual Midland route to Ashchurch. Brunel took his proposed route south following what later became the through route from Stratford to Cheltenham between the points from Gotherington and Bishops Cleeve. This connected with a junction with the then proposed Cheltenham & Oxford Railway running on into Cheltenham St. James. Only two main engineering features were planned for the route ie:–

   - a 60 ft span bridge over the River Avon and
   - a 430 yard tunnel, some 6 miles from Cheltenham at Dixton Hill near Gotherington.

2. Redditch & Honeybourne Bill, 1860. This route pre-empted the Evesham & Redditch Railway of 1863 (as shown on the map). The line was opposed by the Evesham people. They were a major source of funding for the scheme. It was then withdrawn and later amended to its final form.

3. Ashchurch, Evesham, Winchcomb & Honeybourn Junction. Railway. Bill 1860. N.B. Both the latter places spelt without the 'e'. Also note that the line did not connect with Honeybourne

   This scheme consisted of 3 lines:–

   - a line from Evesham to Ashchurch a distance of 11 miles 4 furlongs 6 chains. This was again a similar plan to that of the eventual Evesham – Ashchurch route but it left Evesham via a Junction to the east of the town.
   - a line from Winchcomb to a junction with the Evesham to Ashchurch line at Beckford a distance of 5 miles 5 furlongs 2 chains.

   - a triangle junction formed at Beckford consisting of a 7 furlong spur.

   The only engineering feature on the Winchcomb branch was a tunnel of 900 yards on an incline of 1 in 188 at Greet, similar in position and length to the eventual tunnel on the Cheltenham to Stratford line. This branch was again proposed in 1865 under the Winchcomb & Midland Railway Bill, this time the line was to be 5 miles 6 furlongs 2 chains in distance having no tunnel, but there was an incline for 2 miles at 1 in 71.

4. Andoversford & Stratford Upon Avon Railway Bill 1898.

   Engineers: R Elliot-Cooper and S F Burke

   This scheme consisted of two lines, the main one running close to the Cheltenham and Stratford being a distance of 25 miles 7 furlongs from Andoversford to a junction with the proposed Birmingham & North Warwick line. A short 3 furlong spur from the main line connected to the Stratford to Broom line.

5. Midland & South Western Junction Railway (Northern Section) Bill 1898.

   Engineer: R Elliot-Cooper

   The main line of this route was planned to run a distance of 14 miles 6 furlongs 4 chains from Andoversford to Ashchurch with a short 2 furlong spur added at Andoversford. The only feature of note being a tunnel at Charlton Abbots of 300 yards on a 1 in 87 incline.

   The last two schemes are dealt with in the following chapters in more detail. They forced the GWR to promote their own line as we shall see.

ANDOVERSFORD AND STRATFORD ON AVON,
MIDLAND AND SOUTH WEST JUNCTION

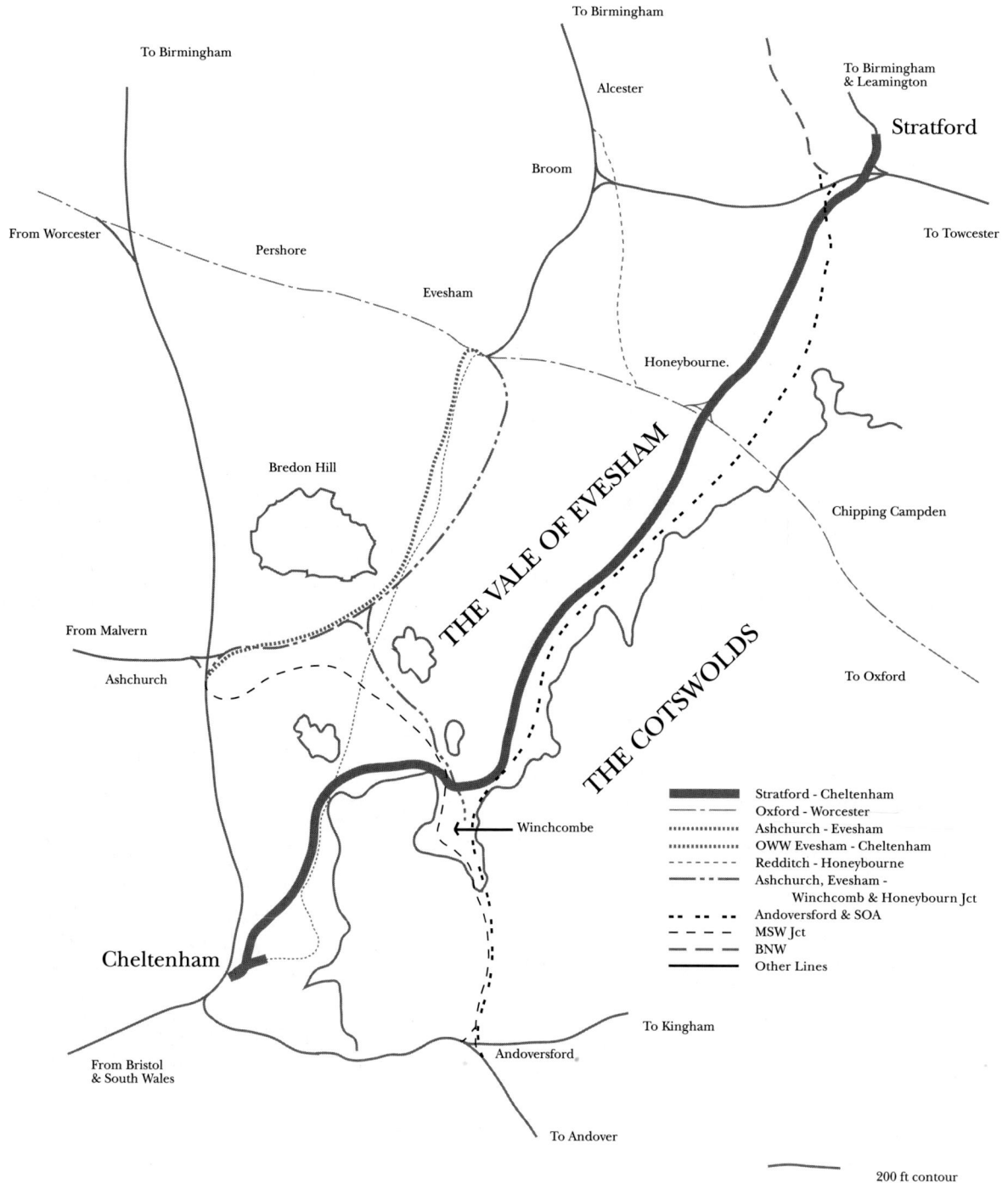

To Birmingham

To Birmingham

Alcester

To Birmingham
& Leamington

Stratford

Broom

From Worcester

Pershore

To Towcester

Evesham

Honeybourne.

Bredon Hill

THE VALE OF EVESHAM

Chipping Campden

From Malvern

THE COTSWOLDS

To Oxford

Ashchurch

Winchcombe

	Stratford - Cheltenham
	Oxford - Worcester
	Ashchurch - Evesham
	OWW Evesham - Cheltenham
	Redditch - Honeybourne
	Ashchurch, Evesham - Winchcomb & Honeybourn Jct
	Andoversford & SOA
	MSW Jct
	BNW
	Other Lines

Cheltenham

To Kingham

From Bristol
& South Wales

Andoversford

To Andover

200 ft contour

5

Under Pressure

The land in the southern end of the Vale of Evesham was considered an area well worth serving but for one reason or another all the proposed schemes and routes fell through, and therefore the Vale with its plentiful harvests of fruit and vegetables, lay largely untapped until the turn of the century. The OWW had bisected the region with its Oxford and Worcester route in 1853 and a branch of the Midland Railway had skirted the southern side of Bredon Hill to join the OWW at Evesham from Ashchurch in 1864.

The Great Western Railway had considered from time to time filling this void, but had not done anything positive. It was not until the Birmingham, North Warwickshire and Stratford On Avon Railway (BNW) of 1894 was proposed, to be met by the Andoversford and Stratford Upon Avon Railway (ASOA) of 1898, that the GWR was forced to declare its intentions and promote its own line from Honeybourne to Cheltenham and link with the BNW Railway at Bearley. The existing line from Honeybourne to Stratford was also to be doubled, thus completing and creating a new through route for the GWR from Birmingham to Bristol.

Both the ASOA Railway, and the GWR schemes went before Parliament simultaneously. Both were passed in the Commons but the ASOA Railway was defeated in the Lords, the GWR arguing that it would serve the area better than its rival. It is also interesting to reflect that the ASOA Railway (which was to be worked by the Midland & South Western Junction (M&SW) Railway) ran into much opposition from local people especially when it was proposed to run close to Sudeley Castle near Winchcombe. So the GWR won the day, the Royal Assent being given on the 1st August, 1899. Yet it was not until three years later that the GWR board gave its consent (21st November 1902) for the construction of the first section.

In the mean time the M&SW did not take its defeat too lightly, it promoted its own scheme in 1898 under its Northern Extension Bill. This line proposed to run from Andoversford via Winchcombe to the Midland Railway (MR) at a junction south of Ashchurch station, some 14 miles in length. This was very much a political move on behalf of the M&SW rather than a serious proposal to build the line, it was designed primarily to secure several important concessions from the GWR

and MR about working arrangements at Cheltenham. The concessions allowed the M&SW to fix its own rates over the route of the GWR from Andoversford Junction to Lansdown Junction. The GWR also undertook the doubling of the above route (28th September 1902) on the understanding that the M&SW also widened its route southward to Cirencester. The M&SW received concessions from the MR for preference of the M&SW route for through traffic from the MR to the London & South Western Railway. With this the MR received running powers over the GWR's route from Cheltenham to Andoversford Junction and indeed over the whole length of the M&SW. The MR even went as far as a loan to the M&SW £200,000 that was subsequently increased by £50,000!

The BNW soon abandoned the thought of being linked with the M&SW after their failure with the ASOA scheme. Their Bill of 1894 proposed to link Birmingham and Stratford via independent stations at both ends of the route. This naturally did not please the GWR but eventually both parties came to terms with one another. The BNW&SOA putting forward its Act of 1899 to authorise the abandonment of its independent stations at both ends of the line, and join the GWR system at junctions at Tyseley and Bearley. The GWR had endeavoured to improve its service to Birmingham from Stratford having eventually opened its Hatton North Loop on 1st July 1897. Then suddenly the GWR found itself having the Order to Construct passed over to them in July 1900, due to the lack of finance to support the BNW&SOA Railway's venture.

This was a new and exciting period for the GWR. Having rid itself of the broad gauge (1892), it was now setting about expansion and development of the new routes with a vengeance. No longer to be nicknamed the 'Great Way Round', it sought more direct routes. In the first decade of 20th century it improved its 3 main routes:–

1903 London to South Wales (Badminton cut off)
1906 West of England via Patney to Westbury, Castle Cary to Curry Rivell Junction and Athelney to Cogload Junction.
1910 London to Birmingham via Ashendon Junction and Aynho Junction.

But the new route to appear in the decade was of course the Birmingham to Bristol, which eventually became fact in 1908.

The old route between Bristol, Didcot, Oxford and Birmingham was 140 miles, although the Great Western's new route (98 miles 80 chains) was 10 miles more than that of the Midland Railways route via the Lickey Incline.

Having identified the need for a new route and to meet pressure put upon the GWR by other schemes as previously mentioned, the railway set about planning the route in earnest. Back in 1892 the GWR employed as its Chief Engineer James Inglis. It was Inglis who had a profound effect upon the future of the Company for the next nineteen years. As Chief Engineer it was he who planned the route of the new line and saw it through the various Parliamentary Committees. He became the General Manager in 1903 and at the same time remained Consulting Engineer, both offices being held until his death in December 1911.

His initial survey took in the most direct route but as usual the route chosen ended as a compromise avoiding any difficult terrain. High speed running was uppermost in the mind of the surveyors with gradients no steeper than 1 in 108 and curves with a minimum radius between 1/2 mile and 1 mile radius, all this being achieved only by massive embankments and cuttings. Tunnels were built longer than first projected as at Winchcombe (Greet) where the tunnel was planned to be only 375 yards long and finished at 693 yards. No tunnel at this stage was planned for Hunting Butts, but which when eventually built was 97 yards long.

The Board of Trade (BoT) required that all new stations be laid on level ground where possible and that sidings should be on a gradient no steeper than 1 in 260. No level crossings were projected, since they were a hindrance to the operation of the railway and expensive to man. Bridging was extensively used although some occupation crossings were inevitable.

For the 'pleasure' of giving up this land, landowners received compensation for the compulsory purchase of their property. If they disagreed with the amount, then they could appeal in two ways; if the sum was under £50 settlement was by Justices of the Peace, larger sums were taken to a jury or to arbitration.

The Bill was drawn up and presented to Parliament in November 1898 and given the Royal Assent the following year; 1st August 1899 for all three lines viz:-

- 20 miles 6 furlong 6.12 chains, Honeybourne East Junction to a point near to the old Cheltenham shed forming a Junction with the existing line into St. James.
- 1 furlong 8.4 chains, Junction spur from St. James to a Junction on the above line, north of that Junction – forming a triangle.
- 2 furlong 8.25 chains, North Junction to West Junction, Honeybourne – forming a triangle.

The second line was rendered unnecessary, the abandonment Act came before Parliament and was granted in 1903.

In passing the Bill, Parliament usually set a time limit for the completion of the line, on this occasion the limit being five years. At this time the GWR were building new lines and were a little slow in releasing the capital for the new contracts.

Pressure was then brought to bear and to get things moving more swiftly Mr H Andrews of Toddington threatened to introduce a Private Bill into Parliament to enable him to construct the railway himself. Shortly after this the contract was awarded to Messrs Walter Scott & Middleton of Westminster!

By the end of November 1902 a temporary siding had been laid at Honeybourne to facilitate the movement of plant and machinery for the construction of the line. This was started from the Honeybourne end of the line because at Cheltenham the town was already in enough mess with the laying down of its own tramway system.

Navvy camps were set up along the course of the line. Sixteen men would sleep in a hut, and for about 2s (10p) a week pay a hut keeper for board and cooking the food. The hut keeper in turn hired the hut from the contractor.

Having marked out the centre line for the route, the land was fenced off, the GWR supplying all the materials required. Steam navvies then set about the work in the cuttings and tip wagons would take the spoil to the embankments over crudely laid track. If more spoil was needed, then cuttings were dug wider. The nature of this spoil (mainly of a clay base) would often dictate how settlement came about on the embankments. Because they were also built quicker than in previous decades due to the use of the steam navvies, it was often to be found that the BoT would implant a speed restriction until the embankments had fully settled. Several methods were tried to ensure quicker settlement on the line.

The first involved trenches filled with slag some 10 to 20 yards apart, this went down to ground level and was bounded by timber shuttering, gradually the shuttering was removed thus causing the clay to cling to the slag that in turn stabilized it and greatly helped the drainage. Another method was to burn the clay before it was dumped but this proved to be costly.

Small streams were a nuisance, requiring culverts and small bridges that had to be erected before any of the heavy plant could gain access further down the line. Of the road bridges the girder type were nearly always used but several three arch overbridges were however constructed, Toddington being one such example.

As the bridges and earthworks were completed so the laying of the permanent way could begin. The standard for this time was bullhead rail of 44 ft 6 in length,

weighing 97$\frac{1}{2}$ lbs per yard with the chairs some 52 lbs each.

Mileposts and gradient posts were then added and the slopes of the embankments and cuttings were then sown with grass seed. This helped to thus bind the soil further and lessening the chance of a slip.

Having installed all signals and telegraph posts etc., the BoT would finally inspect the section and inspect all the works. Once permission was granted for the opening, notices were issued detailing the route and all the signals, that the footplate crews would encounter along the line.

Generally the opening day for new lines on the GWR fell on the first day of the month, this coinciding with the issue of the new timetable, but if the line was not ready for passengers then it would open to goods only, as was true when the line opened to Broadway, goods being extended to Toddington.

6

Seasons of Labour

The Great Western Railway Board gave consent for the construction of the first section of the new line on 21st November 1902. The contract being awarded to Messrs Walter Scott & Middleton, Westminster, who in turn sub contracted out the stations to Messrs Bloxham of Banbury and all the steel work went to Messrs E Finch Co. Ltd., of Chepstow. The two tunnels for the new line were later sub-contracted out to Mr R W Hallam of Stalybridge. The resident engineer for the GWR was Mr J C Blundell.

Messrs Walter Scott & Middleton soon set about their task, the line from Honeybourne to Cheltenham being constructed in two sections:–

1. Honeybourne to Winchcombe (Greet)

2. Winchcombe to Cheltenham

Altogether the GWR gave their consent to four separate contracts at the following agreed prices;

Honeybourne to Toddington	£110,474	4s	4d
Toddington to Winchcombe	£32,330	6s	11d
Winchcombe to St. Pauls Road Cheltenham	£175,295	16s	5d
St Pauls Road to Malvern Road	£21,217	15s	7d

The land for the last section was still in the process of being purchased so the contract had not been set. However it was awarded to Messrs Walter Scott & Middleton being passed by the Board on 1st June 1905.

6.1   Spring 1903

The first sod was cut in November 1902, the time being set for completion of the contract was June 1904 (to Winchcombe). By November 1902 an estimate for the extension of the line to Cheltenham from Winchcombe had not yet been set, but the land was in the process of being purchased. Work by the Spring had progressed well on the 12 mile section; having laid 7 miles of temporary track for the contractor's engines etc. Of this first section the main features were as follows:–

- A bridge under the GWR line at Honeybourne.
- A cutting near the proposed station at Weston Sub Edge.
- A cutting where the line crosses the Broadway to Evesham Road.
- The raising of the Honeybourne to Broadway Road (Buckle Street).
- A viaduct at Toddington.

Only the first was being worked upon in April 1903.

The line was only connected with the Stratford on Avon branch line at a point a few hundred yards after the main line over bridge, (later known as East Loop Junction). The loop (north to west) line was added later. The Station at Honeybourne at this time had not been altered but it was already planned to extend and add platforms. Therefore the GWR purchased land to the north of the station for the projected extension, which did not occur until 4 years later.

The contractors brought in 4 steam navvies which had scuttle buckets on their booms. These buckets were 3 toothed, and enabled 1 ton of earth at a time to be moved, which greatly reduced the amount of manpower that was required for the project. By the Spring of 1903 the contractor had 5 steam locomotives in use. Tip wagons would be filled by the steam navvies or men, and then hauled to the position along the line where the embankments required building up. Where no machines could be used horses were employed, being given various tasks of haulage and supply, especially if there were no contractors' lines laid.

Vague speculation existed at the time about the final position for the stations on the section especially at Weston Sub Edge and Broadway, these were Buckle Street and Pendlum Bank respectively.

Messrs Walter Scott & Middleton had twelve locomotives at work on the line during the construction. They were all with one exception 0–6–0's, being built by Manning Wardle and Co. Ltd. of Leeds, and were probably not all at work upon the line simultaneously. By the turn of the century the GWR declared that all industrial locomotives should be registered with the company thus enabling their inspectors to trace them and keep records of them, so they then had Great Western plates attached. They were as follows:–

GWR No.	Works No.	Name	Type	Built
Authorized Working;				
Broadway to N&E Junctions				
31	—	*	0–6–0ST	1888
Authorized Working;				
Cheltenham to Honeybourne				
49	1525	*Pallion*	0–6–0ST	1902
50	899	*Bradford*	0–6–0ST	1884
51	1425	*Stublick*	0–6–0ST	1898
Authorized Working;				
Honeybourne Station to East Loop Box				
52	678	*Ruby*	0–6–0ST	1877

GWR No.	Works No.	Name	Type	Built
53	1047	*Disley*	0–6–0T	1888
54	971	*Corea*	0–6–0ST	1885
55	1447	*Sirdar*	0–6–0ST	1899
56	1059	*Bertha*	0–6–0ST	1888
57	583	*Ciceter*	0–6–0ST	1876
58	892	*Luli*	0–4–0T	1883
Authorized Working;				
Honeybourne to Stratford				
59	1502	*Buller*	0–6–0ST	1900

* May have been named *Disley*
52–58 were later authorized to work to Stratford.

0-6-0 Saddle Tank Pallion *shunts wagons to the work site. c. Summer 1905. Note the blocks inside the buffers, these corresponding with solebars on the contractors wagons. On top of the chimney is what appears to be an early spark arrestor.*

Photo: C H Giles

The navvies of Messrs Walter Scott & Middleton seem to have lived up to the 'folklore' that surrounded the nomadic labour force. The main core of these men would have appeared to be 'regulars' following the firm from contract to contract. They (about 500 men) consisted of a good cross section of the country, with the majority being from north of the border. It would appear that these faithful were not sufficient to make up the numbers required for the construction of the new line, so the contractors had to turn for help from the local districts, it came as somewhat as a surprise to find the authors' great grandfather was one of these labourers!

Those that could not find lodgings in the local villages were accommodated by the contractor in huts along the line. These huts were generally one or two roomed, being made of wood, with a corrugated pitched roof. Within the limits of the first contract (Honeybourne to Winchcombe) there were several sites for these 'shanty villages' namely:–

Weston Sub Edge (Buckle Street)

Broadway (Broadway Road)

Toddington (Newtown/Didbrook)

Hayles

Winchcombe (Greet)

When Toddington yard was at its busiest the contractors depot had a surgery, engine shed and even its own mission room. Work commenced for these men at 6.30 am and finished at 5.30 pm. The navvies worked hard, even on Good Friday, when they were observed by large crowds at Weston Sub Edge and at Broadway. It would appear that the public were especially interested in the steam navvies at work, which must have appeared to be a novelty at the time.

The contractors employed at most 1,200 men at some stage during the construction. Each man had deducted from his wages 1d per week, which was used for Doctors' fees should they become ill. This fund was found most useful, for not only were the Doctors of the region kept busy through injuries but diseases such as smallpox and scarlet fever were rife at the time and many were the navvies that had to be isolated.

Although conditions for all concerned were harsh it would appear there was a certain amount of stable labour. These men and their families were content and

evidence of the attempts to settle in with the surroundings comes through when we discover that they had an active cricket team.

The team did not win many games, but at least they participated, most games being played on a Sunday and 'away' from home. In 1904 they were known as 'Toddington Railway Cricket Club' and the following year as the 'Gretton Railway Cricket Club'

As the railway opened in sections so the navvies moved home much to the relief of the local communities and the constabulary !

Navvies toil beneath the towering jib of a steam navvy near Folley Lane, Cheltenham. c. 1905.   *Photo: C H Giles*

6.2   Summer 1903

The work on the line was progressing well and high was the speculation that the line would be open from Honeybourne to Winchcombe for the 1904 fruit season. It is interesting to note that it was envisaged that large amounts of fruit were to be transported from the Toddington area. Towards the end of June work commenced on Toddington Station.

It was hard at this time to contain some of the navvies for frequently, until the completion of the line they were before the Police Courts. Winchcombe and Broadway were particularly affected and even Evesham was not devoid of their attention. As an example the Police Charge Registers for Winchcombe reveal:–

1902	20 charges	No navvies	Nil%
1903	78 charges	46 navvies	59%
1904	77 charges	44 navvies	57%
1905	62 charges	36 navvies	58%
1906	47 charges	5 navvies	10%
1907	62 charges	Nil	Nil

The types of offences were various and are recorded in the offence books of that period; drunk and disorderly, assault on police, vagrancy act, drunk on local premises, sleeping out, stealing a goat/fruit/fowl, wilful damage, damage to straw, larceny of coal, breaking windows, begging, game trespass, offensive language, poaching and stealing 2 ferrets!

Some of these men must have been characters. From these records some of their nicknames have been preserved, examples being; 'Brum', 'Happy thoughts', 'Gloster', 'Harmpur', '3 finger Cockney' and 'Cheeky Teddy' to name but a few.

The punishment for most of these offences was a heavy fine or a sentence of hard labour for a time, which was spent at Gloucester Gaol.

August saw the first accidents on the railway. The first being at Broadway where a man was pinned down by an iron girder that caused him to sustain a fractured jaw and cuts and bruises to the face. The second fellow was less fortunate. The accident happened near Stanway Grounds. One of the men from the huts at Toddington yard was working with his horse, shunting wagons to and fro from the steam navvy (presumably this work was in the cutting north of the present station). The horse caused the man to slip underneath a moving wagon, which passed over his stomach. He did not last long and the body was removed to the surgery on the Toddington site. Clearly the yard was well equipped and afforded many facilities that the other sites along the line did not have.

6.3   Autumn 1903

The line was a hive of activity with the contractors' engines being kept fully busy. Not only did they carry most of the spoil to where it was required, they also conveyed the men from the makeshift shanty homes to their place of work. Special trucks were constructed for this purpose, but on the evening of 21st September none of these trucks were available, so the men had to be conveyed home in the normal ballast trucks. One man tried to alight from the moving train as it approached Buckle Street. Hanging on by his hands his legs were run over by the truck. Both legs were broken, one of which was later amputated followed by severe shock, the poor fellow passed away the same night at the Cottage Hospital, Evesham.

Toddington Viaduct

This viaduct (sometimes known as Stanway) was the major feature of the new line, its 15 arches spanning a small stream at the height of 42 ft. It was 210½ yards long with each arch having a 36 ft span and being 27 ft in width. The whole structure was built on a curve of 80 chains, on a 1 in 150 gradient. The contract for the structure was due to be completed in June 1904.

Construction commenced from the northern end in March 1903 and the 50 or so regular men soon set about sinking the foundations into a depth of 12ft. Work was well advanced in the Autumn of 1903, with all the piers and arches nearing completion. On the morning of Friday 13th November at 8.15 am, No. 10 arch collapsed without warning. Having been completed the previous week, it had just had its wooden supports removed, the other arches to the south were still thus supported. When the ring of the arch collapsed it brought down with it a 14 ton steam crane, which was used in bringing up the supporting ribbing and bricks etc. from ground level. This was scattered over a wide area and thus being totally dismembered. After the crescendo of noise and dust had settled down, (which was heard over a mile away) the rescuers set about their task in earnest, with men coming from all parts of the line.

The crane driver, a man by the name of Smith came down with this first collapse. He somehow managed to survive this and was placed underneath No. 9 arch, while his rescuers tried to get at another fellow who was under the crane. However No. 9 arch fell without warning burying Smith again along with four more men. Just 40 minutes later No. 8 arch fell in. Smith was again picked from out of the ruins only to die later that night at the Cottage Hospital Winchcombe. Another man from under No. 9 was removed to the Union Hospital Winchcombe and subsequently died that night. The poor fellow under the crane and another man who was found at 2.30 pm under No. 9 were removed to the contractors' surgery at Toddington yard where they remained until Wednesday, when they were buried at Wormington and Winchcombe. The other two men were also buried locally on the Tuesday at Didbrook and Tewkesbury. The navvies worked through the night for it was not known if anyone else was trapped under the arches. They formed lines for the hand to hand clearing stopping occasionally to listen for any of the injured under the debris. By the Saturday morning no one else had been found and the casualty figures were 4 dead, 7 injured. This

could have been much higher, for the men generally took breakfast about 8.30 am underneath the same arches that collapsed. It is also interesting to note that on the morning of the accident that some 20 casuals had sheltered under the arches during the night and had moved off about 8.00 am.

One man had a remarkable story to tell. While standing on top of the viaduct near to the crane, he felt the arch begin to move underneath him. He grabbed the nearest thing to hand which turned out to be an iron water pipe that ran along the top of the structure, he found himself suspended in mid air, while all about him collapsed. He eventually fell some 30 foot when the pipe suddenly broke. He too like Smith was placed underneath No. 9 arch which subsequently fell in, but unlike Smith he survived to tell the tale being only badly shaken and bruised.

The following day being a Saturday saw crowds gather to view the spectacle, so much so that the constabulary had to enforce some degree of crowd control. It is as

Toddington Viaduct (i) looking north on the Cotswold hill side (east). Nos. 10–7 arches can clearly be seen and the wooden rib formers still in place on the remainder to the south.
Photo: M Shorland

Toddington Viaduct (ii) looking north from the west side. The temporary shoring can be seen against arches 6 and 5. On this side of the structure lines were run alongside in order to get all the materials to the site. One of the contractors 0–6–0 Saddle tanks can be seen in the view taken shortly after the collapse. Photo: P Christie

well they did for at 4.00 pm the ring of the No. 7 arch collapsed without any warning just like the others had and No. 6 arch developed a severe crack.

With this fatal occurrence a deep sense of grief was felt throughout the district, speculation grew about the cause. One suggestion was that the boggy state and condition of the land was the cause, others saying the recent bad weather was to blame. However the inquest on the accident took place on 28th November 1903 the verdict being returned as 'accidental death'. The inquest also added a rider;

1. That considering the state of the weather, sufficient time was not allowed for the lime mortar to set before the supporting centres were removed.

2. The arches of this type should be set in concrete mortar during the winter construction period.

3. The steam crane was carried further on the centre of No. 10 arch than was advisable. This

being not supported due to the cranes track having not been extended to the next pier.

The Board of Trade's Report issued in January 1904, concurred with the inquests findings, and laid no blame on the design or the materials used. Criticism was levelled at the contractors for not issuing special instructions to the foreman with relation to the position of the crane. Still, it was pointed out that 54 ribs had been lifted out without any hint of mishap, so it was reasonable to assume that all was well. The reason none of the other arches had not fallen was due to No's 11 and 12 to the south still being supported by their ribs and that those to the north No's 6, 5, 4 etc. were supported/shored up before anymore damage could occur. Subsequently the contractors paid compensation for the loss of life, and those injured in the accident.

One of those injured men remained in hospital for the next seven months, so severe was the extent of his injuries but he was well looked after for on his release he married the Matron!

The contractors soon set about the rebuilding, not repeating the mistakes that had already been made. The viaduct was near completion in the summer of 1904 although it did not open for passenger traffic until the line was opened to Toddington on 1st December 1904. Goods were conveyed from Toddington upon the opening of the Honeybourne to Broadway section on 1st August 1904 this being an agreement between the contractors and Mr H Andrews of the Toddington Orchard Estate.

6.4 Spring 1904

By the beginning of March reports started to circulate that the line would soon be open, it was envisaged and provisionally fixed for the 1st June. It had been hoped that the opening would have occurred on the 1st May but this was deemed to be impractical due to the large amount of work still required to be done. The telegraph posts were being put in along the line and it was hoped that everything would be working by the above date for passenger and goods trains alike.

Injury and sickness continued throughout this time. In early April one young lad had his foot severed clean off, when he got his foot stuck in the rail and an engine drawing ballast was unable to stop in time being so close.

At this time it was discovered that some workers were suffering from smallpox they being removed to the Isolation Hospital, Enfield Cottage, Langley Hill, Winchcombe. The disease caused uproar in the town, so that all the drains were thoroughly flushed and disinfected with chlorine of lime and carbolic acid and everything was done to prevent the spread of the disease.

The Winchcombe Workhouse and the Cottage Hospital were kept busy, indeed the figures were like those of the police. The work of these establishments did not go unnoticed, for a letter dated 25th February 1904 to the Cottage Hospital from the contractors' wife (Mrs Scott) wished to express the thanks of herself and husband for the kind treatment of their injured work people.

May saw another tragic accident at Toddington where a lad was pinned between the buffers of the contractors engine, *Sirdar* and some wagons in the yard. He

later died from his injuries in the Cottage Hospital, Winchcombe. The incident brought to light a witness to the accident, a one Charles Clark, fitter, who saw the incident having come out of the engine shed. There is therefore evidence to suggest that the contractors had their own engine shed although of a temporary nature. If this was not enough the workforce were going down like flies with suspected smallpox, 11 men were placed in quarantine for a fortnight in a hut placed to one side away from the remaining navvies and their families. So crowded was this situation that a new isolation hut was set up near the Stanton Road.

6.5 Summer 1904

The summer saw the big effort being made for the line from Honeybourne to be opened as far as Broadway. At Broadway a considerable amount of the ground had to be made up due to the levels involved with the goods yard and shed, thus clay was brought from all parts of the line.

On 6th July a train arrived from Didbrook. As it slowed a coupling broke causing 10 trucks to charge down the slope of the yard. They overran the track at the bottom, ploughing through the new weighbridge damaging two sides and the roof. The first few wagons managed to come to an eventual halt before they met the Evesham Road but only just for the first one finished up in the ditch!

About this time a small fire occurred at Weston Sub Edge Station, a telegram was sent to the nearest fire brigade which was at Broadway, upon arrival some 43 minutes later the fire was all but extinguished. This length of time was apparently considered good for the $3^{1/2}$ miles, due to the men being all volunteers and the time taken to catch the horses!

Between Honeybourne and Broadway the work was relatively light the total excavating amounted to 200,000 cubic yards. This was comparatively small when considering that between Broadway and Winchcombe some 637,800 cubic yards were removed. There were 9 bridges over the line and 3 under on the section from Honeybourne to Broadway. All the abutments and culverts were of brick being faced in South Staffordshire brindle brick. The majority of the spans were entirely constructed of steel.

Excursion train to Stratford, 2nd August 1904. Passengers queue at Broadway. To the left of the view no goods shed or signal box can be seen and just beyond the last coach can be seen some of the contractors huts.   *Photo: Hereford & Worcester Record Office*

6.6 The Opening of the Line to Broadway

The double tracked line was inspected by the BoT opening on 1st August, then a Bank Holiday Monday. The section was worked by absolute block.

It came as a great surprise to the public when it was announced at very short notice. From the outset the intention of the GWR was to operate the services with the new steam railmotors, but at the time they were in heavy demand elsewhere on the system and as yet had not been built in large quantities (at this date only 19 were in service). The services were run with normal coaching stock.

The first train from Honeybourne, the 07.14 am comprised of six all third class coaches. This new service was officiated by Mr Cooke, Traffic Superintendent, Mr Dixon, Locomotive Superintendent and Mr Turk,

Chief Inspector all from the Worcester Division. The first train left Honeybourne with only 15 passengers, yet all was not lost for several more were added at Bretforton & Weston Sub Edge, then the only stop between Honeybourne and Broadway. At Broadway there was a large crowd to greet the arrival of this first train.

The return leg of the trip yielded 76 passengers making the return journey to Broadway, still they felt that they should celebrate upon their arrival at Honeybourne and hastily made their way to the refreshment rooms at the Station. They were not open and as the turn round time was short, they had to wait until they were back at Broadway to afford any sort of celebration.

Then and for several more years services ran from the existing platforms at Honeybourne, until the Station was enlarged. The traffic returns for the day were as follows;

Broadway	637 people
Bretforton & Weston Sub Edge	253 people
Honeybourne	234 people

The new service to Broadway immediately had an effect on the local population. The newspapers arrived now on the morning service which had until then arrived in the afternoon around 3.30 pm unless the Birmingham papers were posted (arriving in the morning's mail).

It only took the Broadway people a day to realise the new lines potential, and an excursion was arranged to Stratford on Avon. The local children from Willersey and Broadway together with their families and teachers plus friends took advantage of the cheap fare. They all assembled in Broadway and the procession set off for the Station accompanied by the local band. There were so many of them (623), that there were not enough coaches, so a fair number had to await the arrival of the next train and pay the full fare. The children were subsequently entertained to tea in a large marquee adjacent to the Swans Nest on the banks of the River Avon. All the sights of the town were taken in and the party eventually arrived at Broadway at 9.30 pm. All the fares and teas for the children being paid for by subscription.

The passenger service consisted of 10 trains in each direction between Honeybourne and Broadway. There were two goods services from Honeybourne at the time leaving for Broadway at 8.30 am and 2.30 pm (arriving at 8.58 am and 3.00 pm respectively). The 8.30 am was worked by one of the Honeybourne banking engines arriving back there at 9.43 am having left Broadway at 9.15 am. The 2.30 pm was worked by the 1.20 pm ex Worcester goods engine which then worked back from Broadway at 3.40 pm. This then went through to Worcester connecting with the fruit and vegetable freight for Crewe. The contractors were meeting these two trains carrying out their undertaking that they would convey all the fruit from Toddington to Broadway.

Work had commenced on fencing off a piece of land by the new station at Broadway for the proposed new market. Messrs Harvey Hunt Ltd., Evesham set about opening a fruit and vegetable market, this sale yard eventually opened on 4th July 1905. Today the site is still in existence, in use as the Station garage opposite the goods yard.

The first Station Masters for the new line were;

Bretforton & Weston Sub Edge	Mr G Merrett
Broadway	Mr G J Fifield

The Halt between these two stations, Willersey opened c. October 1904. It was unstaffed from the outset and was constructed from timber.

6.7   Autumn 1904

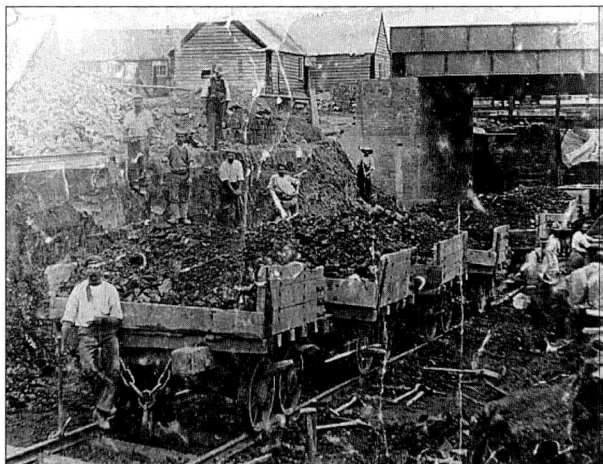

Winchcombe bridge (Greet) dominates the foreground and overshadows the navvies to the west of it in the cutting, beyond it can be seen the temporary bridge to allow traffic over the gap while the new one is built. The curve of the Up platform of Winchcombe Station can just be seen underneath this. Navvies huts abound at this location, the view being taken in the Autumn of 1904.   *Photo: P Christie*

By the start of September speculation was high as to when the next section of the line to Greet would be open, at this stage there was only some embankment work at Broadway and some excavation at Greet to be completed. It was hoped (somewhat prematurely as it turned out) that Greet would be reached by November, Toddington Station was having its finishing touches applied by the painters and decorators and construction at Greet Station (Winchcombe) had commenced. It was at this time that the second contract was signed for the Greet to Cheltenham section of the line and again this went to Messrs Walter Scott & Middleton. This section of some 8 miles presented several engineering problems, the greatest of which was the tunnel at Winchcombe which cut through a spur of the Cotswolds at Greet. The original plans for the line showed a tunnel of 375 yards, this was eventually amended and became 693 yards! There was another tunnel, at Hunting Butts some 2 miles from Cheltenham. Even this was originally planned as a deep cutting, but having received objections from the racecourse which insisted on keeping its gallops

Looking towards Winchcombe cutting (Greet tunnel not yet started) can be seen two steam navvies at work, these being served by temporary lines. The slope on the right is virtually complete in the view and the line to the left was laid in to serve the two shafts for the tunnel and to carry away any resulting spoil. c. 1905.   *Photo: M Shorland*

intact and so the GWR agreed to make a tunnel of 97 yards. It would appear that a bridge was not adequate, perhaps even at this early stage the GWR had its eye on the future potential that the famous racecourse had to offer and therefore did not want to upset future good relationships.

The section also required many bridges, cuttings and embankments much more so than the northern section because it ran much closer to the hills. There were to be Stations at Gotherington and Bishops Cleeve. The work for this section commenced on Monday 3rd October with the laying of the contractors' temporary line to run over the Gretton bank through which the tunnel was to be bored.

Although the section beyond Broadway was not open to the public at the time the contractor ran a special train to convey the navvies and their families from Winchcombe to Toddington. On the evening of

20th September a concert was held in the Tythe Barn at Stanton in aid of the Toddington Railway Cricket Club, presumably an end of season dance.

The GWR were attracting more passengers onto the line especially through the introduction of the railmotors. To assist the public, new stations were opened, these were not exactly stations for they were wooden platforms of one or two coach lengths and were known as 'Haltes'. There was already one of these haltes at Willersey but three new ones were opened (17th October 1904) on the Stratford on Avon branch; they were Broad Marston, Clifford Chambers Crossing and Evesham Road Crossing at Stratford. Local speculation grew in the Vale of Evesham for if Clifford Chambers could warrant such a platform, then there should be haltes at Aldington and Bretforton Crossing on the old OWW route west of Honeybourne. Neither came about although Aldington had its own sidings which

The east face of Greet Tunnel Winchcombe, showing evidence of the use of horses by the contractors in 1905.   *Photo: P Christie*

conveyed local produce and fruit. The new railmotors did not materialize until 1st October, whereupon two were sent to Honeybourne. They were immediately put into service causing some trouble within the first few days. One had a leaking steam pipe (not uncommon in later years) and the other broke down at Long Marston through a defective nut giving way, the passengers being conveyed by another train sent from Honeybourne. The railmotors were soon back in service having undergone repairs at Worcester.

These railmotors took over from the old passenger trains which consisted of nine round trips. Two freight trains still worked to Broadway at this time plus the provision for a Broadway to Oxley (Birmingham) fruit service, 'running when required'.

In October an interesting situation occurred at Greet. A wealthy young lady turned up on site seeking employment. When the men eventually stopped rolling about in laughter, peace was returned and the contractors called in the local constabulary, who subsequently discovered that she had run away from home. Clearly this is not so on the railway at Toddington today; no one is turned away (including wealthy ladies)!

The contractors had commenced work at the Cheltenham end of the line at this time. Work was hindered by the decision of the Cheltenham Street and Highway Committee, who ruled that the contractor would only be allowed to operate 12 trains per day, each way. No trains were allowed between 8 to 9 am and 1 to 2 pm and that within 18 months of the laying down of their tracks, they would be lifted. This decision was reached because it was thought to inconvenience the large bodies of men moving to and fro at lunchtimes.

By the end of the Autumn the contractors had laid their temporary lines over the Littleworth Lane, Greet and to appease the local councils, lowered the roads at Buckland, Laverton and Didbrook.

6.8 Winter 1904/1905

The line to Toddington was opened to public traffic on 1st December 1904. The first train being the 06.43 am ex Honeybourne arriving at 07.10 am. This was the first of nine round trips per day, returning at 07.32 am. All services were run by steam railmotors. By the end of the year the contractors had cleared the site and work was concentrated at Winchcombe. The police recorded that 500–600 navvies were in the area, adding that in view of these numbers not so much trouble had been encountered. Although the contractors moved onto Winchcombe the shanty village remained at Toddington for some time due to the large numbers involved, accommodation being at a premium.

The tunnel at Winchcombe presented a substantial barrier to the contractor. He sub-contracted the tunnels to Mr R W Hallam, many men Hallam employed being ex-miners. Two shafts were sunk into the hill, and a steam winch set up above each of these, which were capable of hauling up 15 cwt at a time. Several men who worked upon the tunnel were involved in fatal accidents. Gunpowder licences were issued and the storage of this took place near to the work, in a stone building. The gunpowder was extensively used, for the clay was very difficult to break up.

Beyond the south end of the tunnel, large quantities of spoil were tipped making up the embankments for the next section to Bishops Cleeve. Just outside the southern portal a large portion was also tipped in a dump still easily recognizable. At this time (December 1904) the bridges at Gretton and Prescott had been commenced. Work could now commence in earnest at the Cheltenham end of the line. The contractors started at a point known as Folley Lane on the outskirts, working back towards Bishops Cleeve. They soon laid 1/2 mile of working rails between Folley Lane and Chestnut Farm.

Railmotor No. 41 stands in the Down platform at Winchcombe on opening day, having arrived from Honeybourne. The temporary shelter for the omnibuses can be seen to the rear of the brick built aceteylene hut and weighbridge. Note also the bricks behind the platform fence. Contractors at this time had use of the Up line.   Photo: T Petchey

This view shows a steam navvy working on the western face of Greet tunnel. All the temporary lines can be seen where the navvy itself is moved up to the workings. The horse drawn wagons were for taking away any spoil dug out by the navvy and also a means of moving bricks etc to the working face. c. Winter 1905 *Photo: P Campion*

A second view of the working taken the same time as the one above. *Photo: P Campion*

A steam navvy was soon brought in, being transported in sections from Toddington via road, hauled by traction engine. It was quickly reassembled at the Cheltenham end where it was soon put to work.

It had been hoped that the line to Winchcombe would be opened by 1st January 1905, but like all the speculation this was not to be. The line was inspected on 26th January by Colonel H A Yorke and his staff, who found the section satisfactory, so 1st February 1905 saw Winchcombe linked with the outside world by its own railway. Although the station was some distance from the town and at Greet, it was known as Winchcombe (not Winchcomb as it had been spelt previously). The first train arrived at 07.18 am. There was no public celebration yet many people journeyed to Toddington to catch this first train (railmotor) there being 30–40 passengers travelling on it. Ten trips per day were made.

With the tunnel taking a while to construct, the GWR ran from 1st February an omnibus service from Winchcombe to Cheltenham calling at Bishops Cleeve, Gotherington and Gretton (thus avoiding Cleeve Hill). The journey time was 1 hour 20 minutes. A temporary shed for the motorbuses was erected on the Winchcombe site. The two motorbuses had been used on the Helston to Lizard trips, having a seating capacity for 28 inside and 2 at the front. Power came from a 20 HP Milnes Daimlar engine. Not withstanding the solid tyres, which must have been uncomfortable, the top speed was 30 mph. Only 14 passengers were carried on the first trip on the 1st February with 19 on the return. There was room for luggage and parcels on the top with lighting provided internally by a central acetylene lamp. Within the next 15 months these vehicles carried some 35,000 passengers, thus giving a foretaste of the route and service to come. From 1st June 1906 when the line was opened to Bishops Cleeve the service was cut back running between there and Cheltenham, and two months later even this service was terminated upon the opening of this last section.

Apart from the normal amenities at the station at Winchcombe two other establishments came into being with the opening of the railway. On the 13th February 1905 the Cheltenham Original Brewery Co. opened a Hotel in place of two public houses in the district. Today this is the Harvest Home tavern. The Winchcombe Co-Operative Auction Market was inaugurated on the 15th by Mr C Castle, in close proximity to the Hotel.

Timetable for the motor omnibus service 4th February 1905

	am	pm	pm
Winchcombe (George Hotel)	8.40	1.20	5.15
Winchcombe Station	8.52	1.30	5.25
Gretton (The New Inn)	9.05	1.45	5.40
Gotherington (The Forge)	9.20	2.05	6.00
Bishops Cleeve (The Old Elm Tree)	9.30	2.10	6.05
Pittville (Corner of Evesham Road)	9.55	2.30	6.25
GWR Office (14 Colonade)	9.58	2.33	6.28
Cheltenham Station	10.00	2.35	6.30
Cheltenham Station	10.30	3.45	7.00
GWR Office	10.32	3.47	7.02
Pittville	10.35	3.50	7.05
Bishops Cleeve	10.55	4.10	7.25
Gotherington	11.00	4.15	7.30
Gretton	11.25	4.40	7.50
Winchcombe Station	11.45	4.58	8.13
Winchcombe	11.52	5.05	8.20

'All Change' Omnibus outside Winchcombe Station awaits to meet a train. 1st February 1905. *Photo: T Petchey*

6.9 Spring 1905

With work commencing along the Winchcombe to Bishops Cleeve section the navvies moved their shanty huts to new locations; Gretton, Gotherington and Southam being three of these. Smallpox still plagued the workforce, placing an inevitable strain on the local communities. Accidents still abounded. One of these

The timbers are still in place supporting the bridge at Gretton in this view and the brickwork is still to be finished. However it is safe to allow one of the contractors locomotives over it in this scene taken c. Spring 1905. Photo: P Campion

navvies was crushed between the buffers of wagons at Winchcombe, while another chap got himself so drunk that he fell into a ditch and drowned!

With the line passing through the old cricket ground at Gretton it was decided to hold a dance in order to raise much needed funds for the new pitch. The princely sum of over £10 was raised.

It should be noted that then there were 35 licensed houses (14 alehouses, 16 beerhouses, 3 beerhouses – off licensed and 2 grocers licensed) in the Winchcombe division. The population for the division was 8,074, therefore one license to every 230 inhabitants.

Of the 28 parishes making up the division, 18 had no license. From this it is easy to gather that to obtain a drink the navvies did not have to go very far from Winchcombe.

Newtown (Toddington) was being developed by Mr Hugh Andrews in connection to his estates. He employed a large amount of labour, the majority of which he set up in houses adjoining the estate. These cottages can easily be recognised today by the insignia of their owner above the doors of these houses thus showing that the environment around the railway was beginning to grow with it.

The New Line Through Cheltenham 1905

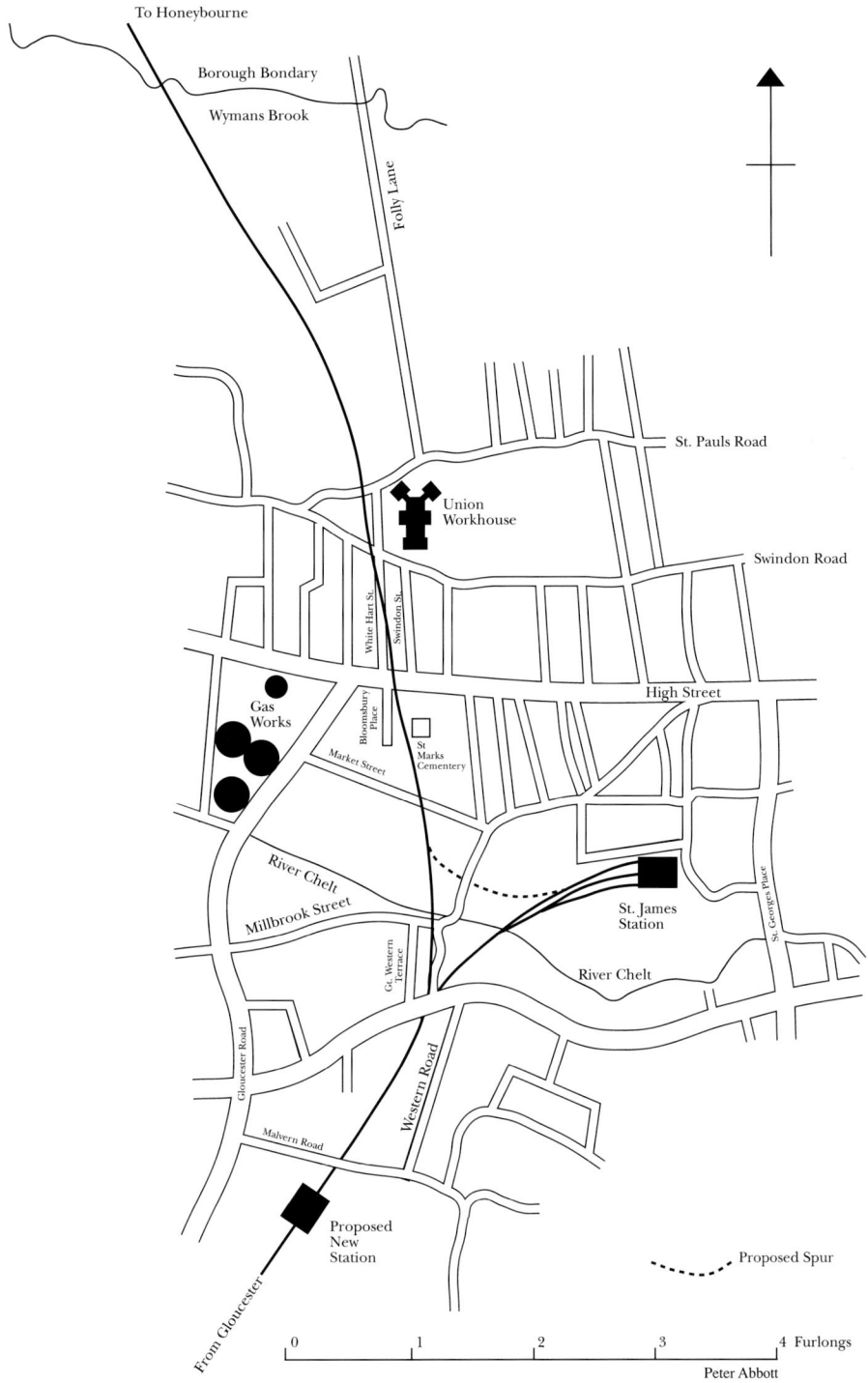

To Honeybourne

Borough Bondary

Wymans Brook

Folly Lane

St. Pauls Road

Union
Workhouse

Swindon Road

White Hart St.

Swindon St.

Gas
Works

Bloomsbury Place

High Street

St
Marks
Cementery

Market Street

River Chelt

Millbrook Street

St. James
Station

St. George's Place

River Chelt

Gt. Western Terrace

Gloucester Road

Western Road

Malvern Road

Proposed
New
Station

From Gloucester

Proposed Spur

0	1	2	3	4 Furlongs

Peter Abbott

6.10 Summer 1905

The Summer realised the full destruction caused by the alterations required inside the Borough of Cheltenham. It was one of the last major upheavals made by such a scheme to an urban area, with roads being closed and buildings demolished.

The line crossed the Borough boundary at Wymans Brook, close to the Folley Lane Brick Co. In order to reach the St. Pauls Road an old cemetery had to be crossed, this being achieved only by the reinterment of some 300 bodies.

This section was made up of embankment through to St. Pauls Road (which was spanned by a 31 ft bridge). From here the line ran on a viaduct, with some arches underneath being used as lock ups. To make this viaduct the houses to the west side of Carlton Place were demolished. The next bridge to be encountered was the 30 ft span over the Swindon Road. Thence to reach the 25 ft span bridge over the High Street the route ran parallel to White Hart Street and here again houses were demolished. Further to the south the railway crossed Bloomsbury Place before another bridge was encountered at Market Street (again a few houses were done away with). Three more bridges then followed in quick succession; those over Millbrook Street, the River Chelt and finally St. Georges Road at the junction with the existing line to St. James Station. More razing to the ground of houses took place on the west side of the Great Western Road leading from Millbrook Street to St. Georges Road. Replacement houses were put up in Alstone Avenue to account for the loss of dwellings. Just for good measure a new bridge was thrown over the railway; known as Malvern Road it was a little to the south of the proposed junction being on the existing line.

The original GWR plans showed a line/spur from Market Street to pass south east over the Alstone Baths to the St. James Square Station and thus form a triangular Junction. This was abandoned, but legal authority was retained to construct this part of the route, should this be required at some later stage.

On 14th August a new halt was opened at Laverton between Broadway and Toddington. Trains called there 6 minutes after leaving the former in the Down direction and 7 minutes after leaving Toddington in the Up direction.

6.11 Spring 1906

With the completion of Winchcombe tunnel in the winter of 1905/6 the line was ready generally to be opened to Bishops Cleeve. On the 19th May advantage was taken by 75 members of the Gloucester Engineering Society to travel from Cheltenham to Winchcombe, permission being sought from the GWR via the Assistant Superintendent at Swindon. The train consisted of the contractors' open wagons, which were hauled by *Pallion*. The train departed from the bridge in St. Georges Road, the journey took about an hour for the 9 miles, for they stopped at all the engineering works along the route. Thus the society achieved the distinction of traversing this section before the inspecting officer for the Board of Trade was able to do so. The inspection between Winchcombe and Bishops Cleeve was carried out by Lieutenant Colonel H A Yorke on the 30th May. The section opened to traffic two days later, on the 1st June. The first service was run by steam railmotor No. 64 and a clerestory trailer coach.

6.12 Summer 1906

The final section from Bishops Cleeve to Cheltenham was all but complete, bar for tidying up at the Cheltenham end, with a view to opening on 1st August.

Members of the Gloucester Engineering Society board the contractors wagons for their special journey to Winchcombe at the St Georges bridge, Cheltenham, on 19th May 1906.
Photo: T Petchey

Most of the land needed for the new station at Malvern Road (some 1½ acres) was purchased from the adjoining Ladies College. A build up of some 600 navvies were in the area and it was found a necessity to plant a quick growing hedge plus adding a six foot fence to prevent them from watching the young ladies playing. The line was slewed some 3 ft between Malvern Road and Queens Road Bridges on the Down side only to accommodate the area for the new station. The permanent way men moved in, in earnest on the 8th July. Some 85 men worked from 4 am to 9 pm remodelling and installing 12 crossovers and 6 switches. The following week (15th) saw 72 men work a similar shift of 4 am to 7 pm installing a compound crossing and switches under the Malvern Road Bridge. Over 60,000 tons of spoil had been removed by the contractors trains to Honeybourne, so that 3 transfer sidings and 2 mileage sidings could be created alongside the proposed Malvern Road Station.

A new engine shed was to be constructed in the yard replacing the earlier broad gauge shed situated near the St. Georges Road bridge. The contract for this work was undertaken by Mr L Jones of Wolverhampton. Several buildings that occupied the site were razed to the ground, including a weigh house and an old slaughter house. 15th July also saw the mass removal of contractors equipment via special trains from the Gretton area to Honeybourne. The plant was positioned to start work on the South Loop to East Loop contract (which connected the Stratford branch from Honeybourne via a south to east connection from the Oxford to Worcester line), and the doubling to Stratford.

The Malvern Road East Signal Box at this time (15th July) was coupled up to the points and several contractors trains also ran over this new section (Bishops Cleeve to Cheltenham). The Signal Box replaced the old Bayshill Signal Box alongside the St. Georges Road bridge. The previous day had been an historic one for the line because it was inspected by non other than the Great Western General Manager, J C Inglis who travelled as far as Toddington from Cheltenham where upon he visited his friend Mr Hugh Andrews at Toddington House.

The line from Bishops Cleeve to Malvern Road East Signal Box was then inspected by the Board of Trade on 26th July. It passed and services duly commenced on the 1st August. The 20 miles 62 chains opened to the public from Honeybourne through to Cheltenham, there being no ceremony for the occasion. The first train to arrive at Cheltenham from Honeybourne was with steam railmotor No. 2. Thus the contractor had completed the main bulk of the task a few months ahead of schedule.

Until this time the line from Honeybourne had come under the control of the Worcester Division but from the 9th August 1906 the line as far as Honeybourne West Loop to the south came under the Hereford Division. Later the Hereford Division in this area became the Gloucester Division which also saw the boundary alter again, falling between Cheltenham racecourse and Bishops Cleeve. To the north of this boundary the line reverted to the Worcester Division.

1st August 1906 Timetable:–

Down Services

Honeybourne	07.46	10.26	11.15	12.49	2.14	4.39		6.12	7.34
Bretforton & Weston Sub Edge	07.53	10.33	11.22	12.56	2.21	4.46		6.19	7.40
Willersey Halt	7.57	10.37	11.26	1.00	2.25	4.50		6.23	7.44
Broadway	8.04	10.44	11.32	1.06	2.32	4.56		6.29	7.50
Laverton Halt	8.10	10.50		1.12	2.40	5.02		6.35	7.56
Toddington	8.17	10.57		1.19	2.45	5.09		6.42	8.02
Winchcombe	8.24	11.04		1.27	2.55	5.18	5.45	6.51	8.10
Gretton Halt	8.30	11.10		1.33	3.01	5.24	—	6.57	8.15
Gotherington	8.35	11.16		1.38	3.06	5.29	5.52	7.02	8.20
Bishops Cleeve	8.40	11.22		1.43	3.11	5.34	5.58	7.07	8.24
Cheltenham St. James	8.51	11.34		1.54	3.22	5.45	6.11	7.18	8.35

Up Services

Cheltenham St. James	08.05	10.01		12.38	2.35	3.38	5.10	6.08	8.40
Bishops Cleeve	8.17	10.13		12.50	2.47	3.50	5.25	6.20	8.51
Gotherington	8.22	10.18		12.55	2.52	3.55	5.30	6.25	8.56
Gretton Halt	8.27	10.23		1.00	2.57	4.00	—	6.30	9.01
Winchcombe	8.32	10.28		1.05	3.02	4.05	5.39	6.35	9.06
Toddington	8.40	10.35		1.12	3.10	4.13		6.43	9.13
Laverton Halt	8.47	10.41		1.18	3.17	4.20		6.50	9.20
Broadway	8.55	10.49	11.35	1.26	3.24	4.27		6.57	9.26
Willersey Halt	8.59	10.53	11.39	1.30	3.28	4.31		7.01	9.30
Bretforton & Weston Sub Edge	9.03	10.57	11.43	1.34	3.32	4.35		7.05	9.34
Honeybourne	9.10	11.03	11.50	1.40	3.40	4.42		7.12	9.40

NO SUNDAY SERVICES

No times are shown for Malvern Road Station because it was not completed until 1908, until then all local services reversed at Malvern Road Junction back into St. James Station and vice versa.

6.13   Winter 1906/7

The winter saw the enlargement of Honeybourne Station and the modification to the existing layout. This coupled to the doubling of the original branch line to Stratford on Avon and the new South Loop to East Loop (thus allowing trains to run directly from the Oxford direction through to Stratford). The contractors were kept fully busy.

The first section to be doubled on the branch was that of the Long Marston to Milcote on 3rd March 1907. This might appear out of sequence but the nature of the terrain was very flat and therefore easy to complete. The East Loop Junction was on the old branch to Stratford and was the eventual junction for the 3 routes; Honeybourne, Cheltenham and Oxford.

The Honeybourne East Loop Junction to Long Marston portion of the doubling was completed on 28th April. This followed more blasting in the cutting near the East Junction as had occurred nearly 50 years earlier. The bridges in this section were widened. Though the ones at Pebworth and Long Marston have since been replaced, the surviving bridge near to the site of the North Loop Signal Box on the road to Pebworth from Honeybourne still shows this widening of the original branch line bridge of 1859. Land for the widening of the line to Stratford from Honeybourne, was purchased. All the subsequent widening taking place to the west of the existing track bed, this doubling of the line cost £25,228 4s 2d.

The South Loop was connected to the line via the East Loop box on 28th June 1907, finally bringing about the loop that had originally been proposed by the West Midland Railway way back in 1862! This small connection cost £13,482 to construct and again Messrs Walter Scott & Middleton carried out the work.

6.14   Spring 1907 to 1909

The last portion to be completed was that from Milcote to the East & West Junction Signal Box at Stratford (to the south of the Evesham Road Crossing Signal Box) on 9th February 1908. The engineering on the bridges over the Rivers Stour and Avon requiring some attention. This section had been slightly held up because on an accident on the bridge which spanned the River Avon.

On 12th August 1907 a girder which was being hoisted fell, blocking the single line for about 24 hours. The passengers were conveyed between Milcote and Stratford by road vehicles. The metalwork for the River Avon bridge was supplied, like that of the southern portion, by Messrs E Finch & Co. Chepstow, costing £1,703 4s 3d. Nine brick arches were provided on the approaches to the bridge, to deal with the floods from the River Avon. The span over the river at this point (known locally as Stannals) was 114 ft 6 in which like the old bridge it replaced was built on a skew. The remaining work for the structure cost £3,060. The short section from the East & West Junction to Stratford station had previously been doubled in May 1902.

Further to the north work had commenced on the North Warwickshire line, from Tyseley to Bearley West Junction. The 17 miles 67 chains presented a few problems to the contractor Messrs C J Willis & Son, who had started the work at Henley in Arden on 5th September 1905. This was completed in 1907 and opened for through goods traffic on 9th December, opening for passengers on 1st July 1908. Advantage was also taken to double the line from Stratford Station to Bearley East Junction.

Ever mindful of the future for through long distance running, the GWR Traffic Committee proposed the provision of water troughs between Long Marston and Milcote (this being fairly level ground). This proposal of June 1907 seems to have come to nothing and was rejected by the Great Western Management. Perhaps it was felt that with an abundant supply of water at Stratford and Cheltenham where most of the trains stopped, these additional facilities were superfluous.

At the southern end work had still been going on at Cheltenham to such an extent that the 700 ft island platform at Malvern Road was opened on 30th March 1908. This meant that all principal services could call there, with a connection from St. James. The bay platform at the north end of the station enabled all local steam railmotors from the Honeybourne direction to call here and then reverse into St. James and vice versa, instead of doing this at the junction as they had previously.

By April 1908 the other principal station on the route that of Stratford, had its Up platform extended to 600 ft and the Down to 550 ft. The main station building also received a new booking office and a tea room and bicycle shed was added.

With the completion of the Birmingham & North Warwickshire line the first through service was run from Wolverhampton to Cornwall on 1st July 1908. The Midland Railway which had given the GWR running rights over its route south of Gloucester made through services go into Bristol over its own route (via Mangotsfield). The subsequent case went before the courts and

The earliest known picture of Stratford on Avon station showing the new buildings plus the old 1891 waiting and refreshment rooms on the Up platform. 0–6–0 '1854' class No. 1753 stands in the Down platform with a local train. Notice Boards are laid up against the building awaiting fixing in place. c. 1908.   Photo: Shakespeare Birthplace Trust Record Office

The new waiting and refreshment rooms beyond the footbridge on the Up platform at Stratford on Avon. Stratford on Avon East Signal Box can be seen in the distance and to the right can be seen the water tank on top of the coal stage over by the engine shed. Many adverts adorn this splendid view c. 1908.   *Photo: Shakespeare Birthplace Trust Record Office*

the GWR lost the judgement but undeterred that company proceeded to take it to the Court of Appeal in October, where this time the High Court was overruled in favour of the GWR. From 2nd November 1908 all the GWR trains left the Midland's line at Yate and ran on into Bristol over the GWR route via Filton.

With the North Warwick open, freight services that had until then used the Gloucester to Ledbury route to get merchandise from Gloucester to the Midlands were diverted over the Cheltenham to Stratford line.

In line with improvements to the south of the city, the GWR greatly extended its principal stations in Birmingham (Snow Hill), and built Moor Street (opened in 1909). So extensive was this work that they were never extended again, since they met all its anticipated traffic demands.

7

Stations and Junctions

7.1 Introduction

Along the line no two station layouts were the same although most of the buildings were identical, standardisation being adopted within several designs. Very often the terrain dictated the final position of the goods shed in relation to the station. Buildings were single storey, the main buildings being split into:–

Station Masters Office

Booking Hall

Ladies Waiting Room

Gentlemens Toilet

Both Broadway and Winchcombe had an extension to the roof at the end of the building forming a shelter leading to the footbridge. On the opposite side a waiting room and gentlemens toilets were provided.

These buildings were constructed from red brick, the main structure being gable roof design while the smaller waiting rooms on the opposite side were of the hipped roof design. Bishops Cleeve and Gotherington were built from Cleeve Hill stone with pea grit quins and plinths. The guttering was set back into the top of the wall, thus completing the smart appearance. The windows were narrow and tall to let in plenty of light into the small rooms and were fitted with openings at the top.

None of the stations along the line had a front entrance to the booking hall, so access was gained via the platform and a gate at one end of the building usually the end nearest the footbridge, so that one man could check the tickets at this point.

The platforms were 400 ft long. At first some were constructed of timber due to the ground not settling, but these were later built with brick facings and concrete edging slabs, the remaining platform surface received a 4 in layer of gravel. 'Spear' fencing was added along the backs of the platforms together with the planting of fir trees finished the screening and blending in with the surrounding area.

The goods sheds were to a gable design built of brick (except for Bishops Cleeve, which was built in Cleeve Hill stone). Gotherington was also built of the same stone yet it was much smaller being of hipped roof design. Most of the goods sheds except Gotherington and Weston Sub Edge had roof lights and Winchcombe also had two side loading doors.

Often the rest of the fixtures and fittings such as cattle pens and loading docks were fitted wherever the lie of the land would permit.

Track layouts of the various stations differed one from another (see individual stations), but access was provided from both running lines to the goods sidings, the lead from the line furthest from the yard being via a slip point incorporated in the main crossover. In some layouts refuge sidings were incorporated.

The line had several different designs of signal boxes, constructed of brick, stone or wood, the latter being built on unstable ground. All the boxes were of GWR hipped roof design (except Honeybourne West Loop and Evesham Road Crossing both being replacement boxes dating from 1960, both had flat roofs).

By the turn of the century the Board of Trade still laid down the maximum distance for mechanical operation of points from a signal box. The distances were 200 yards for facing points and 300 yards for trailing, and thus we find that most of the signal boxes were placed in the middle of the station layouts.

Level crossing signal boxes had to be continuously manned but most of the others were provided with block switches, enabling closing at weekends or nights. When the route was fully open then the line was worked by the 'Absolute Block System'. Where a section was long and to enable trains to be kept moving, boxes that were normally closed would open on busy Saturdays such as Weston Sub Edge, Gotherington and Cheltenham Race Course.

Just after the turn of the Century automatic train control was introduced by the GWR but due to the World War I progress was slow and it was not until 1931 that this route was fitted, oddly enough Stratford was the last place to retain a GWR ATC ramp.

The first halts appeared along the line with the opening in 1904. These early platforms were not very high but to help the passengers the steam railmotors had retractable steps. The later platforms were of standard height built of sleepers. The halts were often extended to save the pulling up twice by a railmotor with a trailer coach attached. These halts were provided with waiting shelters, generally of the 'Pagoda' design.

These halts had a porter to book tickets, the halts being attached to the wing of the nearest Station. The attendants/porters were dispensed with under the economies of 1908, so staffing levels would have been at their highest levels before this date.

The steam railmotors could handle extra vehicles if required, up to 24 wheels besides the actual car could be pulled between Honeybourne and Cheltenham. This could be compiled of any of the following:–

1 – converted coach to count as 8 wheels (ordinary coaches converted to trailers).

1 – 59 ft 6 in Trailer to count as 10 wheels

1 – 70 ft Trailer to count as 12 wheels

They of course proved of great value in doing light shunting movements at various times along the route and it was not uncommon to see them with at least one additional coach.

Note for station gazette; the layouts show the capacity of sidings (except where expressed in feet), shown in wagon lengths of 20 ft exclusive of engine and brake van. Plans not drawn to scale.

Total tonnage figures are combined together reflecting both those forwarded and received. All distances on the northern section are measured from Honeybourne station to Stratford and those on the southern section measured from Honeybourne East Loop to Cheltenham (as per the building of the respective lines).

Keys and Symbols used in the station layout diagrams in the following chapter:

A.H.	=	Acetylene Hut
C.P.	=	Cattle Pens
G.F.	=	Ground Frame
G.S.	=	Goods Shed
O.S.	=	Oil Store
P.W.	=	Permanent Way Hut
S.B.	=	Signal Box
W.B.	=	Weighbridge
W.Col.	=	Water Column
W.S.	=	Waiting Shelter

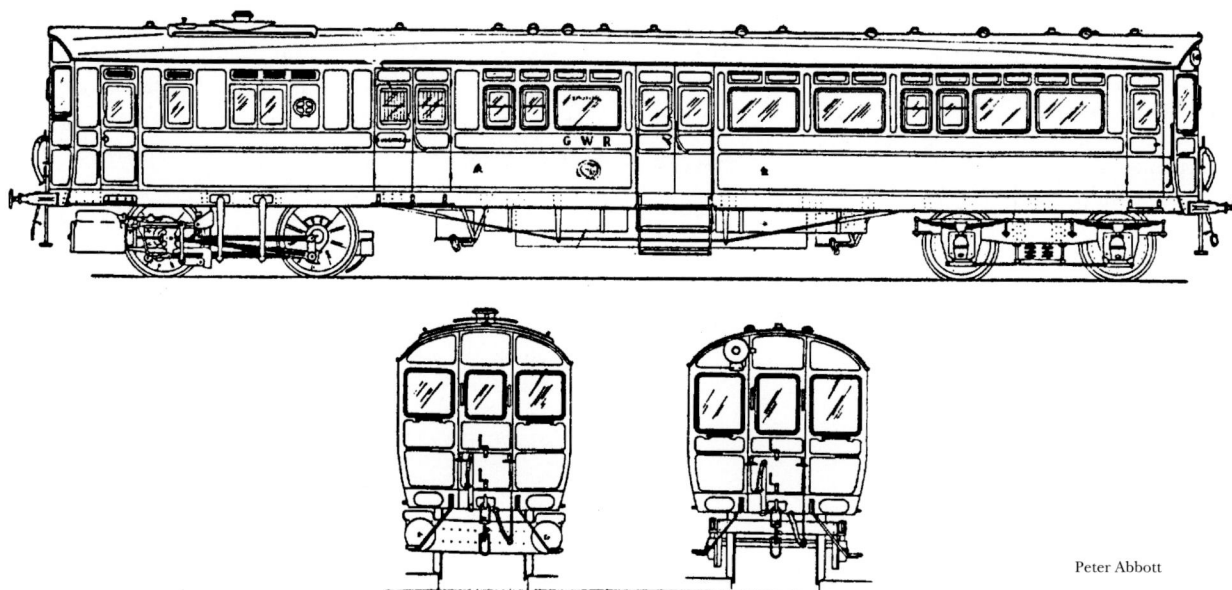

Peter Abbott

A typical layout of a steam railmotor that worked the majority of local services over the line.

7.2

G.W.R.

STRATFORD-ON-AVON

Road. Unlike the OWW line the independent Stratford On Avon Railway Company was mixed gauge and not narrow like that of the OWW. From its opening in 1860 the line was worked by Great Western Railway engines and stock. The station had all the usual facilities including an engine shed with a mixed gauge turntable. Eventually the two separate systems were joined and opened to traffic on 24th July 1861 and from 1st August through services commenced between Leamington and Malvern.

After a meeting held at the Town Hall on 17th September 1861 it was voted that a new station be built beside the Alcester Road at a field called 'The Stile Ground', the site at the Evesham Road being narrowly turned down. From the 1st January 1863 all trains used the station beside the Alcester Road, it was 8 miles 76 chains from Honeybourne. This station was of a temporary nature and the town had to make do with this 'Shed' until after the passing of the Tercentenary celebrations (300 years celebrating the Bards birth) in April 1864. These Tercentenary celebrations were greatly assisted by the railway which played its part with the laying in of extra sidings at both Birmingham Road and Alcester Road, sufficient to take up to 300 extra carriages.

The Traffic Committee of the GWR sanctioned the expenditure for the additional festival sidings but it was not to exceed £400.

The 'new' station duly arrived towards the end of 1865 not having come too far, for it was the original building of the SOA Railway Co. from the Birmingham Road. The station was yet again single sided with buildings and approach road on the side of the then expanding town. The overall roof spanned the adjacent run round/storage line however the station was put at the

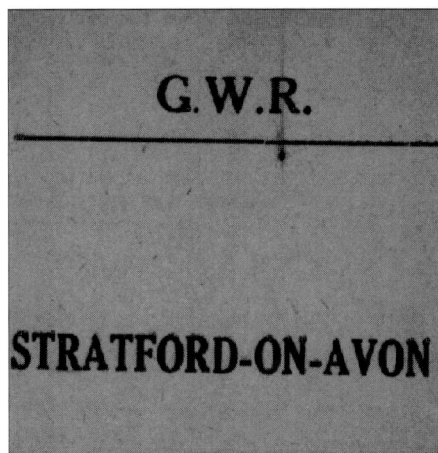

With Stratford being the home of the legendary 'Bard' and since the educating of the English speaking public, people have flocked to the town to see the tranquillity of its setting that gave inspiration to that tongue. It was therefore only natural that railway companies should want to reach it. Upon their arrival the relative 'peace' of the town was shattered but as previously mentioned the railways had taken their time to arrive. The first line was opened from Honeybourne (July 1859) on the OWW system, terminating in Sancta Lane (original name) at 8 miles 35 chains, in a field called Ladye Meadow. It was of a simple layout with engine shed, 40ft turntable, goods shed and single sided platform and like Honeybourne it was provided with a turntable.

The next line that arrived came from Hatton, a line of 9 1/4 miles, which terminated beside the Birmingham

Stratford
Sancta Lane
1859 -1863

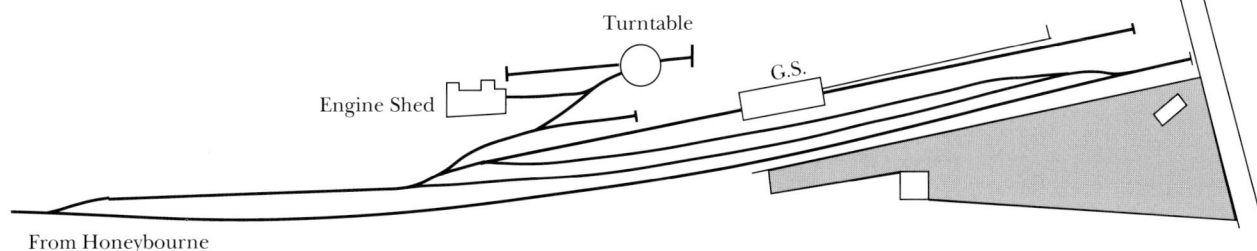

Turntable

G.S.

Engine Shed

From Honeybourne

To Hatton

SOA
Goods Jcn SB

Stratford
Locations

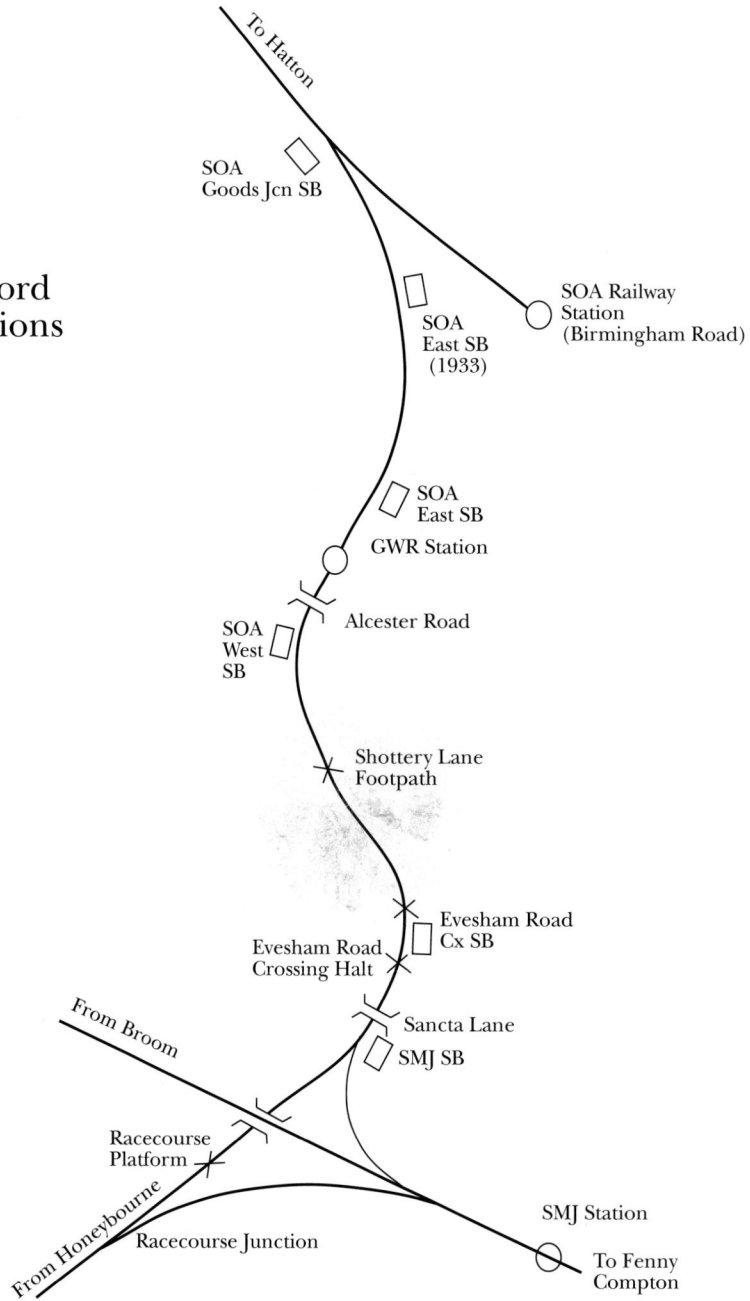

SOA
East SB
(1933)

SOA Railway
Station
(Birmingham Road)

SOA
East SB

GWR Station

Alcester Road

SOA
West
SB

Shottery Lane
Footpath

Evesham Road
Cx SB

Evesham Road
Crossing Halt

From Broom

Sancta Lane

SMJ SB

Racecourse
Platform

From Honeybourne

SMJ Station

Racecourse Junction

To Fenny
Compton

middle of a reverse 'S' giving the building a bad reputation amongst the Stratford populous.

The curve to the north was eased in 1908 and the original alignment can still be seen to this day. The overall roof would appear to have lasted some time. It was damaged in a gale in January 1886 and although a new separate Up platform was added in late 1891 it would appear that the overall roof was still in situ in May 1894 (a fire at Warwick station in that month destroyed a similar structure there). When doubling of the line took place it had been dispensed with and new refreshment and waiting rooms were added to the Up platform c. 1908.

A footbridge had been installed when the Up platform was built in 1891. An Up bay was later added, which was extended to become a loop line on 1st April 1911. This loop reverted to a bay in May 1969 with the withdrawal of the Worcester, Honeybourne, Stratford and Birmingham services on 5th May. The Up platform was 585 ft long. The Down platform was 563 ft with a bay platform at the northern end (which at one time contained a wagon turntable) the longest edge of which was 160 ft long.

The Birmingham Road station site continued to be used by broad gauge stock for excursions and horse boxes, proving very popular with 1/2 day excursionists and with the notorious 'mops, circus and runaways'. The 7 ft 0¼ in system lasted until 1st April 1869 although the 'Third' rail was not taken up immediately due to excess materials causing compensation arguments between the GWR and SOA companies.

Just a little further to the north where the two systems joined, a junction had been formed and would appear not to have been partially interlocked (as other WMR junctions were at that time). Upon inspection, Colonel Yolland strongly recommended that the arrangements adopting signals and points be adopted at this junction (later to become Goods Junction). As late as November 1865 mixed gauge trains were still being run from Hatton causing oversights by the staff resulting in derailments at this point. When the junction had a permanent box is unclear, but a structure was replaced in 1891 by a new 17 lever box. This structure lasted until 1908, being replaced by a 29 lever box.

Stratford's third line came with the opening of the East & West Junction Railway (Stratford to Kineton) on 1st July 1873. The East & West Junction ran its

Sunday engineering (i) Busy scene looking south at the junction leading around from the Stratford and Midland Junctions Station on the left. c. 1935. This was the site of the original Sancta Lane terminal.
Photo: A T Locke

Stratford on Avon

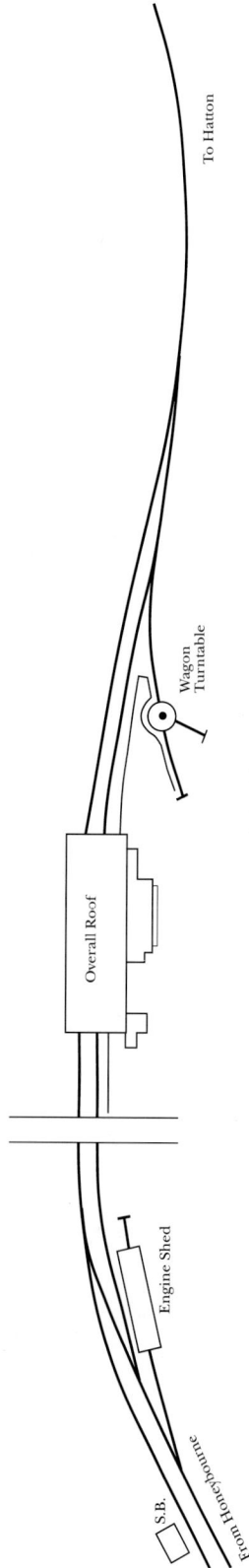

To Hatton

Wagon Turntable

Overall Roof

Engine Shed

S.B.

From Honeybourne

c. 1885

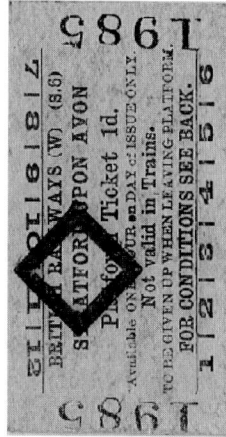

STRATFORD-UPON-AVON

BRIT... RAILWAYS (W) (S.6)
STRATFORD UPON AVON
Pl... for Ticket 1d.
Available ON ...UR ...DAY ... ISSUE ONLY.
Not valid in Trains.
TO BE GIVEN UP WHEN LEAVING PLATFORM.
FOR CONDITIONS SEE BACK.

1985

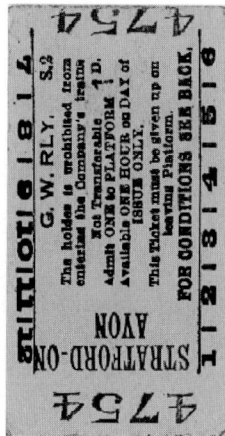

4754

G. W. RLY.   S.2

The holder is prohibited from
entering the Company's trains.
Not Transferable.
Admit ONE to PLATFORM   1 D.
Available ONE HOUR on DAY of
ISSUE ONLY.

This Ticket must be given up on
leaving Platform.

FOR CONDITIONS SEE BACK.

STRATFORD-ON-AVON

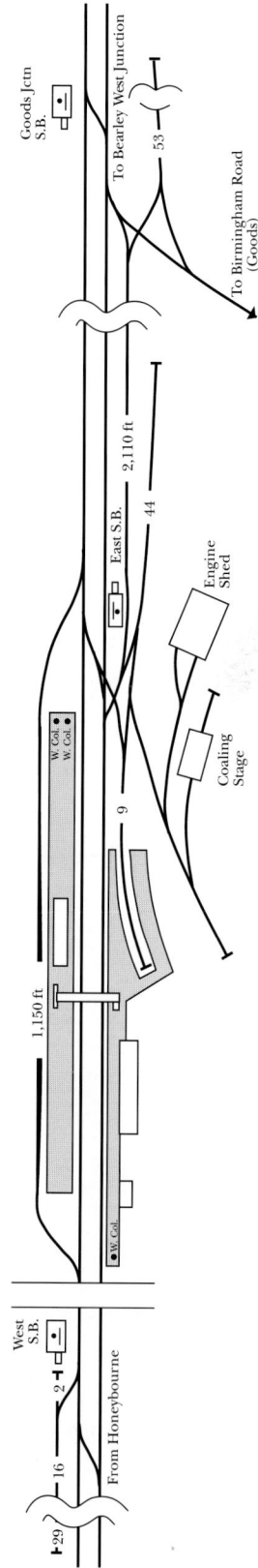

Goods Jctn S.B.

To Bearley West Junction

53

To Birmingham Road (Goods)

East S.B.

2,110 ft

44

Engine Shed

Coaling Stage

W. Col.
W. Col.

9

1,150 ft

W. Col.

West S.B.

2

16

29

From Honeybourne

c. 1920

In the late evening sun Mogul No. 4397 drifts into Stratford at the head of a local train, on 21st May 1935. The engine was later condemned in March 1936. Parts of the locomotive were used on No. 6805 Broughton Grange *(built 15th September 1936) see page 49 for sighting of this locomotive.* Photo: L T Parker

ROD No. 3038 shunts in the Birmingham Road goods yard on 4th March 1935. Built in May 1918 it was withdrawn from service in July 1956. Photo: L T Parker

Mogul No. 6338 stands alongside Austerity No. 90483 outside Stratford shed on 5th January 1960.   Photo: G England

'Such things dreams are made' 2-8-0 No. 2879 stands outside Stratford engine shed on a summers evening near to the water column on 16th August 1959.

Photo: G England

trains into the Alcester Road Station causing further chaos at the already overcrowded situation. This lasted only briefly, for the East & West Junction's own station was ready the following year. In order for its trains to run into the Alcester Road Station a junction was formed with the Honeybourne line at the site of the old Sancta Lane Station. Under the 1873 Act of the Evesham, Redditch and Stratford Upon Avon Junction Railway, the East & West route was extended by 7³/₄ miles to the west to meet at a junction at Broom with the Redditch to Evesham line. This section of line was opened in June 1879. The new line crossed the Honeybourne branch at a point about ¹/₂ mile south of the junction at Sancta Lane. A bridge was thrown over the branch but not until the GWR had secured an agreement for the new line to construct a double width bridge, which meant that the GWR would not incur any further expense when the time came to double their line.

At the old site of Sancta Lane some facilities would still have been in use after the opening of the Alcester Road Station in 1863. The engine shed and facilities were still there although all goods were going on to the Birmingham Road terminus.

The engine shed that appeared later to the south of the Alcester Road on the Down side of the line is of unknown construction date. It shows up on a map of 1885 and could be as early as 1873, when the East & West Junction had opened. This shed was taken out of use c. 1908 and replaced by a larger two road shed (at a cost of £4,970) to the north of the station that lasted until closing on 10th September 1962.

The telegraph had been installed soon after the opening of the line from Honeybourne. The lines to Stratford were worked by staff & ticket. By 1871 the Honeybourne to Stratford staff was square in shape and the ticket was white in colour and the Hatton to Stratford section was round in shape and had a red ticket.

With the whole of the line into Stratford from the north being doubled and realigned with the opening of the North Warwick line (1st July 1908) a further signal box to the north of the station was added; Stratford on Avon East Signal Box opened around this time containing 35 levers. This box was replaced on 13th August 1933 by a new East Signal Box a little to the north and half way between the old East and Goods Junction, thus replacing the old Goods Junction Signal Box at the same time. This new East Box of wooden construction contained 55 levers, and had previously been at Acton West. Today it remains Stratford's only signal box. When the Ministry of Food opened its depot to the west of the station on 20th July 1942 it was this box that controlled the exit of the two sidings.

The new Stratford on Avon East Signal Box (ex Acton) August 1933. Photo: A T Locke

By 1885 a signal box had been provided to the south of the station, opposite the engine shed. This box was replaced in 1891 by a new box called the Stratford on Avon Station Signal Box. The frame was of 21 levers, but this was lengthened to 29 levers by February 1911, meanwhile it had been renamed Stratford on Avon West Signal Box in 1908. This box lasted until 18th May 1969. It was this box that became well known throughout the area as 'The Palace' for it was kept in pristine condition by its regular signalmen. Any important visitor to the station would be escorted by the Station Master to the box to be shown just how things should be kept!

Just behind the box was one of Stratfords dominant features, a tall water tower. Built in 1886 it lasted until May 1970.

Shottery Footpath Signal Box was a small signal box working 14 levers of which 4 were spare. The box was of a temporary nature and was situated on a footpath leading from the town to nearby Shottery, between the station and Evesham Road crossing. The existing loop to the south of Evesham Road Crossing was extended through that crossing to a point 300 yards further north (the level crossing at Evesham Road had to be widened). This work was

Mogul No. 9314 passes the adjacent Stratford engine shed with a Down freight on 29th April 1958. In June of the same year the locomotive was renumbered into the 73xx series.   *Photo: G England*

Mogul No. 5336 passes Shottery footpath south of Stratford with a Down evening goods train on 20th August 1959. A banking engine awaits in the headshunt for its next duty by the West Signal Box.   *Photo: G England*

Sunday engineering (ii) More than one gang would be involved in the slewing outside Stratford on Avon West Signal Box. Taken from the Alcester Road bridge looking south. c. 1935.   *Photo: A T Locke*

carried out to the west of the existing single line and Shottery Signal Box was opened c. September 1899 to control the northern section of the double lines south to East & West Junction. It was subsequently closed c. May 1902, when the Up line was again extended to meet the old siding running out of the station. A new siding was added next to the old one, on the west side of the line.

The road system within the town crossed the line in several places with bridges being built at Sancta Lane in 1864 and Alcester Road in October 1861. This means that for a short time both roads would have had to have been gated in some way like that at Evesham Road that lay between. A cabin was presumably provided for the gatekeeper at the latter but probably no levers nor signals existed. The Evesham Road structure was replaced c. 1891 this new Signal Box having only 13 levers.

A 6 in high railmotor halt (at 8 miles 41¹/₂ chains) of 100 ft length was opened on 17th October 1904. This was situated just to the south of the Evesham Road level crossing and was closed to traffic on 14th July 1916.

Evesham Road Crossing Box with signalman L Emms taken 8th August 1937.   *Photo: A T Locke*

Austerity No. 90403 heads a train towards Broom while in the foreground the new connecting curve awaits to be opened (12th June 1960) the line to the left being the Stratford to Cheltenham line. The Racecourse Platforms are just visible on the left. This marvellous panoramic view was taken on 29th May 1960.   *Photo: G England*

It is unclear whether the box at the junction of the East & West system and the old Honeybourne branch was in position upon the opening of the East & West line. Some form of control existed and once the East & West had its own station, traffic over the junction became very light. The connection became gated and was used as an exchange siding. Later the signal box on the GWR line was known as S&M Junction Signal Box and later still London Midland Railway Junction Signal Box.

Both the old Evesham Road Crossing Signal Box and the old East & West Junction Signal Box were replaced on 12th June 1960. The new Evesham Road Crossing Signal Box contained 50 levers plus a gate wheel and controlled the new running junction facing to the south. This junction was built to aid the running of South Wales to Banbury ironstone traffic (which had previously gone via Hatton and Bearley) and allowed

the closure of the Stratford to Broom line. Yet this was shortlived for the traffic did not materialize and the new curve closed to traffic on 5th July 1965. The box was last regularly manned on 22nd September 1976 and the line to Long Marston severed by 10th August 1980.

The line to the south crossed the River Avon by Stannals bridge running along a short embankment, this bordering on the adjacent Stratford racecourse. Racing had taken place in the meadows here as far back as c. 1770, but it took the GWR until the 6th May 1933 to realise the potential. The platforms were opened to serve the course, though no shelters were provided upon the 550 ft platforms.

The new junction (known as Racecourse Junction) was created in June 1960 making its connection with the Milcote to Stratford section just to the south of the halt.

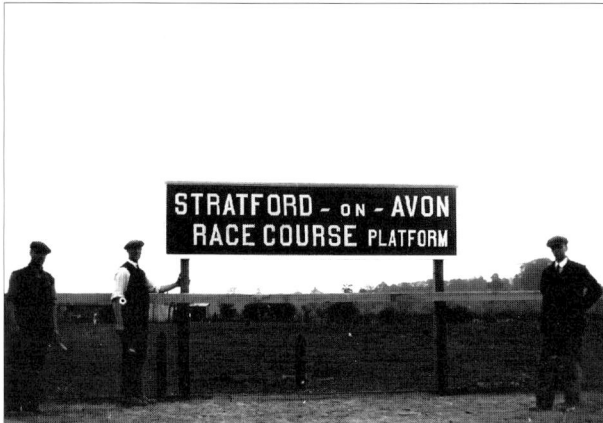

The finishing touches being added to Stratford on Avon Race Course Platform. It was usual practice to hang a separate board underneath this proclaiming the date of the next race meeting. The photo was taken just prior to the Platform opening on 6th May 1933. Photo: A T Locke

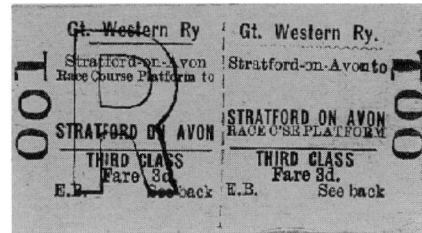

Some of the very first tickets issued from Stratford to Stratford on Avon Race Course Platform. Courtesy: A T Locke

Pannier No. 3775 accelerates away with the ex 1.47 pm, Stratford to Evesham local. The location is the racecourse junction but more interesting is the fact that the date is 11th April 1958 some two years before the junction opened. Photo: G England

Great Western Railway

STRATFORD-ON-AVON STEEPLECHASES

First Race 2.0 p.m. each date.   UNDER NATIONAL HUNT RULES.   Last Race 5.30 p.m. each date.
Admission Charges (including Tax) Course 2/-, Grand Stand and Paddock 12/-.
TOTALISATOR MEETING.

On SATURDAYS, MAY 6th and 20th
EXCURSIONS TO
Stratford-on-Avon

FROM	Depart				RETURN FARES To Stratford-on-Avon Station or Racecourse Plat.		RETURN TIMES SAME Day	
					First Class	Third Class	Stratford-on-Avon Racecourse Plat. Depart	Stratford-on-Avon Station Depart
	p.m.	p.m.	p.m.	p.m.	s. d.	s. d.	p.m.	
Wolverhampton (L.L.)	—	—	12 40	—	7 0	4 0		
Bilston (G.W.)	—	—	12 47	—	6 0	3 6		
Wednesbury	—	—	12 53	—	0	3 6		
West Bromwich	—	—	1 2	—	0	3 0	6 0	
Handsworth (G.W.)	—	—	1 6	—	0	3 0		
Soho & Winson Green	—	—	1 12	—	5 0	3 0		
Hockley	—	—	1 15	—	5 0	3 0		
BIRMINGHAM (S.H.)	—	—	1 25	—	4 6	2 6		
Bordesley	—	—	1 30	—	4 6	2 6		
Small Hth & Sparkbrook	—	12 31	1B 10	1 26	4 6	2 6		
Tyseley	—	12 35	1B 7	1 30	4 6	2 6		
Acocks Gn. & Sth Yardley	—	—	12B 59	—	4 6	2 6		
			noon					
Dudley	—	—	12F 0	—	6 0	3 6		
			p.m.					
Stourbridge	—	—	12F 48	—	7 0			
Stourbridge Junction	—	—	12F 54	—	7 0		6F 0	
Lye	—	—	12F 34	—	7 0			
Cradley Hth & Cradley	—	—	12F 38	—	6 0	3 6		
Old Hill	—	—	12F 44	—	6 0	3 6		
Rowley Regis & B'heath	—	—	12F 49	—	6 0	3 6		
Langley Gn. & Rood End	—	—	12F 53	—	0	3 6		
Leamington Spa	12 50	—	—	—	2 0			
Warwick	12 54	—	—	—	2 0	1 3		
Hatton	1 2	—	—	—	1 9	1 0		
Claverdon	1 7	—	—	—	1 0	9		
Bearley	1 11	—	—	—	1 0	9		
Spring Road	—	12 38	—	1 33	4 6	2 6		
Hall Green	—	12 41	—	1 36	4 6	2 6		
Yardley Wood	—	12 45	—	1 40	3 6	2 0		
Shirley	—	12 49	—	1 44	3 6	2 0		
Grimes Hill & W. Plat.	—	12 54	—	1 49	3 6	2 0		
Earlswood Lakes	—	12 57	—	1 52	2 6	1 6		
Wood End	—	1 1	—	1 56	2 6	1 6		
Danzey (for Tanworth)	—	1 5	—	2 1	2 6	1 6		
Henley-in-Arden	—	1 15	—	2 9	2 0	1 3		
Alcester	12C 50	—	—	1E 50	2 3	1 6		
Great Alne	12C 57	—	—	1E 56	2 0	1 3		
Olton	12H 20	—	—	—	4 6	2 6		
Solihull	12G 35	—	—	—	3 6	2 0		
Knowle and Dorridge	12G 41	—	—	—	3 6	2 0		
Lapworth	12G 46	—	—	—	2 6	1 6		
	a.m.							
Banbury	11J 52	—	—	—	7 0	4 0	5D 40	

		p.m.	p.m.	p.m.	p.m.
Stratford-on-Avon Station	arr.	1 20	1 31	—	2 25
Stratford-on-Avon Racecourse Platform	„	1 42	1A 42	2 12	2 28

A—Change at Stratford-on-Avon Station. B—Change at Bordesley. C—Change at Bearley. D—Change at Stratford-on-Avon Station and Leamington Spa. E—Stratford-on-Avon Station arrive 2.15 p.m. F—Change at Birmingham (Snow Hill). G—Change at Hatton. H—Change at Solihull and Hatton. J—Change at Leamington Spa.

In the event of the Races being postponed or abandoned, the special facilities announced on this bill will not be given.

CONDITIONS OF ISSUE OF EXCURSION TICKETS AND OTHER REDUCED FARE TICKETS
Excursion and other tickets at fares less than the ordinary fares are issued subject to the Notices and Conditions shown in the Company's current Time Tables.
Children under Three years of age, Free ; Three and under Fourteen, Half-price.

LUGGAGE ARRANGEMENTS
DAY AND HALF-DAY EXCURSION TICKETS.—Passengers holding day or half-day excursion tickets by special trains are not allowed to take any luggage except small handbags, luncheon baskets, or other small articles intended for the passenger's use during the day. On the return journey only, passengers may take with them, free of charge, at Owner's Risk, goods for their own use, not exceeding in the aggregate 60lbs.

For any further information respecting the arrangements shown in this Bill, application should be made at any of the Company's Stations or Offices ; to
Mr. W. E. HART, Divisional Superintendent, Snow Hill Station, Birmingham. *Telephone Central 7944* (extension—" Enquiries ") ; or to
Mr. H. L. WILKINSON, Superintendent of the Line, Paddington Station, W.
Paddington Station, April, 1933.   JAMES MILNE General Manager.

B.H. 31/155. B.H. 15,000.   Printed by Joseph Wones Ltd., West Bromwich ; also at Birmingham and London.

Notice giving details of the first excursions to Racecourse Platform.

Courtesy: S Webb

Out of gauge loads became a common sight at Stratford, for it was an ideal route to get these bulky items from the builders in Birmingham to the South Wales docks for transhipment overseas, this taking place mainly on Sundays. Examples are as follows:–

14th June 1936	4 sleeping cars for China Railways.
4th July 1937	3 diesel loco cars for Argentina.
4th October 1937	7 GPO vans for India.
1st October 1939	7 double deck sheep vans for India State Railway.

With all the excursion traffic and other workings Stratford received many unusual locomotives. Members of the 57xx class that were built by outside contractors saw passage over the route on their journey to Swindon for checking. On 19th February 1931 examples noted in a 'raft' of these locomotives were; Nos. 7770–4 ex North British Locomotive Co. and 7775–6 ex Armstrong Whitworth. The first sighting of a Grange locomotive came on 16th October 1936 when No. 6805 *Broughton Grange* was seen on an Up fast goods from Cardiff to Banbury.

The majority of through passenger trains stopped at Stratford with some services running in 4 parts on summer Saturdays. The Up services were impeded by the Wilmcote bank (1 in 75) to the north, which meant that engines would have to help fully laden holiday trains returning from the south coast, by double heading to Earlswood (this was not a success due to time lost uncoupling the assisting locomotive) or on through to Birmingham. Tyseley shed would send out sufficient locomotives for this purpose and on Saturday evenings as many as eight would be awaiting these expresses. The initial climb out of the station going north was often banked between the West Signal Box and the East Signal Boxes starting signal.

Local services consisted of Leamington and Birmingham trains from the north (the latter over the North Warwick line running out of Moor Street, although most of the through trains came from neighbouring Snow Hill Station) and from the south local services came from Worcester or Evesham via Honeybourne.

In 1903 staff totals for the passenger station was 17 with passenger receipts amounting to just over

Hall No. 6948 Holbrooke Hall *passes to the south of the racecourse junction with an evening Birmingham Snow Hill to Worcester service on 14th April 1960.*

Photo: G England

£12,000, throughout the 1920s and 1930s 36 men were employed with an average £24,000 in receipts per year. On the goods side (Birmingham Road) 14 men were employed by 1913 on the site that brought in £29,000 this representing 86,449 tons in merchandise. During the 1920s about 20 staff were employed this figure being slightly reduced in the 1930s to around 16 (1932) averaging £35,000 every year throughout this period, which in turn represented an average of 58,000 tons. The (1907) weighbridge at the station had been of 15 ton capacity but was renewed to a 20 ton variety in 1930.

At the end of the summer timetable (9th September 1962) through scheduled services ceased from the West of England and South Wales, yet summer Saturdays to the West of England continued until September 1966. The withdrawal of the Gloucester to Leamington DMU's took place on 23rd March 1968. Finally the local service from Worcester and Evesham via Honeybourne was withdrawn on 5th May 1969.

7.3   Wilcox & Raites Siding

At approximately 7 miles 10 chains from Honeybourne a private siding was installed for Messrs Wilcox & Raites. It was built to hold 6 wagons for the construction of the nearby Stratford Sewerage Scheme. This gated siding was controlled by a ground frame of 2 levers, locked by keys attached to the electric train staff. The siding was completed by the end of November 1904 and it is believed to have been taken out of use in January 1907.

7.4   Chambers Crossing Halt

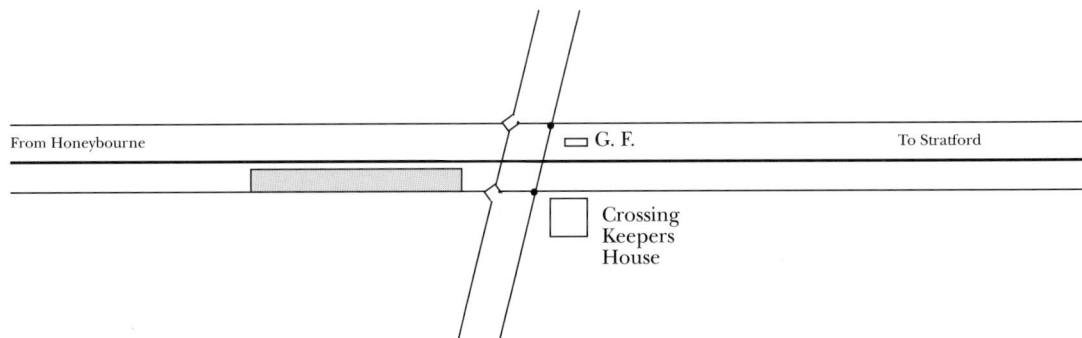

Like the other two halts along the Honeybourne to Stratford line Chambers Crossing Halt was opened on 17th October 1904 for steam railmotors, and closed on 14th July 1916. At 6 miles 34 chains the original halt was a single platform, situated to the south of the crossing and on the eastern side of the line. The lane that crossed at this point ran from Clifford Chambers to Weston on Avon. There had been a crossing keepers house here from about c. 1899 and when the halt was built the

> *gates were worked by a ground frame and protected by signals.*

This ground frame was situated on the west side of the line to the north of the crossing when first open, but when the line was doubled (opening for traffic on 9th February 1908) the frame was moved to the opposite side of the line next to the keepers cottage. It was on this date that an additional platform was added to the Up side at a cost of £75. The 100 ft platforms lacked any form of shelter but were provided with lamps and nameboards.

7.5   Pearces Crossing

Just to the south of Chambers Crossing Halt and some 520 yards north of Milcote level crossing was a small occupation crossing (at 6 miles 16½ chains) that was protected by warning bells. In both directions these warning bells were activated by treadles.

Chambers Crossing Halt

From Honeybourne   ▭ G. F.   To Stratford

Crossing Keepers House

7.6

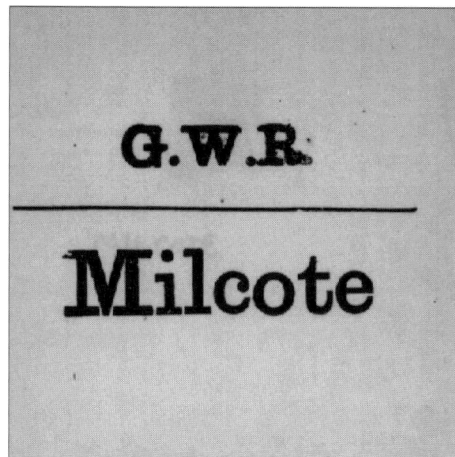

pleted to the north to Stratford (East & West Junction) on 9th February 1908.

Milcote's first Station Master was Mr G J Priday. His station only had the one platform to the south of the crossing, being of 196 ft long until the above doubling. The new platforms of 400 ft on the Up and Down sides (at 5 miles 78 chains) were added to the north of the level crossing, being completed on 7th May 1908. The

Milcote Signal Box interior taken in the mid 50's. Signalman Keith Hopkins poses along with a friend beside the level crossing gate wheel. Photo: K Hopkins

Milcote, Weston and Welford (as the 1861 timetable shows the name) served as mentioned the above villages. The station was situated 5 miles 72 chains from Honeybourne. The level crossing here was not doubled (like that at Long Marston) until the widening scheme of 1907. The double line was opened from Long Marston on the 3rd March of that year and com-

Milcote

c. 1896

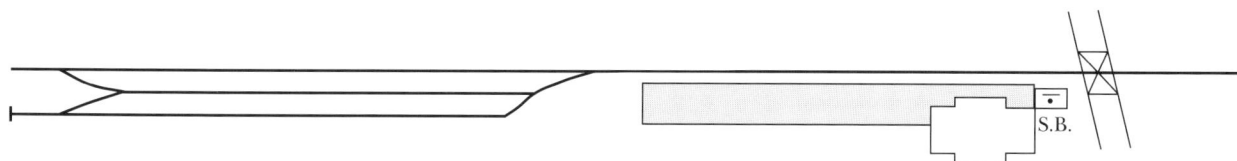

c. 1909

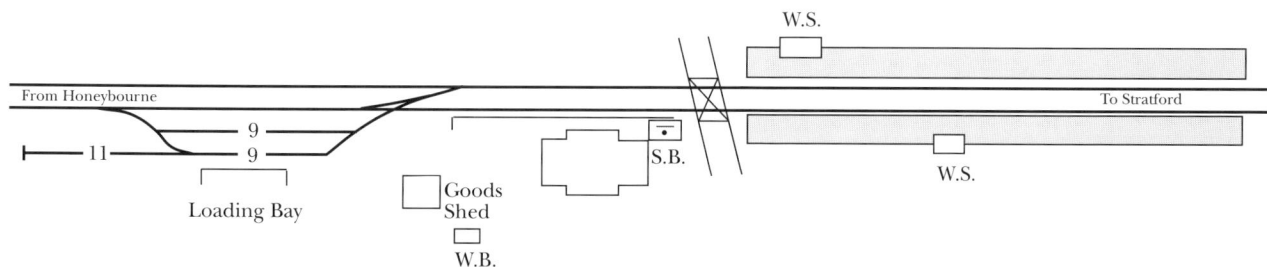

The platform edge has already been removed by the time this photograph was taken (c. February 1966). Having closed the previous month to passengers no time has been wasted in obtaining clearance for high speed running through the platform. An Up service in charge of a DMU speeds through Milcote Weston & Welford on a wet winters day. Photo: G H Tilt

Milcote Down local passenger behind No. 1014 County of Glamorgan. Photo: K Hopkins

original 10 ton weighbridge was replaced in 1932 by a 15 ton version that lasted until June 1964.

Although no record exists of a signal box until c. 1891 some form of control must have been here before then, perhaps a cabin with duties carried out by a gate-keeper and then a porter signalman. The 1891 box contained 21 levers 2 of which were spare and in addition had a gate wheel and 2 wicket levers. The frame was renewed c. 1903. This class 4 box was eventually relegated to a crossing frame (ie no longer a block post) on 29th June 1973, closing in late 1976. No block switch was provided due to the level crossing.

By 1903 the staff numbered 4 and by 1931 had risen to 5 and now came under the control of the station master at Long Marston. Total receipts averaged £1,500 with tonnage being in the region of 1,800 tons per annum throughout the 1930s. There was a coal merchant here but towards the end this did not generate much traffic. Latterly the only traffic that was forwarded being sugar beet and then only during the season.

It was during World War II that the station received attention from the German Airforce (Luftwaffe). A train was attacked while in the station area. Little damage resulted but a bullet found its way into the woodwork of the Down platform waiting room side window and the subsequent hole remained until the station closed.

On the 1st March 1956 the station became unstaffed and was closed to goods on 1st July 1963, passengers following on 3rd January 1966. The empty Station Masters house adjoining the main building (similar to that at Long Marston) became the home of the then

Winchcombe signalman who commuted daily.

The signal box lever frame was obtained by the Birmingham Railway Museum, Tyseley and the brickwork went to the Great Western Society at Didcot. Long after the rails had been lifted the ones on the level crossing remained in situ, until eventually they were taken out by private contractor on 19th November 1984.

The area has since been landscaped and a small car park has been made to accommodate walkers who can traverse the track bed. The Long Marston to Stratford Racecourse section having been made into a ride and walk way with Milcote falling half way between these points.

Castle No. 5046 Earl Cawdor *heads the Down 'Cornishman' past the yard at Milcote on 31st May 1961. This locomotive was withdrawn some 16 months later.*   *Photo: G England*

7.7

G. W. R.

Long Marston

At 3 miles 32 chains north of Honeybourne lay the station of Long Marston, it served both its namesake and Quinton to the east. This latter place became much bigger in population due to the housing of the staff for the War Departments camp built adjacent to the station during World War II. The road from both these places ran across the line at this point thus causing the need for a level crossing.

The station was opened with the opening of the branch from Honeybourne to Stratford on Avon on 12th July 1859. It then consisted of only one platform and the usual station building, it is doubtful that a signal box existed during these early years but there probably was some kind of cabin. A gatekeeper would be charged with the working of the crossing that would have been operated by hand with all the other fittings.

By 1868 cattle pens were added at an authorized cost of £14. In 1872 the station layout enjoyed the luxury of becoming a crossing place, a staggered platform arrangement was added (costing £212), and the Up platform being located to the south of the Down platform. The level crossing still remained single. The cost of rearrangement of the points and the installation of the locking gear came to £975 10s. This work was duly inspected on 3rd April 1872 from which date we can assume that a signal box came into being.

The staggered platform arrangement was short lived, in 1892 the Up platform was done away with and a new one built opposite the Down platform which was lengthened simultaneously, becoming 405 ft as opposed to 402 ft of the Up. The crossing loop was extended to the north of the level crossing which therefore required double gates and a new box came into being with 19 levers and 6 spare. A ground frame (released from the box) of 5 levers controlled the south end of the yard.

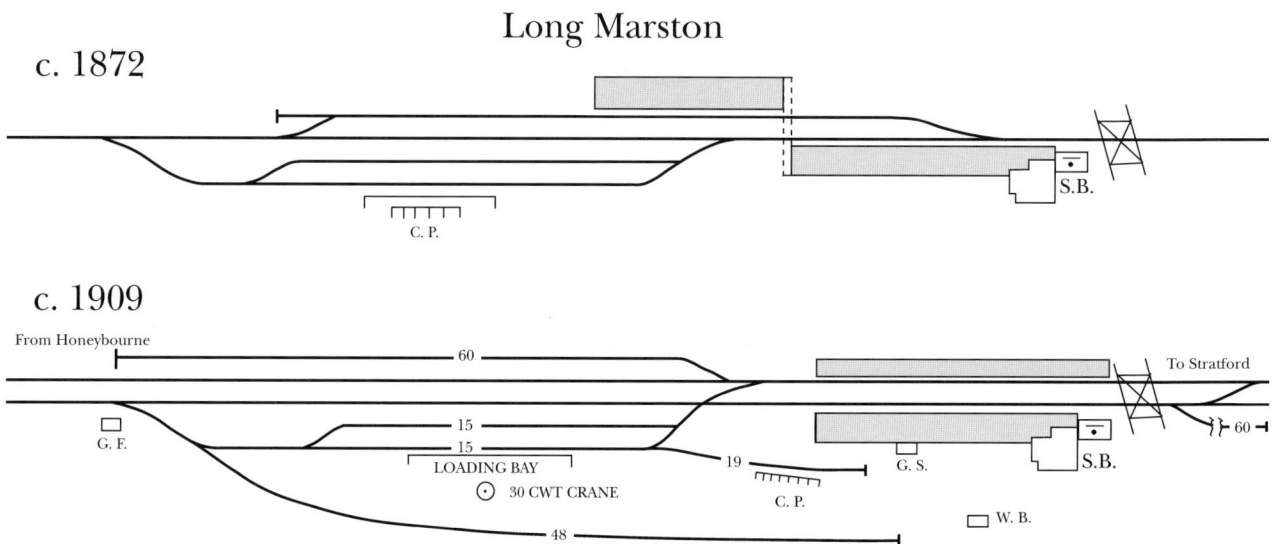

Long Marston

c. 1872

C. P.

S.B.

c. 1909

From Honeybourne

60

To Stratford

G. F.

15
15
LOADING BAY
⊙ 30 CWT CRANE

19

C. P.

G. S.

S.B.

60

☐ W. B.

48

Like the house and signal box at Milcote, Long Marston was very similar in design. This shot was taken at the turn of the century looking north. The steps on the box were later altered to accommodate a toilet for the Signalmen. Milk churns await collection on the Down platform. *Photo: Shakespeare Birthplace Trust Record Office*

Originally the line was worked by staff and ticket. Absolute block was installed in 1890–1, this was considered money ill spent for in 1893 Electric Train Staff was put in for the working of the line. The telegraph had been at the station since its early days but in November 1897 it was extended up into the village to the then Post Office.

The line was eventually doubled to Milcote on 3rd March 1907 and Long Marston to Honeybourne East Loop Junction followed on 28th April 1907, the former being the easiest to construct due to the level terrain. This second set of rails was laid on the Up side throughout from Honeybourne East Loop to East & West Junction except for the existing passing loop at Long Marston.

In September 1936 the signal box frame was increased to 32 levers at a cost of £500. This 1892 box was a class 4 in 1923 and by 1937 had become a class 3 duty. Du-

ring and after World War II the box was continuously manned, before this it had been closed Sunday morning to Monday morning. No block switch was provided because of the level crossing.

The first Station Master here was one William Tyler, the Station Masters house adjoined the main station buildings on the Down platform. Other railwaymens houses were to be found in nearby Wyres Lane. By 1903 the staff numbered 7 with total receipts amounting to just over £2,000, the goods tonnage handled being near to 6,000 tons per annum. During the 1920s staff increased to 8 and average receipts had risen to £7,000 and the goods tonnage went up to 12,000 tons. In 1931 all the staff at Milcote came under the Station Master, making up the total to 12. The early 1950s saw the staff levels peak around 20.

The original 10 ton weighbridge was renewed in 1926 by a similar 10 ton capacity version. This only lasted

Looking south from the footbridge at Long Marston the exchange sidings and MOD yards can be seen to the left. Note the remains of the connection from the Down sidings to the Up line. c. February 1966. Photo: G H Tilt

until 1936, being replaced by a 20 ton variety, which was withdrawn from service on 31st December 1965. This was still in situ at the entrance to the coal wharf until c. 1988. A footbridge was added in the 1930s.

The majority of the freight traffic came from one source and that was from Mickleton to the east of the line. Here Webb's the market gardeners grew cauliflowers in quantity; on average some 1¼ million were grown locally.

If Long Marston could not handle all this traffic then some would be taken to Milcote and sometimes to Weston Sub Edge. By the early 1960s this traffic had ceased, this decline being due to several factors, in that Webbs started to sell their excess plants to the Offenham and Evesham areas, that effectively cut their own throats. Anything that was left of this traffic, which did not go to market via road was centered on Evesham were bulk loading facilities were available.

With the onset of World War II and the mass evacua-

tion from France a need arose to create an Engineer Stores depot in the United Kingdom. Long Marston was chosen as the site for the first such depot. There was easy rail access and the surrounding terrain gave good camouflage from the air. In 1940 the running of the depot was taken over by a detachment from 154 Railway Operating Company Royal Engineers. Covering 455 acres several hundred men were needed to man the depot and its rail system of 45 miles. This was reduced a little and now still boasts 20 miles of track. The depot had seven of its own 0–6–0 locomotives during the hostilities and was handling up to 300 wagons per day in transportation to various ports.

An airfield (like the one at Weston Sub Edge) was constructed to the north east of Long Marston, which brought in more activity to the area during this period.

With 'The Camp' being set up and the War effort in full swing the figures for Long Marston station make interesting reading for the duration of World War II:–

Year	Staff	Pay Bill	Coaching Receipts	Total Tonnage
1939	12	£2,033	N/A	8,020
1940	12	£2,477	N/A	10,189
1941	12	£4,242	£5,460	227,698
1942	12	£6,690	£7,087	391,140
1943	12	£8,749	£8,951	482,538
1944	12	£10,097	£8,302	458,688
1945	12	£9,043	£12,905	357,299

The War Departments extensive sidings ran parallel to the GWR line. A 'West ground frame' (opened June 1941) was installed on the Down line, consisting of 4 levers electrically released by the No. 9 lever in the signal box. There was also another ground frame, the 'East ground frame', which let out traffic from the GWR's own Down sidings, again electrically released from the box (by No. 10 lever). The points giving access to the Up goods loop (nearly 1,100 yards from the signal box) was worked by point motor operated by No. 8 lever in the box.

The decline in traffic resulted in a staff investigation. Carried out towards the end of 1962, this found that over manning existed, economies set in with staff reductions thus meaning an annual saving of nearly £2,000. This only staved off the inevitable, with closure to normal goods traffic coming on 7th September 1964 and passenger services being withdrawn on 3rd January 1966.

With the closure of the through route a way was sought of minimising signalling staff. Long Marston Signal Box was reduced to a ground frame on 24th March 1980. The Ministry of Defence (MOD) and the scrap yard were still served by the Monday–Friday local trip freight from Worcester, and to do away with both Honeybourne West Loop and Long Marston Boxes the layout had to be altered to eliminate reversal at both

Britannia 4-6-2 No. 70045 (formerly Lord Rowallan) *heading a southbound (Saturdays only) express passing the Down yard c. July 1965.*
Photo: G England

Birds eye view from the footplate of Castle No. 5096 Bridgewater Castle, *storming through Long Marston with an Up Swansea to Birmingham Snow Hill express on 20th April 1962.*   Photo: G England

places (at the latter the train had to go over the level crossing and set back into the connection at the south end of the old Down platform into the MOD sidings). So the old North to East Loop curve was reinstated at Honeybourne (13th September 1981) and the track at Long Marston slewed into the south end of the yard, making a direct line into the sidings by 16th November 1981. Long Marston became the last signal box on the old GWR main line to remain open closing on the 16th November 1981.

The long siding of 2 miles 70 chains from the ground frame where the line leaves the Oxford to Worcester route at Honeybourne to the MOD sidings was soon brought up to standard after being singled and slewed, a bridge at Long Marston being totally replaced in July 1985. The actual lifting out of the old bridge (1907) did not take too long but the hire of a 200 ton capacity crane at the rate of £2,000 a day did seem a little excessive, for during its 8 days on hire the heaviest item it had to lift was only 9 1/2 tons!

With the conflict in the Falklands in 1982 the depot remained open 24 hours a day, seeing much activity. Traffic for Birds Commercial Metals Ltd. in the old 'F' yard along with the MOD traffic, remained the only lifeline for the existing section of the route. Birds incidentally was the final resting place for many ex–British Rail engines and coaches. In 1987 the MOD staff numbered 10.

In October 1987 the Corps of Royal Engineers celebrated the granting of the Royal Warrant (1787). This culminated in two days activity centered on Long Marston with its own MOD steam locomotive No. 98 *Royal Engineer* working around the complex with all the other diesels stabled at the site. This was further enhanced by the appearance of 8F 2–8–0 No. 8233 which represented the type of locomotive that did so much during World War II. It was this locomotive that ran to Honeybourne and back with passenger stock on both days (3rd/4th October). This latter date saw the connection made at Honeybourne with a special that was run behind ex Southern Region 4–6–2 Merchant Navy No. 35028 *Clan Line*, that in doing so broke the ban on steam on the Oxford to Worcester line which had been in force since 1975.

The signal box was eventually demolished in November 1989. The last local trip working took place on 29th May 1992, from 31st July of that year the Railway Detachment and branch from Honeybourne was mothballed. Two special workings were run over the branch on 2nd May 1993 in connection with the Worcester Open Day.

7.8 Broad Marston Halt

Broad Marston Halt at 2 miles 9 chains from Honeybourne served the villages of Pebworth, Mickleton and its namesake. It was opened as a railmotor halt on 17th October 1904 with a single platform to the east of the single line, 6 in above rail level and 100 ft long.

The residents of nearby Mickleton appealed to the General Manager, asking provision for accommodation of goods traffic here. However the Traffic Committee met on 10th May 1905 and voted against the request.

Upon the doubling of the line between Honeybourne East Junction and Long Marston on 28th April 1907 another platform was added on the Up side at a cost of £75. No shelter was provided but nameboards and lamps were in existence.

The halt closed as a wartime economy on 14th July 1916.

7.9 Pebworth Halt

To the south of the old Broad Marston Halt at 1 mile 76 chains from Honeybourne a new halt was opened called Pebworth Halt on 6th September 1937. The platforms were 150 ft long and 8 ft wide and both had a small waiting shelter. It was not inspected by the Board of Trade until after 9 years had passed (26th November 1946). In the preceding September the halt had entrained 876 passengers.

This halt faired better than the old one at Broad Marston, managing to stay open until the withdrawal of passenger services on 3rd January 1966. Both Broad Marston and Pebworth Halts came under the control of the Station Master at Long Marston.

Set on embankment between Long Marston and Honeybourne stands lonely Pebworth Halt. Taken in February 1966, looking south. To get to either platform a large flight of wooden steps had to be negotiated.
Photo: G H Tilt

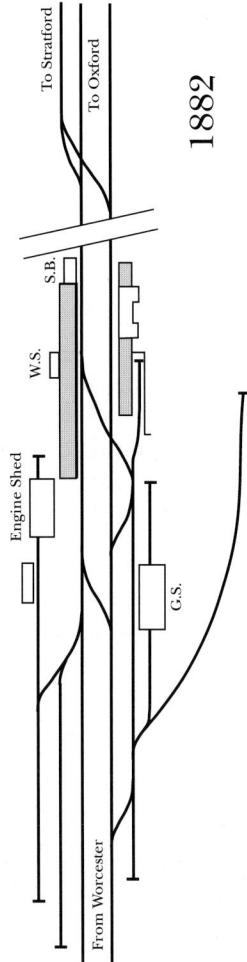

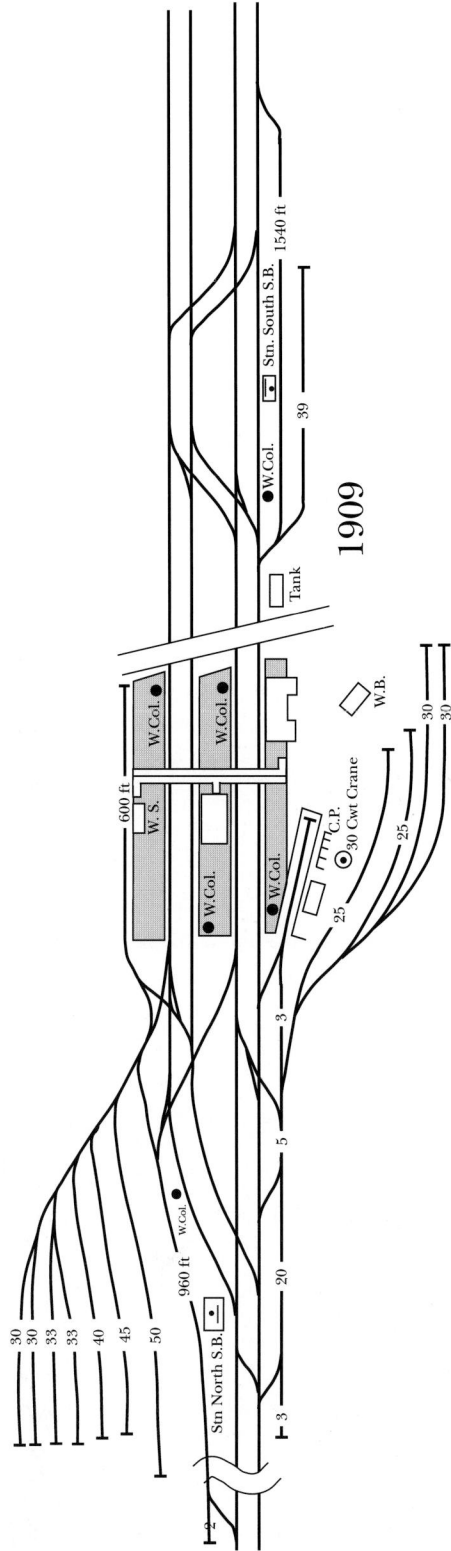

Honeybourne

1882

To Stratford

To Oxford

S.B.

W.S.

Engine Shed

From Worcester

G.S.

1909

Stn. South S.B. 1540 ft

W.Col.

39

W.Col.

Tank

W.Col.

W.Col.

600 ft

W. S.

W.Col.

W.Col.

W.Col.

C.P.

30 Cwt Crane

W.B.

30

30

25

25

3

5

960 ft W.Col.

20

30
30
33
33
40
45
50

Stn North S.B.

3

7.10

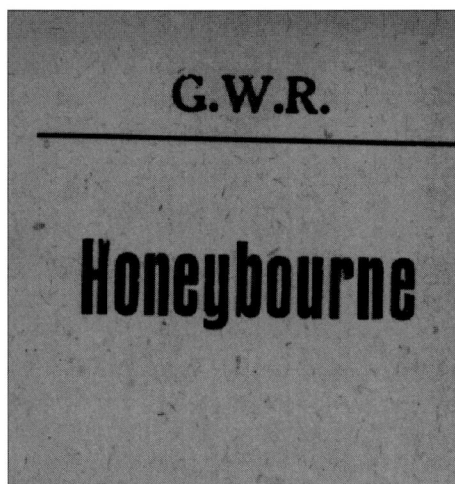

To write of Honeybourne merits a book of it's own. The growth from a humble mixed gauge single line to a very active junction station requires more space than the author (regretfully) can include in this work. Honeybourne is situated on the old Roman road of Icknield Street (sometimes known as Buckle Street), the original village lies to the east of the present one. Today the village is split by the line of the old Roman road and centred around the stream at the crossroads. The village had a population of 336 persons in 1801 rising to 455 by 1851 and with the opening of the line and the branch to Stratford, rose steadily to 502 over the next decade.

When the Oxford, Worcester & Wolverhampton (OWW) was laid out a way had to be found to get off the Cotswolds as effectively and as cheaply as possible in order to descend into the lucrative Vale of Evesham and on to Worcester. Brunel was fortunate

All destinations are mentioned on the nameboard but within two days of this photo being taken (5th March 1960) the last three mentioned were deleted.

Photo: D Bath

to find an outcrop of the Cotswolds that gave access to the Vale just above Honeybourne, it enabled him to plan the line but only via the aid of a tunnel, (Campden tunnel otherwise known as Mickleton) could this be achieved. The line then descended at 1 in 100, being the gentlest gradient available, which proved of great significance in the future of the development of Honeybourne station.

The OWW originally planned to construct a line to Stratford by branching a line off at a junction near Mickleton, this would have meant a junction on the incline and proved even more difficult to operate from a railway point of view than Honeybourne did. Had this plan come to fruition then Mickleton would have become the busy junction but sense prevailed. With Honeybourne at the bottom of the incline it took on a great importance, banking engines worked from here, assisting trains up to Campden or on to Moreton in

Marsh, an arrangement that lasted until the end of steam traction. Other lines were projected realising how important this centre might be, at one stage Honeybourne was being hailed as the 'New Swindon' with all manner of grandiose ideas being projected.

After much adventure the single line of mixed gauge was open from Evesham to Wolvercot Junction (near Oxford) on 4th June 1853. The Board of Trade inspection train had been the only train of broad gauge to traverse the line as far as Evesham just two days previously. At that time the line was worked by pilotman. The 20th March 1855 eventually saw the line double tracked from Evesham to Campden and the section from Honeybourne to Campden worked by electric telegraph. This section was so worked because of the incline and the length of the section (4 miles 87 chains) including the Campden Tunnel (887 yards

Honeybourne (i) c. 1883 This photo shows many features which are referred to in the text. However the double slotted semaphores are worthy of note along with the inside keys on the rail. The engine is running around its train in the Down platform having just arrived from Stratford, the original box overshadows the scene.　　　　　　　　　　　　　　*Photo: C N Clemens*

Honeybourne (ii) taken in 1959 from the same spot as the previous page. The main station building and road bridge are the only things that remain the same.

Photo: C N Clemens

long). With this exception the remainder of the line was worked by time interval. From this date 'Absolute Block' worked the section via the electric telegraph on the bank and was then superseded by using Tyers instruments.

With the opening of the line to Stratford in July 1859 the branch was worked by one engine or two coupled together in steam at once. Soon after the opening telegraph was installed and staff and ticket were introduced, the staff being square in shape and the ticket was white in colour.

A 40ft turntable was added at Honeybourne it then being a requirement of the BoT to have one at both ends of a branch line. It did not last long and was probably taken up with the construction of the new shed in 1870. It is likely that banking engines had been involved at Honeybourne since the opening of the line

but whether an engine shed existed is unclear. The mention of this 'New Shed', which was authorized at a cost of £1,200 along with appliances for water supply, would suggest that one had existed prior to that date.

When the line here was quadrupled and the branch platforms added it was this shed that was taken down in 1907 from near the west end of the Up platform and a similar replacement put in position near the end of the Up branch platform in 1909. This did not last long for it was burnt down on 13th September 1911 following a very hot summer. It was not replaced, the only facility for the engines was a coaling platform of primitive design, thus no covered accommodation existed for the engines.

The original Brunel 'Chalet' type station on the Down platform was replaced in 1872 in two stages with contracts being set at £650 and £895 respectively.

Driver Ted Ayres awaits instructions in the Up yard, in charge of one of the Honeybourne bankers 0-6-0 No. 2207. The locomotive was built in August 1939 and condemned in April 1961. c. 1953
Photo: K Hopkins

When the service opened to Broadway and much later on further to the south, Honeybourne became very congested for both these trains and the Stratford services still had to use the main platforms together with the other traffic (indeed this must have required smart work by all staff concerned) until the branch platforms were ready. The old Up platform building was done away with and replaced by large waiting rooms and a refreshment room, the licensee being the landlord from the 'local' Gate Inn.

The cost of these new buildings came to £3,056 6s 9d, Mr C A Horton carried out the work. A new shelter was provided on the Up branch platform and this was all joined together by a footbridge spanning the four tracks. The main building lasted until closure of the station on 5th May 1969. Both central and branch platforms were 500 ft in length with the main Down platform being 567 ft.

A 30 cwt crane was provided in the Down yard, one having been in existence as early as 1856. The weighbridge was of a 10 ton variety being installed c. 1907, this was replaced in 1926 by a 15 ton version and this in turn was replaced in 1955 by a 20 ton capacity bridge, which was eventually done away with in 1988.

Looking at the annual returns for the station it would suggest at first glance that it was not very busy, tonnage was not vast but then Honeybourne did not generate much traffic of its own. 1913 saw the tonnage handled stand at 6,515 tons, with 1923 at 4,428 tons and 1933 at 5,092 tons. Naturally when the line to the south was under construction all materials came into the contractors sidings via the station, which then (1903) saw the total stand at 44,874 tons. With the onset of World War II, activity increased further here and in 1944 the total tonnage came to 278,942 tons with a staff of 39.

Although on the edge of the Vale the station handled some produce but nothing like the other stations further down the line. These figures were greatly increased with the movement of the annual 'Lamb Sale' traffic, when on the first Wednesday in August lambs would be handled being taken away by the railway to their new owners.

In 1903 the staff numbered 11, rising to 40 by 1923, although this then declined towards World War II, more staff being needed with the addition of extra sidings to the west (Sheenhill) and Weavings sidings to the immediate south of Honeybourne station. The highest figure recorded for staffing levels here came in 1952 when the figure stood at 64, this included 9 drivers. By this time two banking engines and two shunting engines had to be manned.

The shunting and banking engines were rostered to do the following hours per week in 1960;

No. 1 Shunting engine Up yard   145 hrs
No. 2 Shunting engine
              Down yard   119 hrs   15 mins
No. 3 Banking engine   49 hrs   30 mins
No. 4 Banking engine   62 hrs   30 mins

Honeybourne like that of Evesham was a sub shed to Worcester and it was from the latter that the above shunting and banking locomotives would be swapped. The stabling point remained open until 31st December 1965, this date marking the end of steam on the Western Region of British Railways.

For the staff only one house was provided, that of the Station Masters just to the immediate north of the station.

The track layout for Honeybourne was designed to allow trains to be remarshalled, arriving from both Stratford and Cheltenham branches, and then made ready for despatch. Many of the sidings were used to store wagons for servicing all the lines radiating from this point, which made for a very busy location.

Honeybourne became one of the first junctions in the area to have a signal box that was partially interlocked and was one of the few along the OWW line. The date for its construction is uncertain, but it is probable that it dates from the early 1860s to the mid 1860s period. Other details about it are unknown but a picture of it has survived, showing how tall the structure was thus

Visitor from afar. J25 0-6-0 No. 2071 is seen here on the head shunt at Honeybourne, having come on loan to the GWR from the LNER due to chronic locomotive shortage. Loaned in November 1939 it stayed until it returned to the LNER in November 1946, returning under its new number '5696' which the GWR carried out for the LNER.   *Photo: M Shorland*

giving the policeman/signalman a good view up the bank over the road bridge. It only had control over the station area and it is not certain what it worked. It was situated at the Campden end of the Up platform and was made entirely of wood. Looking at the photograph it would suggest that it was not of GWR design but was perhaps installed by a contractor, perhaps Saxby & Farmer or more likely McKenzie & Holland who were based at Worcester. This structure was replaced around 1883 by a box on the other side of the road bridge, nearer to the junction for the line to Stratford. Again little is known about the box but other boxes were constructed simultaneously along the OWW line. Two from that period are still standing, namely Moreton in Marsh and Ascott under Wychwood, and it can therefore be deduced that they were of a similar design to this second Honeybourne Box. It had 31 levers and at the time of the widening in the station area all of these were in use. At the time of construction Absolute Block was introduced along the main line c. 1882–4.

As early as March 1871 engine whistles were used to indicate to the signalman the direction they wished to go at Honeybourne:–

For the main line	1 Whistle
For Stratford	2 Whistles
For Hatton	3 Whistles

The second box was probably not very tall but it restricted the vision of the signalmen especially with regard to the station area. Most of the goods yard would have been controlled by hand points, only the crossover and junction points plus associated signals being worked from this box. When the widening was completed in 1909 this box witnessed a complete change in its surroundings, no longer a humble country station with a single line junction but a fully quadrupled layout, servicing the surrounding districts. The old 31 lever box was replaced by two boxes at either end of the extensive layout, Honeybourne Station North and Honeybourne Station South Signal Boxes were brought into use in January 1909 and March 1909 respectively. Having quadrupled the station, more sidings had to be laid. Owing to World War II, there was a substantial increase in coal traffic from the London Midland and Scottish Railway (LMS) to the GWR via Honeybourne. In addition due to shipping diversions to the west coast ports the traffic between South Wales area and the LMS also increased considerably until the marshalling facilities at Honeybourne were overtaxed to the limit.

By purchasing land behind the Station North Box all the existing Up exchange sidings had their capacities increased and advantage was taken to add 3 more sidings (giving a 383 wagon capacity), while opposite in the Down yard 2 more mileage sidings were included, making 4 in total (giving a 230 wagon capacity). Later from No. 4 siding a connection was made to private sidings, known as 'Weavings Sidings'. These sidings belonged to the Ministry of Food and consisted of two roads. This MoF depot opened during May 1942 and handled vast quantities of foodstuffs for the war effort. When the yard was pushed for space, wagons full of sugar beet would be stored in the sidings to relieve the bottleneck.

During the war another depot was built, Sheenhill, to the west of Honeybourne. The Sheenhill layout consisted of 4 double ended sidings on a gradient rising towards Honeybourne and connected to the Up goods loop at the station end, also direct access could be gained to the main line at Sheenhill. Each exchange siding was 1,425 ft long, therefore they could hold 68 (12 ton capacity) or 58 (20 ton capacity) wagons. A speed restriction of 5 mph was applied to the exchange siding and connections. The signal box called Sheenhill Signal Box was opened in March 1944. It was of standard ARP (Air Raid Precautions) design and controlled the area that belonged to the American Medical Stores Depot. The box had 30 levers (8 being spare) with the facing connection between the Up main and

Sheenhill

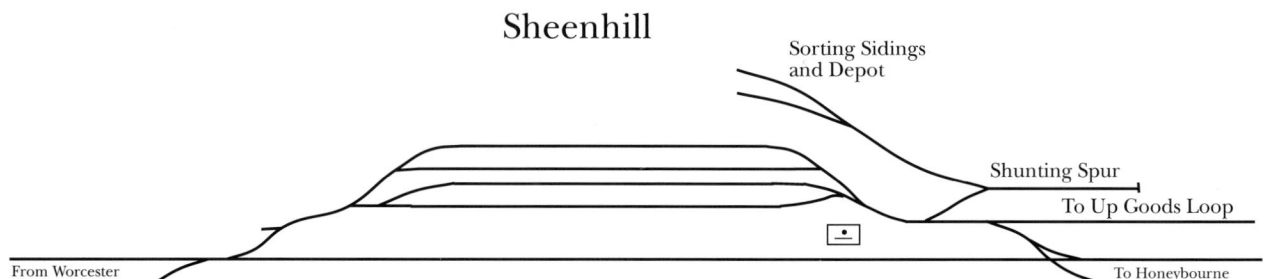

Sorting Sidings and Depot

Shunting Spur

To Up Goods Loop

From Worcester

To Honeybourne

exchange sidings and the crossover between Up and Down main line being operated by electric point motors (actuated through a hand generator in the signal box) since they were approximately 865 yards away from the box. The box was provided with a switch and in its early months only closed on Sundays from 6.00 am to 8.00 pm but by October 1944 it was open continuously. The box was finally taken out of use on 17th July 1951. The depot had its own engine shed which serviced the complex system of sidings (some 10½ miles of track), these gave direct loading to each of the 67 double sheds that made up the establishment. The depot closed in 1963. The sidings lasted a little longer although not connected to the main line they were still in situ in the mid 1970s and at that time there was talk of British Leyland using the system to transport traffic from the depot that they now own.

Honeybourne stalwarts pose for the cameraman outside the Up shunters cabin from left to right Bert Cotton, Harold Smith and Frank Phillips.   *Photo: K Hopkins*

Honeybourne Station North Signal Box was positioned on the north side of the Up main line with the Up goods loop running behind it. This brick built box contained the largest number of levers ever to appear in any Honeybourne box, this was 61 levers when opened in 1909 and increased to 66 working levers in May 1942 as opposed to the 52 in use when first opened. Nos. 40 & 42 were hand generator point levers, 40 being the points for the Up main line to goods loop at approximately 670 yards away, with 42 being the throw off on the Up goods from Sheenhill. The Up goods loop was extended by using these hand generators and when in 1942 completed, could accommodate 100 (12 ton capacity) or 86 (20 ton capacity) wagons plus loco and brake van this being 2,398 ft long on a gradient rising towards the station at 1 in 126. Station North Signal Box was reclassified in January 1913 from a Class 1 to Special Class. By 1923 it was a Class 3 duty.

At the box end of the Up platform a short spur was installed in the 1930s being known as middle siding, it was here that the auto train would simmer during a lull in its hectic schedule. More locally the siding was referred to as 'Curnocks Siding', being named after a well known Station Master of the 1930–40s period. It is in this area of Curnocks Siding that the British Transport Commission proposed to build an early power operated panel box c. 1955. Restrictions and further economies prevented this but it is worth noting that it would have meant the doing away with all the other signal boxes including all the junction ones!

With separate Up and Down shunters cabins the yards were worked by hand points once off the main lines. A bellcode for the telephone was used between the Up yard and Station North Signal Box as follows:–

Call Attention 1

Up Branch to Old Yard or Vice Versa	2 consecutively
Shunting Spur to New Yard or Vice Versa	3 consecutively
Up Loop to New Yard or Vice Versa	4 consecutively
Branch Crossover	5 consecutively

In addition to the normal bellcodes the signalman had to have full knowledge of the engine whistles that were applicable to Station North Signal Box in January 1910:–

For Up Main Line	1 Whistle
For Up Branch Line	2 Whistles

For Up Main		
to Up Goods Loop	2 Short, 1 Long
For Up Goods Loop		
to Up Main	3 Whistles
For Up Goods Loop		
to Up Branch	2 Short, 1 Crow
For Up Goods Loop		
to Up Sidings	2 Crows
For Up Sidings to Up Branch	4 Short
For Down Horse Dock Siding		
to Down Main	2 Short, 1 Long
For Down Siding to Up Main	1 Long, 1 Short

Also by 1950:–

For Up Goods Loop		
to Up Sidings	1 Crow
For Up Sidings to Up Branch	2 Crows
For Up Sidings		
to Shunting Spur	2 Long, 1 Short
From Down Sidings		
to Down Main	1 Short
From Down Sidings		
to Up Main	1 Crow, 2 Short

The box finally closed on 4th April 1965 with consequent loss of the connections at that end of the layout including the crossovers from main to branch platforms. The Down yard was still in use but was padlocked with the key held at Station South Signal Box but later in February 1967 a ground frame controlled the site.

It was in the Down yard that the goods shed was situated, the original shed had been demolished to make space for a canopy at the end of the bay platform at the west end of the station. Next to the goods shed were the cattle docks. At the buffer stops at the back of the Down platform there was an old restaurant coach. It had been acquired to accommodate Mrs C Taylor and Miss D James who served in the 'Canteen'. The canteen had come about during World War II when engine crews and staff alike congregated at Honeybourne. Under the harsh conditions of wartime the staff managed to persuade Worcester to send up some Palethorpe sausages and from then on meals were ordered in advance, being sent from Worcester in vacuum sealed tins. This was greatly appreciated by all the staff and crews alike.

With all this activity of men and trains a control was set up at Honeybourne to govern their movements and

achieve the best out of the system, this was combined with the telegraph office, therefore staff were kept very busy.

The water supply here came from the Campden Tunnel and when low it could be increased via a booster pump that was controlled from Campden Signal Box. This supplied a large tank situated by the road bridge on the Down side. Water columns were provided on the Up and Down main line platforms, Up and Down branch platforms, Up and Down loop lines, garden loop and later both Up and Down yards at West Loop (1960).

The 1 in 100 incline stretching for some 4^{1}/$_{2}$ miles falling from the east and leveling out in the station area made an ideal racing ground for the Down express trains and it was on 31st July 1939 that No. 4086 *Builth Castle* achieved the first 'official' 100 mph by any Great Western locomotive.

The Honeybourne Station South Signal Box was positioned on the south side of the Down main line and had a siding and a loop line immediately behind it. This brick built box controlled all the east end of the station including the entrance to the above Down loop, and the wartime 'Garden' Up loop opened 1st December 1942. The loops were 1,638 ft and 1,480 ft long respectively. The locking frame contained 57 levers of which 41 were in use at the time of opening. With the closure of the North Loop Box in March 1933, the junction was brought under the control of Station South Signal Box by the installation of hand generator worked points working the North Loop Junction, thus bringing about another economy. Levers No. 42/43 controlled the Up branch and Down branch points respectively and later No. 40 controlled the Down main to Down goods loop points and No. 41 the points from the Up branch to main line. By 1937 the box was a Class 3 duty.

Between Station South and Station North boxes freight trains could be propelled on the Down main and Up branch lines between these boxes in the wrong direction, providing that both signalmen were in agreement and that a man rode on the leading wagon.

Like the larger Station North Signal Box, Station South had its own set of engine whistles;

By January 1910:–

| For | Whistle(s) |
| Down Main Line | 1 |

Down Main Line to Branch	2
Down Branch to Station North	3
Down Branch to Down Main	4
Up Main Line	1
Up Branch Line	2
Up Branch Stratford Line	2 Long, 1 Short
Up Branch Cheltenham Line	2 Short, 1 Long
Up Branch to Up Main	4
Down Branch Platform to Up Branch for Stratford	1 Crow, 2 Long
Down Branch Platform to Up Branch for Cheltenham	2 Crows, 2 Short
Down Branch Platform to Up Branch for Up Main	3 Short

By 1950:–

For	Whistle(s)
Down Main Line	1
Down Main Line to Branch	1&3
Down Branch to Station North	2 Short
Down Branch to Down Main	3&1
Up Main Line	1
Up Main to Branch	1&3

Up Branch Stratford Line	2
Up Branch Cheltenham Line	3
Up Branch to Up Main Line	3&1
Down Branch Platform to Up Branch for Stratford	3&2
Down Branch Platform to Up Branch for Cheltenham	3&3
Down Branch Platform to Up Branch for Up Main	2&1

With all the facilities gradually being withdrawn throughout the 1960s the box was reduced to a glorified ground frame on 20th September 1971 when the lever frame was reduced to 21 levers. This date also marks the singling of the Evesham to Moreton in Marsh section of the Oxford to Worcester route. The Station South Signal Box was completely closed on 7th March 1983, and the point for the branch to Long Marston was connected to a small ground frame being released by a token for the section Evesham to Moreton in Marsh. An auxiliary token instrument being provided to allow a train to be 'shut in' on the Long Marston branch siding.

The ex 9.15 am Paddington to Worcester express is seen here approaching Honeybourne Station having just passed Station South Signal Box, with Castle No. 7027 Thornbury Castle *on 28th December 1963. The locomotive was withdrawn by the end of the month.*

Photo: G England

Honeybourne's Junctions

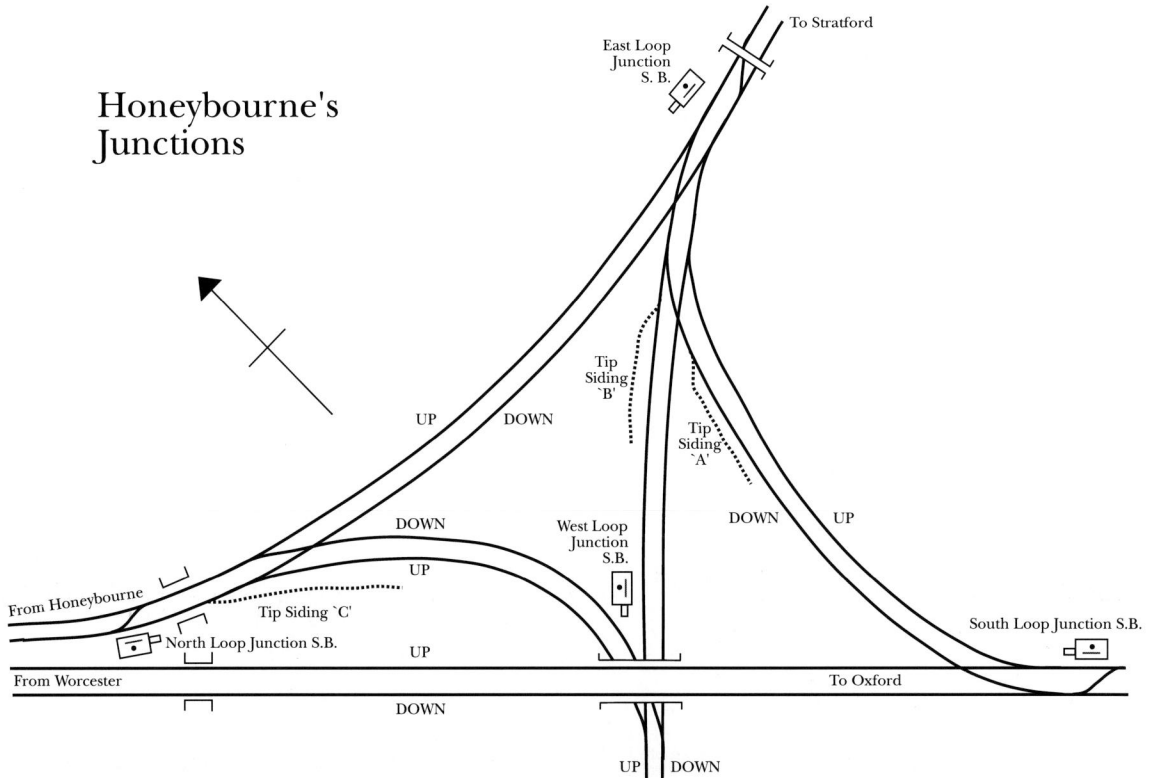

To Stratford

East Loop
Junction
S. B.

UP   DOWN

Tip
Siding
`B'

Tip
Siding
`A'

DOWN   UP

DOWN

West Loop
Junction
S. B.

UP

From Honeybourne

Tip Siding `C'

South Loop Junction S.B.

North Loop Junction S.B.   UP

From Worcester   To Oxford

DOWN

UP   DOWN

From Cheltenham

Contractors Siding 1903

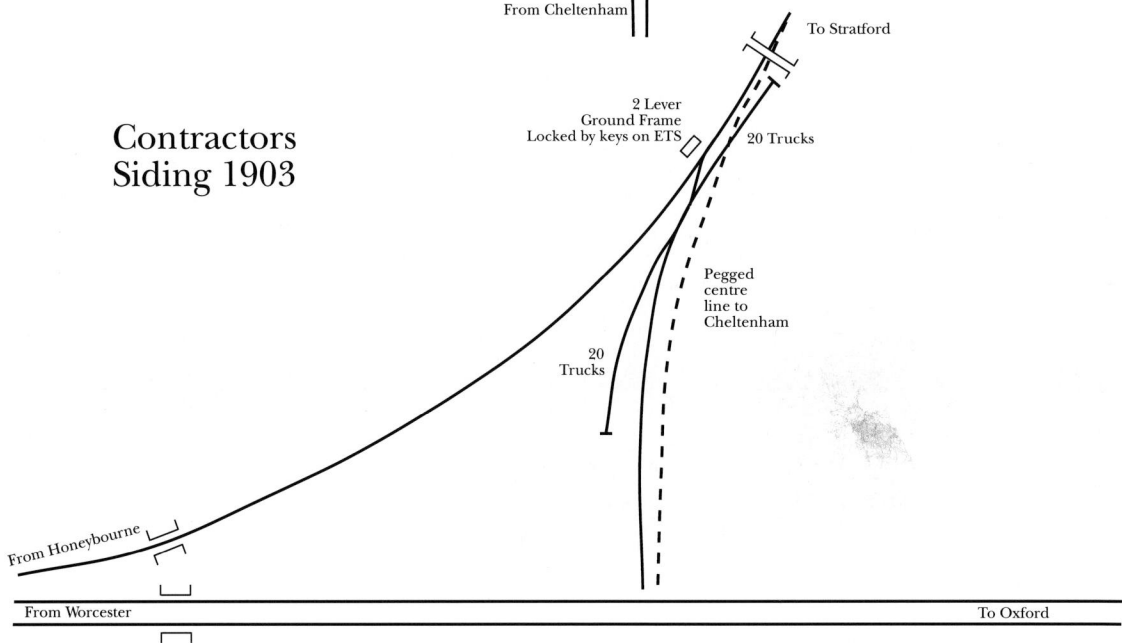

To Stratford

2 Lever
Ground Frame
Locked by keys on ETS   20 Trucks

Pegged
centre
line to
Cheltenham

20
Trucks

From Honeybourne

From Worcester   To Oxford

7.11   Honeybourne and its Junctions

The trio of North Loop, East Loop and West Loop Signal Boxes all opened with the branch line from Honeybourne to Broadway, on the 1st August 1904.

North Loop Box was situated on the south west side of the branch at the double junction where the branches from the East & West Loop Signal Boxes met. This all wooden box was built on 'made up' ground and had 31 levers of which 27 were in use at the time of opening. It cost £222 15s to construct. Although it worked no points on the main Worcester to Oxford line it was a block post for it and by 1910 all 31 levers were in use. January 1913 saw the box reclassified from a Class 2 to a Class 1. It was again reclassified under the 1923 Marks system at which time it had become a Class 4 duty. In March 1933 the box was done away with, the junction coming under the control of Honeybourne Station South Signal Box.

The box structure is still in existence, for a local man brought it and erected it in his garden for use as a shed. After many years adjacent to the main line and not too far from its original site, it was by 1981 no longer required, and was kindly donated to the Gloucestershire Warwickshire Railway at Toddington. The Signal & Telegraph (S&T) department made the most of this for the top was retained and subsequently it was made into the S&T workshops. It was then converted into a classroom in which guise it remains today.

Honeybourne East Loop Signal Box was the nearest box towards Stratford, situated on the Up side at the double junction of the lines to and from North and West Loop boxes. At this remote spot a small cart

Garden sheds do not come much bigger. Here the old Honeybourne North Loop Signal Box resides not far from its original location. Since the photo was taken (c. 1967) it has been donated to the Signal & Telegraph department at Toddington where it is used as a classroom. S&T did not retain the base as it was found to be quite rotten.   *Photo: G H Tilt*

bridge known locally as 'Kill Bridge' ran across the cutting to the north. When opened in 1904 this brick built Class 4 box contained 18 working levers and 7 spare and it cost £239 12s 7d to construct.

Initially both double lines converged into the old single branch at this point and the section to Long Marston continued to be worked by electric train staff until the line was doubled and opened through to Long Marston on 28th April 1907.

On the 1st July 1907 the loop line from South Loop Signal Box was opened, making East Loop Box a very interesting place to work, tucked away from civilisation. Having the 3 routes from the south to contend with meant that all 25 levers were then in use. Two small levers were later added for emergency detonator placers.

With the line opening from the South Loop Box engine whistles were adopted:–

	July 1907 Whistle	By 1950 Whistle
Stratford to South Loop	1	2
Stratford to Cheltenham	3	1
Stratford to Honeybourne	2	3

It was near the East Loop box during World War II that two incidents occurred within a short space of time. On 17th November 1943 the crown of the firebox on Class 'S160' American Austerity 2–8–0 No. 2403 collapsing near the East Box. Both driver and fireman were badly scalded, injuries that proved fatal to the latter. When he later reported to the signalman on duty he was found to have left most his skin from his hands on the banisters of the steps. The engine was taken to Honeybourne whence it was despatched to Worcester but because the boiler had collapsed into the frames it literally had to be chocked

Hall No. 6917 Oldlands Hall *and Castle No. 5046* Earl Cawdor *pass the Honeybourne East Loop Signal Box with a northbound express on 19th June 1961. One of the locomotives would be working back to its home shed. The lines going off to the right are those leading on to Honeybourne Station.*

Photo: G England

A pair of 8F's No. 48385 and No. 48662 pass at Honeybourne East Loop on 28th December 1963. The East Loop Signal Box can be seen on the far right and in the immediate foreground (to the right) is the curve around to South Loop. Photo: G England

and dragged there. It was later repaired thanks to the expertise of the Worcester Works. The following year, 13th October saw a Wellington bomber from Honeybourne Aerodrome crash into the hill beyond the East Loop Signal Box towards Pebworth after hitting electric cables five of the six man crew were killed.

The box finally closed along with the line from the old North Loop junction on 3rd November 1970, the connection from the South Loop having been defunct since the 13th October 1965.

It was in the East Loop area that an exchange siding(s) was planned back in 1914, just to the north of the signal box on the Up side. Perhaps this was a foretaste of the new West Loop of the 1960s? The remote points of the layout would have been worked by a ground frame released from the signal box, since they would have been some 573 yards away. The scheme did not

come about but it was strongly rumoured that it might resurface in World War II, though nothing came of it.

The first signal box at Honeybourne West Loop contained 19 working levers and 6 spare when the line was opened. It was not provided with a switch until 1st July 1908 when through north to south services commenced over the route. Situated in the 'V' of the double junction this all wooden box was like that at North Loop, and cost £240 15s 3d to construct. Although initially 'Temporary Closed' it was opened for the turning of the ballast trains that conveyed the ballast to the contractor who was still at work to the south, being open between 1.00 pm to 2.45 pm daily. If turning was required outside these hours then the Station Master at Honeybourne arranged for a signalman to be on hand for the work. From the opening of the through route the box was open from 8.00 am Monday to 6.00 am Sunday. This Class 5 box was

The scene at Honeybourne West Loop on 7th March 1964. With No. 6910 Gossington Hall *on a northbound freight passes 9F No. 92235 on the stabling line and No. 6944* Fledborough Hall *shunts in the Down sidings.* Photo: G England

Honeybourne West Loop Junction with a diverted Peak No D. 45 heading south having come from Worcester. Beyond the three huts was the site of the old Pre 1960 Honeybourne West Loop Signal Box. c. 1967 Photo: G H Tilt

reclassified by 1937, becoming a Class 4. Due to its position it was literally 'overshadowed' by the overbridge to the south spanning the junction and carrying the Worcester to Oxford line.

It was during World War II that a beacon was constructed nearby West Loop Signal Box and a telephone link was provided to the nearby Honeybourne Aerodrome from the box. The beacon lay on the flight path to one of the runways and when requested the signalman would turn it on.

It was on 24th April 1960 that signalman J Perry had the distinction of closing the old West Loop box and then walking the 440 yds south in the direction of Broadway and opening up the new box of the same name. This was a modern flat roof structure containing a 50 lever frame and at the time 41 were in use with 9 spare. The box was built primarily to control 4 holding sidings on either side of the main running lines. The exit from the Down and entrance to the Up yards plus the crossover to the south were operated by electric motors controlled by a hand generator, these levers being Nos. 31, 36 and 38 respectively. The sidings were opened on the 13th June 1960. The junction points as before were worked from the box. The box replaced two ground frames at the north end of each siding, these had previously been released from the old box for use by the contractors in making the formation for the sidings. Using the new Racecourse Junction opened at Stratford on 12th June 1960, Banbury iron ore trains to South Wales were now routed this way and took water here in each direction. Shunting and crew changing was carried out here plus remarshalling of train formations due to weight restrictions on the line from Stratford to Fenny Compton. With the points within the yards set for No. 1 sidings the Up yard could take 71 (20 ton capacity) wagons and the Down yard 66 (20 ton capacity) wagons. The traffic was shortlived and the sidings were closed on 31st January 1966. On the 3rd November 1970 the Down sidings were reconnected at the north end and the Nos. 1, 3 & 4 were brought back into use; 1 & 3 being runround facility for the local pick-up freight to Long Marston due to the closure of the North to East loop curve as mentioned previously. When that curve was reinstated on 13th September 1981 the line to these sidings ceased. The box had closed on 24th March 1980 with the layout having been simplified from that date and all points connected to hand levers.

The South to East loop connection finally opened along with the signal box named Honeybourne South Loop Signal Box on 1st July 1907. Of brick construction this box was situated on the north side of the Up line at the double junction. It contained 18 working levers with 5 spare when opened but later all 23 were in use. The engine whistles for the box were:–

| For Down Main Line | 1 Whistle |
| For Stratford Line | 2 Whistles |

It was this connection that had for a long time been threatened in strategic planning, in fact back in the old days of the West Midland Railway! It was little used but World War I and World War II saw the box continually open as opposed to night times only, during peacetime. Excursion traffic used the connection until its closure, being very popular for the 1/2 day trips from London and theatre specials from the Southern Region to Stratford which brought many Southern engines over the northern section of the line latterly in British Railways days.

The south curve was known locally as 'The Plantation' due to the planting of ash trees along the majority of its length by the Down line. These were available to the GWR's Carriage and Wagon Department for plank repairs on wagons etc.

Like all the other four junctions a crossover was provided for shunting purposes. The box closed on 13th October 1965 although the curve remained in situ for some time after, having seen the last of any kind of regular freight traffic over it from 1st March of that year.

Honeybourne South Loop Signal box taken shortly after closure, stands forlorn awaiting its fate. Note the nameplate blackened out. c. 1966. Photo: T Petchey

7.12   The Moreton Slips

With the opening of the Honeybourne South Loop Signal Box, traffic started to use the East Loop to South Loop curve from 1st July 1907. At first two Up and one Down freight trains began to use it, those in the Up direction needing banking assistance up the Campden Bank. The curve was on a gradient of 1 in 100 rising towards the box, so catchpoints were placed on the Up line to stop runaways. They were situated 360 yards 'in rear of' the Up starting signal from East Loop Signal Box. It allowed for 44 wagons between it and the South Loop Signal Boxes advance starting signal therefore positioning was vital and instructions were issued to the drivers to draw up their locomotives as near as possible to the advance starting signal.

From the above opening date one of the more unusual workings was introduced over this curve, that of the 'Moreton slips'. The 4.45 pm ex Paddington to Wolverhampton slipped through coaches at Moreton in Marsh for Stratford and Cheltenham. In the reverse direction a 'B' code headlamp service ran from Cheltenham at 4.55 pm, calling at all the principal stations and arrived at Moreton to make the connection with the Up Dining Car Train from Worcester.

To get there the Cheltenham train went through to East Loop Junction where another engine backed onto the train and took it onto Moreton via the South Loop at 5.49 pm. In the opposite direction the train ran with an 'A' code headlamps arriving at East Loop at 6.46 pm. Here it split, the front portion going onto Stratford and arriving there at 7.05 pm. The rear portion then proceeded onto Cheltenham with the engine that had started out on the 4.55 pm train, departing East Loop at 6.52 pm, Cheltenham St. James being reached at 7.35 pm. The train stopped at Broadway and Winchcombe and called at all the other principal stations upon request.

By 1911 the 4.55 pm Up train went into Honeybourne Station whence it then proceeded up the main line but the return still ran over the South to East Loop curve splitting at East Loop Junction as before. This routine finally ceased from 22nd March 1915. The through coach facility continued via Honeybourne until the end of services in March 1960, still called 'The Slips'.

As a direct consequence of the commencement of this service on 1st July 1907 the Honeybourne West Loop Box became more regularly manned being open from:–

11.45 am	–	2.45 pm
5.30 pm	–	7.30 pm
10.30 pm	–	9.30 am

Also at this time ballast trains destined for the North Warwick line (then under construction) were diagrammed from South Wales. By January 1908, 5 Up services including the ex 4.55 pm Cheltenham and 4 Down services including the ex Moreton were using the east to west through route, the rest of the services being freight trains.

By October 1947, 5 freight trains were scheduled in each direction in midweek over the East to South Loop curve. Most trains requiring to go south to Cheltenham having come from the Oxford direction would either reverse the train from Honeybourne Station to East Loop or run round its train having turned the locomotive on the triangles. In the opposite direction from Cheltenham to Oxford, runround would usually take place in the station. However a more unusual move was to take the train to North Junction and reverse it to East Loop and then set off up the Campden Bank via South Loop. This was carried out in the early years by the ex 12.50 am Pontypool Road to Oxford freight, the engine that was attached to the rear at North Junction out to East Junction then became the banker up to Campden.

Speed Restrictions at Junctions 1911:–

Honeybourne Station to/from Stratford, branch to main	15mph
North Loop to/from Cheltenham	20mph
West Loop to/from Cheltenham	20mph
South Loop to/from Stratford	35mph
East Loop – Oxford to Stratford and vice versa	25mph
Stratford to Honeybourne and vice versa	40mph
From overbridge at 102m 64c to 0m 15c on the Cheltenham to Stratford	40mph
From 102m 54c to overbridge at 102m 64c on the Stratford to Cheltenham	40mph

In passing, spare a thought for the poor lampman for several of the signals around Honeybourne were on the tall side, for sighting purposes. One can well imagine this task being given to a young trainee under the lampmans wing! In the days of the one day lamp Honeybourne must have had several of these hardy sons for it would have proved a thankless task for one man versus all those signals!

The oil was stored in lamp huts at every box. When the supplies ran low the lampman would inform the ganger who would arrange for it to be taken on a platelayers trolley to the location required. So many were the lamps here that to save the poor fellow much walking he would often carry two poles of prepared lamps.

Over the years the two triangles created by the embankments at these junctions have been slowly filled in. At first a connection was available to the contractor, Messrs Walter Scott & Middleton from a ground frame in the East Loop area. Since this was in the middle of a single line it meant that any trains with loads for the siding coming from the Honeybourne direction could call but would then have to go on to a signal box to clear the section.

When the contractors had finished the line to the south they used the area to tip unwanted earth in the triangle between the North, East and West Loop boxes. An idea of the amount of traffic caused by this can be judged by the timetable for the earth trains as set out below;

Commencing Monday 27th August 1906, on each day until further notice. Note the trains to be worked by contractors engines and conveying 15 wagons per trip. The earth will be loaded at Malvern Road (West Box) and unloaded on the loop at Honeybourne. Each earth train will have a brake van at front and rear to save reversing.

The locals have turned out in force for the Honeybourne re-opening taken from the road bridge. This shot clearly shows the desolate state, with the main line singled and the branch lines (for runaround purposes) still intact. 22nd May 1981 sees No. 47510 Fair Rosamund *calling with the first train.* Photo: K Hopkins

	1 am	2 am	3 pm	4 SX pm
Malvern Rd. Junction	4.20	8.25	12.50	5.5
Winchcombe arr	4.50	8.55	1.20	5.35
Winchcombe dep	4.53	8.58	1.23	5.38
Toddington arr	5.5	9.10	1.35	5.50
Toddington dep	5.10	9.15	1.40	5.55
Honeybourne	5.45	9.50	2.15	6.30
Return empty trains				SX
	am	am	pm	pm
Honeybourne	6.15	10.35	2.45	7.50
Toddington arr	6.50	11.10	3.20	8.25
Toddington dep	6.55	11.15	3.25	8.30
Winchcombe arr	7.7	11.27	3.37	8.45
Winchcombe dep	7.10	11.30	3.40	8.48
Malvern Rd. Junction	7.40	12.00	4.10	9.27

SX = Saturdays excepted

It was this patch of land that was known locally as 'The Bull Pen' for obvious reasons. At the time of construction it was still fields with local barrow crossings over the line for the farmer near the West Loop Box. This intensive tipping soon ended although the contractor still used the area as a base when widening the station and line to Stratford. The triangle between East Loop,

West Loop and South Loop did not escape tipping, for a siding known as Tip Siding 'A' was in use around c. 1954 (taken out of use in June 1958). Situated on the South Loop to East Loop curve it was controlled directly from the East Loop Box. A second Tip Siding 'B' was then in use on the West Loop to East Loop line. It was worked via a ground frame that in turn was released from the East Loop Box. Lastly Tip Siding 'C' by the North Junction was brought into use on 31st January 1960 and ever since life expired ballast has been tipped here, even to the extent that it has encroached over the old North Loop to West Loop curve, when it was closed on 13th September 1981.

For many years the Yarnton freight traffic from Oxford, was reversed from the Station to East Loop Junction. This operation was obviously fraught with danger and at some stage the powers were considering making another loop, running from South Loop to West Loop but it was found to be too sharp a curve and too steep an incline to contemplate.

Over the years Honeybourne saw most types of locomotives except the 'King' class. It was still only a connecting station with very few 'A' class passenger services calling over the years, perhaps this was due

2-6-2 No. 4110 approaches the Up branch platform at Honeybourne with the ex 12.25 pm Worcester to Stratford train. No. 90485 simmers gently on the coaling stage siding. Taken on 5th March 1960.
Photo: D Bath

Honeybourne Station taken February 1966. The lines on the right being the branch platform and those on the left the main Oxford to Worcester line. The remains of the footbridge which crossed the branch lines are still on the No. 4 platform to the right with services having ceased 6 years previously. The coaling stage can still be seen just beyond the waiting room, having closed to steam at the end of December 1965. The last steam banking duty came on 30th December when BR 4-6-0 No. 75022 was rostered. The shot is taken looking towards Evesham. The branch platforms were finally taken up in January 1993.   *Photo: G H Tilt*

to its location at the foot of the bank. However there was a good connecting service to Evesham and all the other radiating stations. During the height of the season when many parts were run besides the normal service, a large 4–6–0 engine usually a 'Hall' would be positioned at Honeybourne with its chimney facing up the bank. This acted as a standby for both main lines and meant having to be in position from 9.00 pm Friday through to 1.00 am and again on Saturday from 7.30 am to 12.30 pm. Steam ceased here as indeed it did generally on Western Region from midnight on 31st December 1965, although it was still to be seen up to the middle of 1966.

The passenger services from Cheltenham ceased in March 1960, and goods on 1st January 1964. Local services to Evesham and Stratford lasted until May 1969 when the Station was closed with effect from the 5th of that month, However due to the increase in popula-

tion in the area, partly due to the building of Long Lartin Prison, British Rail have been made to rethink and thanks to the Cotswold Line Promotion Group applying pressure, the station (part of the old Down main platform) was reopened (albeit a shelter) for passengers again on 22nd May 1981. The station was 101 miles 62 chains from Paddington, London. The original branch line (reinstated in September 1981) was utilised for a night stop over by HRH The Duke of Edinburgh while visiting the area by Royal Train on the night of 15th May 1985.

Some steam specials were run during the early 1970s along the Oxford to Worcester line but ceased in 1975 until the run of No. 35028 *Clan Line* in connection with the 200th Anniversary Celebrations at Long Marston in October 1987. More recently steam locomotives have traversed the line in both directions on their way from Didcot to Hereford and Didcot to Kidderminster.

Weston Sub Edge Station c. 1908 with Down local passenger train for Cheltenham. Note the Station Masters house and there were no fir trees to the left of the photo at this time.
Photo: Lens of Sutton

Whit Monday, 1919, passengers waiting on the Up platform for a local service.
Photo: Mrs R Wynniatt

7.13

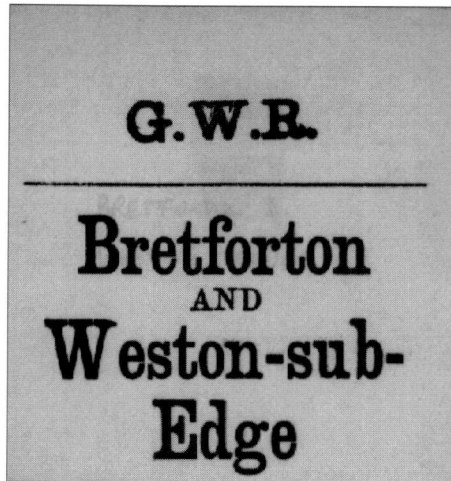

Bretforton & Weston Sub Edge Station at 2 miles 18 chains from Honeybourne East Loop was some distance from the communities it served, although the latter was closer. Passenger services commenced on 1st August 1904 through to Broadway, there being ten trains a day in each direction. At the GWR Traffic Committee meeting of 13th February 1907 it was proposed to shorten this elongated name to Weston Sub Edge, this coming into force on 1st May 1907. However the new signal box nameplate was not ordered until 12th June from the signal works at Reading.

This the first station on the new line had the usual 400 ft platforms, with lamps, nameboards and fencing, a weighbridge and a 6 ton crane was provided. No footbridge was provided, the barrow crossing was sometimes used or access to the Up platform could be gained by a footpath leading from the adjacent road bridge. Mr D G Merrett was the first Station Master, the staff under him consisting of just one Porter/Signalman. The signal box contained 20 levers

in use with 7 spare and cost £253 4s 4d to construct. The box was only open to attach and detach traffic as required and in the early days would have split the section between Honeybourne North Loop Box and Broadway. From 1932 onwards the staff came under the Broadway Station Master after the Station Masters position here had been abolished. By 1934 one Porter and one Porter/Signalman was the authorized staffing. Throughout its life the station was lit by oil lamps. A small lock up goods shed was provided on the Down side.

The signal box closed on 8th October 1950 having been preceded by the closure of the goods yard on 25th September 1950 and when the station became an unstaffed halt, albeit a very large one! Prior to that the only track alteration that took place occurred in the early 1930s when the southern crossover was removed.

The May 1911 timetable shows only 2 goods trains on the Down and 3 on the Up calling at Weston Sub Edge, these were:—

Down		Headcode
05.45 am	ex Leamington to Gloucester	'K'
11.15 am	ex Bordesley Junction to Gloucester	'K'

Up		Headcode
08.30 am	ex Gloucester to Leamington	'K'
10.55 am	ex Gloucester to Bordesley Junction	'E'
5.14 pm	ex Gloucester to Wolverhampton	'E'

By 1947 this had been reduced to 1 goods train on the Down and 2 goods trains on the Up.

During the 1920s tonnage averaged about 3,000 tons per year with receipts in the region of £2,500, but like the rest of the stations traffic started to fall off during the 1930s, although it did pick up during World War II, peaking at 15,366 tons in 1941.

Some milk traffic was sent from here by Tredwell, Broodys and Robinsons and fruit and vegetables by

Bretforton & Weston Sub Edge

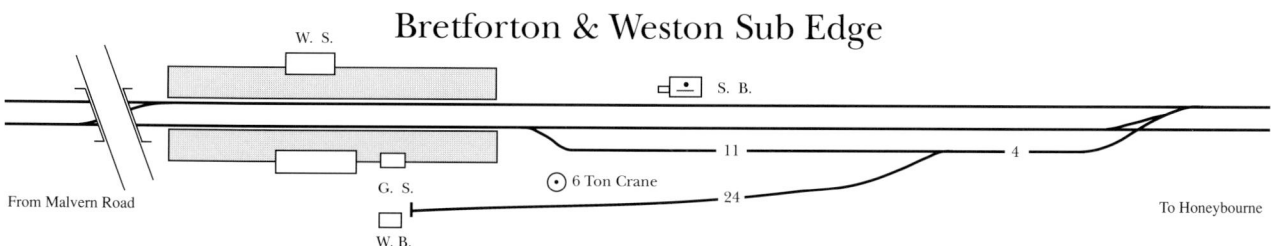

Forlorn Halt, Weston Sub Edge one week before closure taken looking towards Honeybourne on 27th February 1960. The bridge in the distance is the one on Buckle street (see Chapter 6).

Photo: D Bath

Mr J Haydon. Some apple traffic was also generated via the Merevale Fruit Farm, and if Webbs at Mickleton could not get all their cauliflower traffic out via Long Marston they would send some from here to ease congestion.

Not too far from the station was the slaughter house of Mr D Perkins who sent meat regularly up to London in casks. When he had enough bones from the beasts he would fill a 10 ton wagon, to be sent to the Sheppey Glue Chemical Co. Kent where it would be turned into glue (for such items as postage stamps) or used in the making of gelignite. During World War I quantities of horse meat were sent from here to Belgium.

Along with the Station Masters house there were two other houses to accommodate the staff, a ganger and platelayer. When the Station Masters position was done away with a signalman was allowed to use the house. All shared a pump, supplemented by a churn of water sent to each house every day from Toddington on a local train.

Opposite these houses at the entrance to the yard was

the weighbridge, which was supplied by Henry Pooley & Son Ltd., like those others similarly they were of a 15 ton capacity and were known as 'Cart Machines'.

With the onset of World War II many airfields were built on the flat land in the area. One just to the north-west, behind the signal box became known as Honeybourne. Most of the materials which Laings, the contractors brought in came via Honeybourne. When operational (October 1941) some personnel did use the station but Honeybourne saw most of the traffic since that station had a more direct service up to London. The base saw some action during the war, losing many planes by the end of it. Aircraft stationed there included Ansons, Beauforts, Blenheims, Hudsons, Liberators, Lysanders but the bulk of the aircraft were Whitleys. After the war the aerodrome became a storage site for many Wellingtons these planes along with others were later cut up and loaded into wagons at the station and sent away for scrap.

The halt closed to passengers on 7th March 1960.

7.14 Willersey Halt

At 3 miles 47 chains from Honeybourne East Loop, Willersey unlike other halts was quite close to the community it proclaimed to serve. One of the first batch of halts to be opened in the area, it opened to traffic around the beginning of October 1904. Although not inspected until November it was complete by 29th August and the October 1904 timetable shows it for the first time, with a service of 9 Down and 8 Up trains a day, all services utilising the new railmotors.

The halt came under the supervision of the Broadway Station Master. The platforms were originally of 100 ft but soon authorization for their extension to 152 ft was authorized in November 1906 at a cost of £30. Like the later halts of Laverton and Gretton, Willersey was provided with the 'Pagoda' style corrugated shelters. The halt closed on 7th March 1960.

Willersey Halt awaits closure looking north with its pagodas standing guard on both platforms. The temporary signal box was sited beyond the Up platform (see Chapter 8). 27th February 1960.
Photo: D Bath

Willersey

P. W. Hut
W. S.
O. S.
From Malvern Road
To Honeybourne
W. S.

An early shot of Broadway with staff and passengers taken looking north.　　　*Photo: Hereford & Worcester Record Office*

The fireman keeps a lookout for the driver in this view taken from the Childswickham Road. The train is the local pickup and is shunting to and fro into Broadway yard. The engine is Bulldog 4-4-0 No. 3449 Nightingale *taken 2nd August 1947. This locomotive was withdrawn in June 1951.*
Photo: Evesham Almonry

7.15

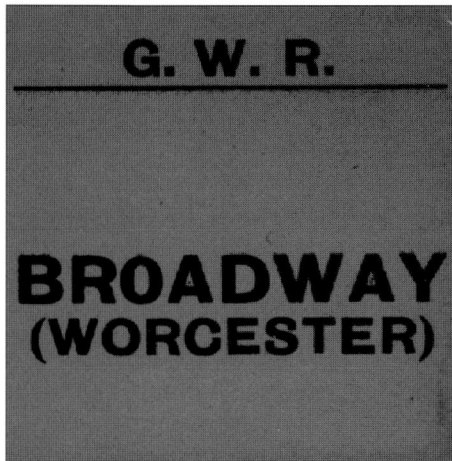

Broadway Station was built 4 miles 73 chains from Honeybourne East Loop and unlike the other stations along the line (except Milcote later) it was split by a road (the main Evesham to Broadway, road) with the main bulk of the sidings and goods yard facilities laid out on the south side of the road and the station proper, lay to its immediate north.

The main station building was situated on the Down side (which was on the eastern side) with the village some 3/4 mile away. The unusual balance was struck here with a large cutting to the north and the yard requiring the level of the ground around the goods shed to be built up, the latter building had to have concrete pillars sunk to give it the footings. The line to the south then ran out onto embankment. Due to the ground being unsettled, the southern end of the 400 ft platforms were placed on wooden supports until the formation consolidated and then some time

later they were reconstructed in brick like that of the remainder of the platforms. At the north end of the main building a verandah/canopy extended from the main building leading to the footbridge that spanned the line. On the opposite side were the usual waiting rooms and gents lavatory.

At the time of opening to traffic, (1st August 1904) the goods shed to the south was still under construction but when completed this standard 60 ft long structure housed a 30 cwt crane having a radius of 12 ft 6 in. In the yard there was also a 6 ton crane (15 ft radius) at the throat of the mileage sidings. The usual cattle pens were positioned on the line that ran through the goods shed. Opposite the main drive leading up to the station lay the entrance to the yard, where was situated the acetylene hut and weighbridge being of a 15 ton capacity, which unlike most others nearly outlived the railway itself.

Initially all the passenger services were locomotive hauled until the introduction of steam railmotors in early October. These services arrived at and departed from the Down platform. When the Up service departed it was crossed over onto the Up line upon leaving the station.

For the duration of the working of ordinary stock a notice was issued to the effect that the distance between the two crossovers was 220 yards, a fact that the staff had to consider due to the clearance when running round the stock. This temporary layout was controlled by a small box (costing £48 19s 7d to construct) positioned at the end of the Up platform. The 12 ft by 8 ft wooden structure had 13 levers of which 12 were in use with 1 spare, these arrangements were temporary with the

Broadway

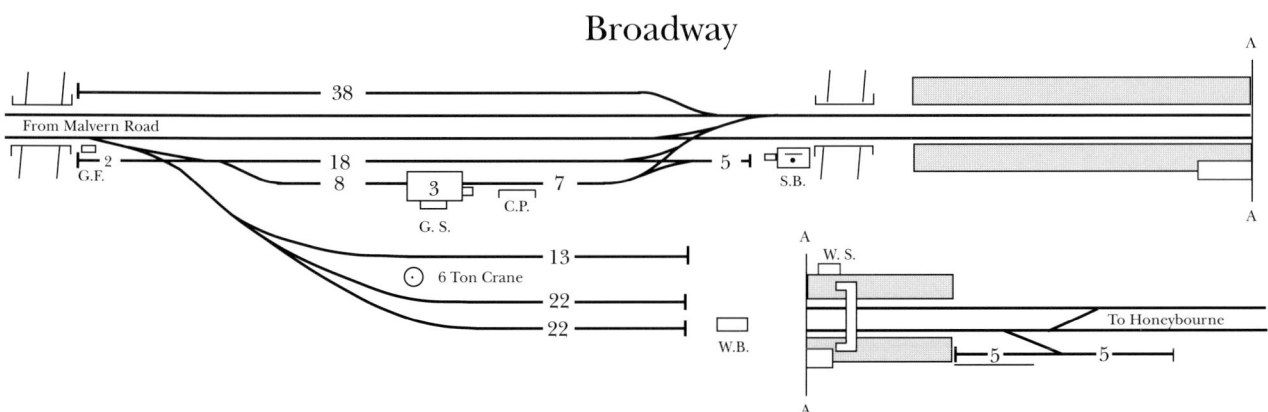

Broadway Station is overshadowed by its surrounding trees in this view looking north. Note the crossover and horse siding had been abolished at the time of this photograph, 27th February 1960.

Photo: D Bath

distant signal being fixed at danger. The box also contained the key for working a small ground frame at the southern end of the layout.

This box was done away with when the line to the south was opened to Toddington on 1st December 1904, and it was replaced by a 37 lever signal box of wooden construction which cost £306 6s 8d to construct and was situated on the Down side immediately to the south of the road bridge. Of its 37 levers 9 were spare. Initially it was a Class 5 box but by December 1924 it had become a Class 4. Upon opening a switch was provided.

The section to the south (to Toddington) was one of the longest sections on the line then (and for some years to come) at 4 miles 49 chains between boxes. The catch points that had been on both lines to the south of the station were dispensed with.

The entrance to the main yard was controlled from a ground frame of 6 levers at the south end and bolted directly from the box being released by No. 10 lever.

With regards to the Down yard, special instructions were issued for its safe working, and in effect read:–

> The entrance from the Down main line at the Toddington end of the yard to the three sidings on the low level is on a gradient of 1 in 50, and that the greatest care must be excercised by all concerned in shunting wagons into these sidings. The engines were to remain attached to the wagons until brought to a stand, a rule that also applied to the goods shed and front road sidings.

With these instructions no accidents should in theory have occurred but there has been more than one occasion when wagons have ended up in the Evesham to Broadway Road!

Two sets of semi detached houses were provided for the workforce plus the Station Masters house, all being situated at the top of the main station drive. The first Station Master here Mr G J Fifield had under him by May 1905:–

1	Signalman
1	Porter/Signalman
1	Porter
1	Checker
1	Machine Lad

By October 1908 another signalman was authorized and by 1932 Weston Sub Edge came under the control of Broadway with the staff becoming:–

1 Station Master Class 4	
1 Junior Clerk	Weston Sub Edge
2 Porters	1 Porter
1 Goods Checker	1 Porter/Signalman
3 Signalmen Class 4	

Broadway took responsibility for Willersey Halt from its opening and later (c. 1941) Laverton also came under its supervision.

The traffic handled at Broadway is as follows:

Year	Staff	Total Receipts	Total Tonnage
1913	7	£6,726	14,053
1923	9	£9,328	11,370
1933	8	£6,299	9,803
		Coaching Receipts	
1942	10	£3,782	14,092
1953	8	£2,792	6,013
1959	6	£2,430	N/A

Castle No. 5015 Kingswear Castle *heads a Down Wolverhampton to Penzance express on 4th August 1950. The location is just to the north of the station. The line on the right is the horse dock, note the original wooden Up starting signal to the left. The Down home Signal has a sighting board to help drivers see it more clearly.*   Photo: Evesham Almonry

Quantities of agricultural produce were handled, being made up largely of grain, fertilisers and cattle feed, plus cattle that were shipped from here to market. The horse siding at the north end of the station saw regular use not least because of the close proximity of the hunt at Broadway. R White, Wallace & Co. and King Bros. were initially the coal merchants then Mr C Collins and the Co. Op. later had the coal wharves here with their separate offices. All milk traffic went on the 07.30 am ex Cheltenham in a siphon to Honeybourne where it was sorted for Birmingham or London and trolleyed over onto the Up platform. The empties returned on the 5.55 pm from Honeybourne.

Staffing levels remained constant at 10 until the end of the 1940s but then gradually tailed off to 6 by 1959.

One of Broadway's main industries was the production of furniture, supplied by the Gordon Russell Co. It was during the 1930s that they supplied wireless cabinets for Murphys at Welwyn Garden, with wagons being despatched at the rate of one a day. The workforce for the company was conveyed from Cheltenham on a 6.30 am works train.

To the nobility of Broadway the railway proved a valuable connection with the outside world even the papers were delivered early instead of arriving in mid afternoon. One of the most regular users of the station was C T Scott, son of the contractor Walter Scott. His family liked the area so much that when the line was completed they looked around for a suitable residence, they found one just to the south of Broadway at Buckland Manor. C T Scott used the Moreton slips regularly, going up to London on business on Mondays and returning on the return working on Fridays. He is well remembered for his tipping, sixpence (2¹/₂p) was a lot in those far off days and this proved a valuable perk to the porters income (who naturally did not wish to share with anyone else their good fortune). Observing this with anticipation one Station Master tried to overstep his position by muscling in on the act but he was told in no uncertain terms by Mr Scott's chauffeur, Mr Roe, that the tip was for the porters only!

This is today as it was then very much hunting country and soon C T Scott became Master of the hounds at Broadway. Point to point races were held with special trains laid on for the event. At first the meetings were held over a course near the Evesham Road over Gorsehill, Collin and Gorse Farms, later this was altered to a course near to Little Buckland becoming known as 'Moco' named after a farm near Laverton. More recently the North Cotswold point to point meetings are held at Spring Hill above Broadway.

After the completion of the blanketing in the area the crossovers were taken out in 1959 together with the two lower sidings in the yard, the horse siding having disappeared in 1957. The box remained open until 10th October 1960.

Signalman Leek looks out in this view of Broadway Signal Box taken in the mid 1930's note the wings on the bannisters, enclosing the top few steps. This was to deter the prevailing SW winds.   *Photo: W Leek*

With the demise of signal boxes along the line sections became longer so intermediate block signals were introduced. This enabled two trains to be in a long section placing a distant and stop signal at a mid way point, being controlled by the box in the rear. Continuous track circuiting from the controlling signal box and colour lights for both home and distant signals were provided. Having closed Broadway Signal Box intermediate block signals on the Up line were worked from Toddington Box, access to the Down yard was still via the ground frame but it was electrically released in this case by the box in advance — Toddington. With the abolition of the crossovers, traffic had to be worked by south bound trains even if the goods were destined to go north!

The station closed to passengers on 7th March 1960, but the goods yard managed to survive until 1st June 1964, all other connections were dispensed with by 15th September 1964.

7.16 Laverton Halt

Laverton Halt at 7 miles 3 chains from Honeybourne East Loop was opened on 14th August 1905, serving the villages of Buckland, Laverton and Stanton. The 100 ft platforms cost £235 and were provided with shelters, nameboards and lamps. Further extension to the platforms was authorized in November 1906 at a cost of £29, these being extended to 158 ft each. An extra footpath was added in the spring of 1909 at a cost of £54. At first the halt was supervised by Toddington but this was later transferred to Broadway. Many was the porter assigned to this halt to tidy up and light the lamps in the depth of winter. These lamps proved somewhat of a task to light in this exposed spot and having run out of matches the porter would have to walk into Laverton and purchase some more. Although season tickets were issued at the larger stations like Toddington and Broadway, many school children used the season tickets to get to Cheltenham schools from this halt, which meant quite a walk from the surrounding villages. The halt closed to passengers on 7th March 1960.

The bridge here was recently lifted out to allow tall machinery access to the Gas Boards pumping station at Wormington. This was carried out in August 1988, it will be replaced by them as soon as is practical, thus reinstating the formation.

Looking north at Laverton Halt with one week to go before closing. 27th February 1960. *Photo: D Bath*

Laverton

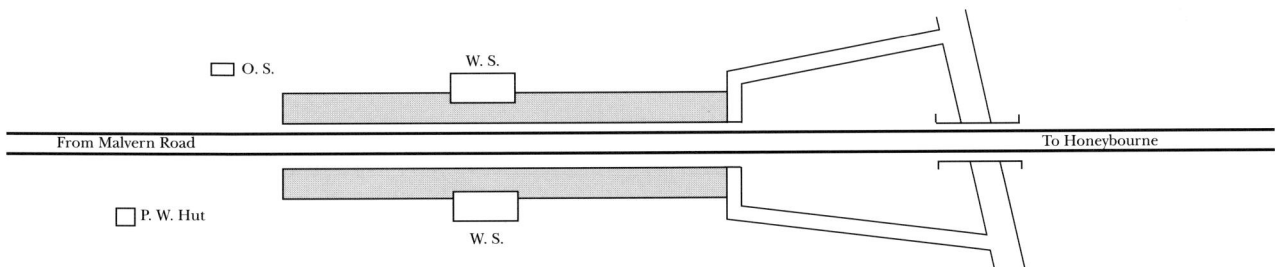

90

One week of local services to go before passenger services are withdrawn. These two views of Toddington show all the fittings and could have easily been taken prior to the 1960 scene.

Photo: D Bath

Looking south from the same platform. 27th February 1960.

Photo: D Bath

7.17

G. W. R.

TODDINGTON

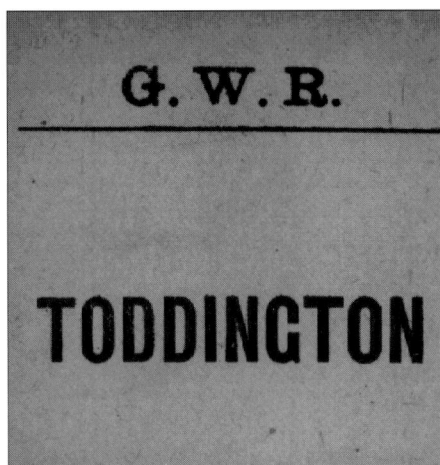

At 9 miles 36 chains Toddington was situated a little to the east of the crossroads of the Stratford on Avon to Cheltenham and Tewkesbury to Stow on the Wold roads. Toddington is today home of the Gloucestershire Warwickshire Railway, one of the most ambitious projects to be undertaken in preservation todate. It must seem some what far removed compared with that first train from Honeybourne, the ex 06.43 am arriving at 07.10 am on the 1st December 1904. Unfortunately no record exists as to the number of passengers carried on that first day. The service was operated by steam railmotors as indeed the majority had been to Broadway since October of that year.

At that time no footbridge existed (erected in 1912) so the barrow crossing at the south end of the 400 ft platforms had to be used by the passengers. The contractors would still have been very much in evidence,

especially as the 'Shanty' huts were still strewn about the yard, although by this time the fruit packing shed and all the other fittings were there. The fruit had, as previously mentioned, been carried for some time (1st August since the opening to Broadway) by the contractors from Mr Hugh Andrews' orchards.

The first Station Master (Class 4) was one Mr Thomas Marsden who was transferred from Presthope to Toddington on 27th July 1904, on the princely wage of £1 13s (£1.65p) per week. He remained here until he retired in March 1931. The first signalman, Mr J B Bowen arrived on 28th November. He was transferred from Stourport to take up his Class 5 duties.

The signal box was opened on the opening of the line from Broadway (1st December 1904) but this must have been a temporary nature since the layout was still partially under the hands of the contractor to the south. When H A Yorke on behalf of the BoT inspected in November 1904, he found 13 levers were in use with 16 spare. At this inspection he also required a couple of immediate necessities to be carried out;

- the temporary catchpoints on the Down line to the south of the station to be moved not less than 200 ft from the existing crossover road and

- that the Down home signal be raised about 6 ft for better sighting purposes for the driver of approaching trains.

When it was again inspected in January 1905 for the expected opening to Winchcombe, the signalling

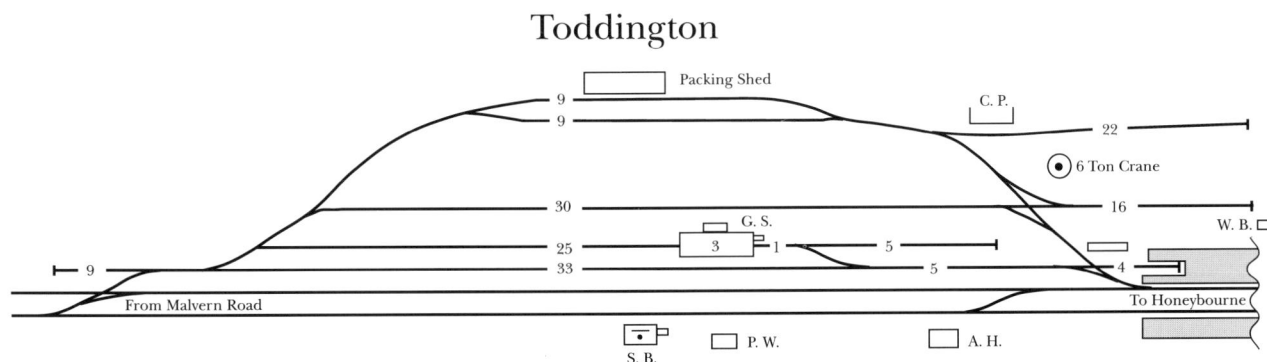

Toddington

Station Master Marsden (2nd from right in main group) stands proudly alongside colleagues and admirers in what is believed to be the opening day from Broadway. 1st December 1904. Note the contractors huts in the background. Photo: Mrs R Wynniatt

arrangements had been completed and the box contained 23 working levers with 6 spare. The construction cost for the box came to £235 10s 2d. The 24th January 1905 saw the second signalman, Mr H Wyatt arrive from Witney, he was the second full time signalman here although there had also been a porter/signalman (Mr C Price) since November. Mr Price was then transferred to Winchcombe.

By May 1905 Mr Marsden had under him:–

2	Signalman
1	Porter
1	Checker
1	Machine Lad

With the opening of the line through to Cheltenham (1st August 1906) the first through passenger excursions appeared along the line. Commencing on 13th August 1906 and to the end of September two excursions ran both 'Mondays Only' from Swansea to Leamington and Wolverhampton to Tintern. Both

these day excursions called at Broadway, Toddington, Winchcombe and Bishops Cleeve, thus affording days out for the locals.

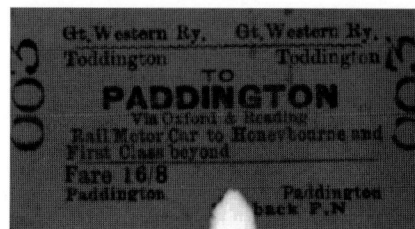

1st Class from Toddington, 25th January 1905. For 2 months only Toddington was a terminus. Courtesy: T Petchey

Through regular running of course did not commence until the opening of the North Warwick line (1st July 1908) when the West of England services commenced. Freight services at Toddington commenced in earnest after the opening from Broadway then later it had its own service, the 11.45 am to Oxley Sidings. The ex

3.20 pm Winchcombe, which went forward to Crewe also called to collect, both these services running when required. Then with the opening of the line to Cheltenham, Toddington was served by:–

Down		Headcode
6.50 am	ex Honeybourne to Gloucester	'K'
12.10 pm	ex Honeybourne to Gloucester	'K'
11.25 am	ex Wolverhampton to Gloucester	'F'

Up		Headcode
6.10 am	ex Gloucester to Honeybourne	'K'
11.45 am	ex Toddington to Oxley Sidings	'E' (RR)
1.30 pm	ex Glos (Cheltenham Loop) to Honeybourne	'E'
3.20 pm	ex Winchcombe to Crewe	'E' (RR)

(RR) = Runs when required.

This last train when run was given precedence over the 1.30 pm ex Gloucester to clear the line first.

Within weeks of the line opening James Taylor & Co. Coal Merchant from Beckford set up depots at Toddington and Winchcombe. The big houses like Stanway House and Toddington Manor had their own coal wagons.

With the Earl of Wemyss in residence at Stanway House, the house had many visitors, one of the most famous being the author of Peter Pan (J M Barrie). It was Mr Barrie who frequented Toddington Station on many a quiet afternoon to have a smoke and a chat with his friend Mr T Marsden, when this happened the porters would be told to make themselves scarce. Another distinguished visitor at the station was the Reverend Allen who resided at Didbrook. He used a tricycle to get along to the station, this was then put into the waiting room awaiting his return from Oxford University where he taught twice a week.

Father and Son. Head Ganger Charlie Caldicott poses with his son Harry, taken just to the south of the station. The trolley is on the headshunt siding known here as 'The Parlour'. c. 1913

Photo: Mrs R Wynniatt

Toddington's second Station Master Thomas Downton Lane whose service there was from 23rd March 1931 until he retired on 14th April 1944. Photo: T W H Lane

Mr Marsden lived in the Station Masters house at the top of the main drive. There were also four other railway cottages on the adjacent side of the line and before World War I were occupied as follows:–

No. 1	C Coldicott	Head Ganger
No. 2	F Coldicott	Ganger
No. 3	H Slatter	Signalman
No. 4	E Cull	Checker

Monday mornings as always brought about washday, and the weekly competition between the station masters wife and Mrs Coldicott would commence, pride and honour being at stake the winner being the first with the washing out on the line!

Although Mr Marsden had larger gardens than the semi detached cottages a way was found to find more land for the staff. Allotments were created on the embankment to the north of the Toddington road bridge. Generally these allotments were 15 yards by 5$\frac{1}{2}$ yards and to this day three plum trees can still be seen on the Down side near the bridge. Later more allotment space was found in the 'dip' to the south of the yard, today this area is where the North Gloucestershire Railway narrow gauge shed is. These allotments were well catered for by using any manure from the cattle/horse traffic that was transported from here. There were further allotments at Stanton and Didbrook according to the Head Ganger's notes that have survived from the early years. It was his job to measure these and collect the rent, this being just one of his jobs together with maintaining a working railway. Mowing of the embankments generally commenced towards the end of June and lasted for about 8–9 days, this grass was then collected up and then sold to local farmers, it making excellent hay. This practice lasted for some time but in more recent years it was burnt off.

Before World War I Mr Coldicott had eight men under him and their section was from 7 miles 70 chains to 10 miles 20 chains. These men worked 47$\frac{3}{4}$ hours during the winter (short time), and this went up to 56$\frac{1}{2}$ hours (long time) during the summer. It consisted of five 10 hour days plus 6$\frac{1}{2}$ hours on a Saturday. Engineering work would bring overtime on Sundays. If it was a big job then all hands were required bringing in many men from adjacent gangs

Front view of the Station Master's house at Toddington, which shows the veranda/conservatory on the end. c. 1935.
Photo: T W H Lane

and of course vice versa; they would go some distance to help others. For the men that lived close to the railway further overtime could be gained by working in the summer evenings loading up the fruit wagons. This work was to be had in August through to the end of October from 6 pm onwards generally for a couple of hours but sometimes this could go through to 10 pm. Winter would also bring a little overtime, lighting the fire devils under the water columns during frosty weather meant a couple of hours for the man who got the job. The permanent way hut was just to the north of the signal box on the Down side.

Upon Mr Coldicott's retirement from the railway in 1929 a testimonial was made to show the appreciation that the local men felt for him, he had held the position of Head Ganger since the opening of the line, the collection amounted to £3 5s (£3.25p). So detailed are his notes that they read like a diary and give a clear insight into everyday life of permanent way men.

Derailments were not infrequent and his notes contain such details as follows:–

> *30th August 1910 Engine No. 210 off the road at catch points No. 17 from 6 pm till 5.15 am single line worked from here to Broadway.*

> *12th August 1912 truck No. 87314 Engine No. 3912 delay of 15 minutes off at 12.15 on again at 12.30. Smart work.*

For a long time the station and surrounding area was well attended to, because Mr Andrews would send his gardeners to the station regularly, they even had a verandah/conservatory put onto the end of the station house.

Mr Andrew's Toddington Orchard Co. purchased horse manure from the GWR stables at Paddington in the early years. This was delivered on Tuesdays and Fridays at a cost of 6s (30p) per ton.

'The Coffeepot' 0-4-2T No. 1402 on a Cheltenham to Honeybourne service at Toddington on 6th August 1947. All the locomotives of 'The Coffeepot' were placed on the Cheltenham side of the carriage(s).
Photo: Evesham Almonry

If the devil could cast his net! This group was taken in the yard at Toddington c. 1919. From left to right:– Walter Wright, Alan Hodges (Examiners), Frank Joyner, Jim C Biggs, Ernie Pearson (Greaser), Harry Carter, Sid E Knight (Lad Porter), Frank Roberts (Signalman), Joe Wilkes (lad Porter) and Frank Grinal (Shunter).
Photo: H Carter

During World War I Toddington was very busy, having its own POW camp of about 150 men, guarded by wounded soldiers, the camp being located to the rear of todays Primary School. Men were set to work all over the area and especially down at the station taking their lunch in a small hut provided at the south end of the packing shed. At about this time large consignments of timber were moved, being brought down from the woods off the surrounding hills and the Stanway Estate. A small saw mill was set up where the Garden Centre is now. So great was the volume being turned out that Gloucester would have to send out its crane to assist in the loading.

Sunday services commenced in July 1909 with two services in each direction, thus enabling the milk traffic to be worked. A large quantity of milk was taken to Toddington being supplied by over a dozen local farms.

The 17 gallon churns would be loaded into a siphon that was stabled in the dock or 'Parlour' as it was known here, and was then attached to the early train for Honeybourne. Some of it went on to London, the rest went to Birmingham with the empties returned via the Down platform, where the porters would show great dexterity by getting the churns over the barrow crossing two at a time! Sundays developed as the busiest day for this traffic being due to Beckford on the Midland Railway being closed and all the milk traffic from there came to Toddington. In the event of no locomotives being available for shunting purposes, Toddington was allowed to use horses for such movements. By way of other local traffic generated, Mr H Smith of Norton Farm sent cattle to Gloucester Market every Monday on the 8.30 am and on Fridays local game birds and rabbits would be sent to Stratford on Avon Market.

By November 1917, two Admiralty coal trains were run from South Wales to Lowestoft, Yarmouth and Parkestone Quay via Leamington (London and North Western Railway), they also ran four such trains to Immingham via Banbury. This volume of coal was required to keep the fleet at sea. Such workings ran through Toddington, all being 'when required', with all locomotives taking water at the station. A special bellcode (3 4 4) was used for such workings.

The GWR was always keen to promote Safety and First Aid knowledge in the staff, and this they duly did every year by organising an annual First Aid competition. Around 1919 Toddington and Winchcombe combined forces and proceeded to win the area knockout, they then went to the 'Shrine' where the finals were held (in Swindon Works 'C' shop) where upon they came third out of the whole of the GWR network. For this achievement each member of the team was awarded a bread knife!

Most freight trains were scheduled to stop here for examination and locomotives to take water. From the outset wheel tapping, examination and greasing took place here, two old carriage bodies (which were situated on the end of the 'Dock') being provided for the men. These carriages of unknown origin, were divided as follows;

First coach had a work bench with a vice and a large box of tools. There were also wooden lockers under the bench, one for lamps and the others for carbide and oil, the other lockers were for the examiners and greasers for keeping personal items in and fitted with a lock each man having his own key.

Second coach/first portion had seats and a desk plus a small stove where the men could have their food and dry their clothes out. These men were not allowed any set meal times but were allowed the luxury of a 20 minute break between the 3rd and 5th hour of each shift. Yet if a train came during this 20 minutes then the food had to be left and the train attended to.

Second coach/second portion was the section where the grease, oil and grease boxes were kept. These were always kept full.

This activity was centred on Toddington because it was a half way point for the Bristol/South Wales to Birmingham traffic that required examination every 45 miles due to the old type grease axleboxes in use. These grease axleboxes used to have a brass bearing which had two feed holes that in turn fed the grease from the axlebox, if these holes became blocked or short of grease then the axle journal used to run hot

and if very hot it could catch fire and in such cases the wagon would have to be put off, causing delay to other traffic. The examiner would carry a stiff piece of wire that was called a 'Pricker' which was used to make sure that the feed holes in the brass bearing were kept clear. The examiner would leave the lid up if the box required greasing, and the greaser would follow along filling the boxes as he went, and during the summer this work required plenty of grease, it not being uncommon to use 8–10 of the 20 lb boxes of grease on one train!

If the examiner found a defect which meant that a vehicle could not proceed, then a red card was attached to the vehicle and it was put off into the yard. Minor repairs could be carried out by the men and these defective wagons were put into the cripple siding by the local pick up. The heavy repairs were carried out by Wagon Repairs Ltd. if privately owned and company wagons came under the district repairers, Ernie Wasley and Sam Coates. Green cards were attached to wagons with minor faults and allowed to continue to their destination for repair after unloading.

The only shot that exists showing the shunters and examiners carriages at the end of 'the Dock'. This view was taken looking south c. 1925. Photo: T Petchey

The Down trains would take water in the Down platform and then draw forward down to the starting signal for examination, the Up trains would stop at the starting signal for exam, the engine going light to take water from the Up water column by the bridge.

> *'When engines of Up goods trains have work to perform at Toddington, requiring water at that place, it must be taken on arrival, so that when the work is completed, the train may leave at once' (Working Timetable 1911)*

The Up trains were only put into the Up refuge siding if there was a passenger train due to pass, in the Down direction trains would be reversed over the

Having reversed into the Up siding to allow following trains to pass No. 5332 awaits while sister engine No. 6333 passes with a Down freight. Taken on 22nd April 1954.   *Photo: R S Potts*

The ill fated Trevithick *shunting at Stratford on Avon c. 1935.*   *Photo: Authors Collection*

south crossover to allow the passing of other trains. Officially no examinations were carried out in the station area, a rule probably enforced by the Station Master who required his sleep and did not want to hear the constant clanging of wheel tappers in the small hours! Examination continued until 5th May 1941, when it was discontinued. The coach bodies lasted a little longer being demolished by the derailment of 'Duke' class engine Trevithick shortly before its withdrawal in December 1949. With a lull in the traffic the greasers would play football or cricket with the local railway children either behind the railway cottages or use the goods shed door as the goal! These occasions of course were few and far between, due to the volume of traffic.

On the Down road here there is a small hut that housed the stations carbide store, acetylene provided all the lighting, supplying the station and lamp standards, this lighting also went into the goods shed office and the two lamp standards down the main drive and the one by the weighbridge. Great care had to be excercised when putting the calcium carbide into the container, thick leather gloves being provided to prevent any burns, with carbide within the container, water was added that let off the gas which in turn was stored until required in a pressurized vessel in which the contents were measured by a pressure gauge. By March 1917 along with Honeybourne, Broadway and Winchcombe, Toddington had to revert to oil lighting due to the shortage of carbide at the time.

The water supply for the station came from the Stanway Estate and every Friday a porter would have to take the reading from the meter situated in the garden of No. 1 railway cottages and carefully record it. A large tank was provided on the Down side by the footbridge. This water was needed further along the line for the railway houses at Weston Sub Edge since they were not connected to the mains until the early 1940s. The GWR made arrangements that, in times of low pressure the station houses at Broadway and Winchcombe, would be supplied with one churn per house per day. These churns were carried from Toddington by the local service. The signal box lacked supply so the signalman had to fetch his water from a tap in the middle of the yard by the cattle pens (where the latrines were also located).

The porters at Toddington as elsewhere along the line, were kept fully employed cleaning the station, along with Laverton Halt and weighing goods on the weighbridge (15 ton capacity) and later attending to Hayles Abbey Halt (opened in 1928) that came under the jurisdiction of the Toddington Station Master. He would send out a porter to light the lamps before dusk in winter and tidy up. Sometimes, if lucky, the porter would be able to get a ride back on a train, getting off before the station and thus grabbing an extra 10 minute break. The lamps at all the halts along the line would be turned out by the guard of the last train of the day. The porters worked early or late turns, swapping each week, their hours of duty being; 6.30 am to 2.30 pm and 12.30 pm to 8.30 pm. Before the introduction of the signal lamp that would burn for 8 days on one filling c. 1907, lamps had to be filled and trimmed every day. This meant the poor porters had to travel 3/4 mile in both Up and Down directions to the distant signals and with all the other signal lamps the task took up a large slice of time. Personal recollections would suggest that the 8 day lamp was not brought into use along the line until at least 10 years after their first introduction on the GWR.

The Goods shed here was 60 ft and contained a 30 cwt crane. The packing shed was independent of the goods shed in that all the traffic handled in it was that of one firm, originally the Toddington Orchard Co. then Marshalls the sweet company and finally it was taken over by Samuel Hanson. Vast quantities of fruit would come in (often imported) and taken to the trading estate, (known locally as the 'Jam Factory', set up by T W Beach & Sons back in 1883) where the fruit was processed and put into tins before being shipped out again. Large amounts of coffee were also handled in this way. All this traffic was literally lost overnight through a strike on the railways in the 1950s when the factory owners found that it was a lot cheaper to convey the goods by road.

A restriction placed on the sidings was that:–

'78xx and 10xx class engines are prohibited from working over the connection north end of the packing shed platform siding'

With the opening of the Cheltenham Race Course Station in March 1912 (which incidentally the Toddington permanent way staff helped to construct), race specials started to be run from all points on the GWR system. The servicing of these trains was partly dealt with at Toddington, up to four being stored and serviced here. Worcester would send out a train conveying the staff to service and clean the coaches of these specials. On the eve of a meeting all the traffic that was not urgently required would be cleared out of the sidings to make as much room as possible. Upon arrival the coaches would be watered in the Up platform then reversed into the sidings where they would be filled with gas if required. A 'Cordon', a specially built mobile pressurized vessel would be used. 'Cordons' were also used at stations where no gas supply existed for lighting purposes or, as in this case, it would be used to replenish the gas tanks on the restaurant cars.

The locomotives would then go on to Honeybourne for turning and upon their return be stored in the sidings awaiting departure time. At Winchcombe a pile of broken crockery existed this corresponding to the location of one of the restaurant cars.

The 11th December 1941 saw the Germans bomb the line at Weston Sub Edge and Stanton Cutting, the former was not very serious but the latter caused wide disruption. The bomb landed near to the aqueduct that crosses the cutting. It was a direct hit on

Specially posed for the camera, the signalman has pulled off the shunt signal on the Down side. Taken in 1967 it is probably the original and therefore at the time the photo was taken over sixty years old. Photo: G H Tilt

the Down line lifting it by 8 ft out of level. The Up line was also badly affected but was brought back into use on the 14th and single line working could resume. The Down line followed a day later after much fill had been tipped into the huge crater. Such was the force of the blast that it bent the rails on the aqueduct walkway, damage that can still be seen to this day. During the same raid bombs flattened the Stoneville Street area in Cheltenham near the site of the old High Street Halt.

The traffic handled at Toddington is set out below:–

Year	Staff	Total Receipts	Total Tonnage
1913	9	£7,144	12,183
1923	9	£6,459	6,849
1933	6	£4,854	7,548

Although the tonnage did increase during World War II peaking at 30,015 tons in 1942, the staffing level by

that time was 10 (at which level it remained throughout the duration of the war) this figure included several women. In 1950–2 staff numbered 14 but declined to 5 by 1959.

When the line opened only one post of signalman existed; his hours for December 1904 were from 6.45 am to 8.30 pm, weekdays and Saturdays. Yet in those early months the box was also required to be open on Sundays, when ballast trains were run in connection with the contractor. A signalman/porter greatly helped the signalman in between his other duties!

On the opening of the line to Winchcombe in 1905 the box was provided with a switch, and the signalmans hours became 6.45 am to 8.40 pm weekdays and Saturdays. When the line opened to Cheltenham in August 1906 the hours were 7.00 am to 9.30 pm weekdays and Saturdays 7.15 am to 9.30 pm. With the opening of the North Warwick the hours were lengthened again so that by 1911 the box was open from Mondays at 7.45 am through to 10.30 am Sunday and then open later in the Sunday afternoon from 5.00 pm to 8.15 pm. During World War II the box was open continuously. The box retained to the end the board mounted on a stand behind the levers describing the function of each lever, not uncommon in 1905 but was replaced in most boxes by individual levers badges. It remained the last box on the southern (ie opened 1904-6) section to remain open, breaking latterly the section on nights from Lansdown Junction Cheltenham via Toddington to Stratford (Evesham Road), with Long Marston switched in and Milcote reduced to a gate box.

Single line working took place on several occasions, in the 1954–55 period. On one occasion the cutting to the north of Toddington was found to be slipping onto the Down line and a retaining wall had to be built to prevent this. Following this in early 1958 single line working took place between Toddington and Laverton Halt in connection with blanketing in the Stanton Cutting area. On 25th December 1967 a slip occurred at Willersey and single line working was instigated on the Down line between Honeybourne West Loop and Toddington this continued until 4th January 1968. In February single line working was again enforced upon the line by the partial collapse of a wing wall at Stanton and the Down line was used between Honeybourne East Loop and Toddington.

At the time of the accident at Winchcombe in August 1976 the Toddington Signal Box was being contin-

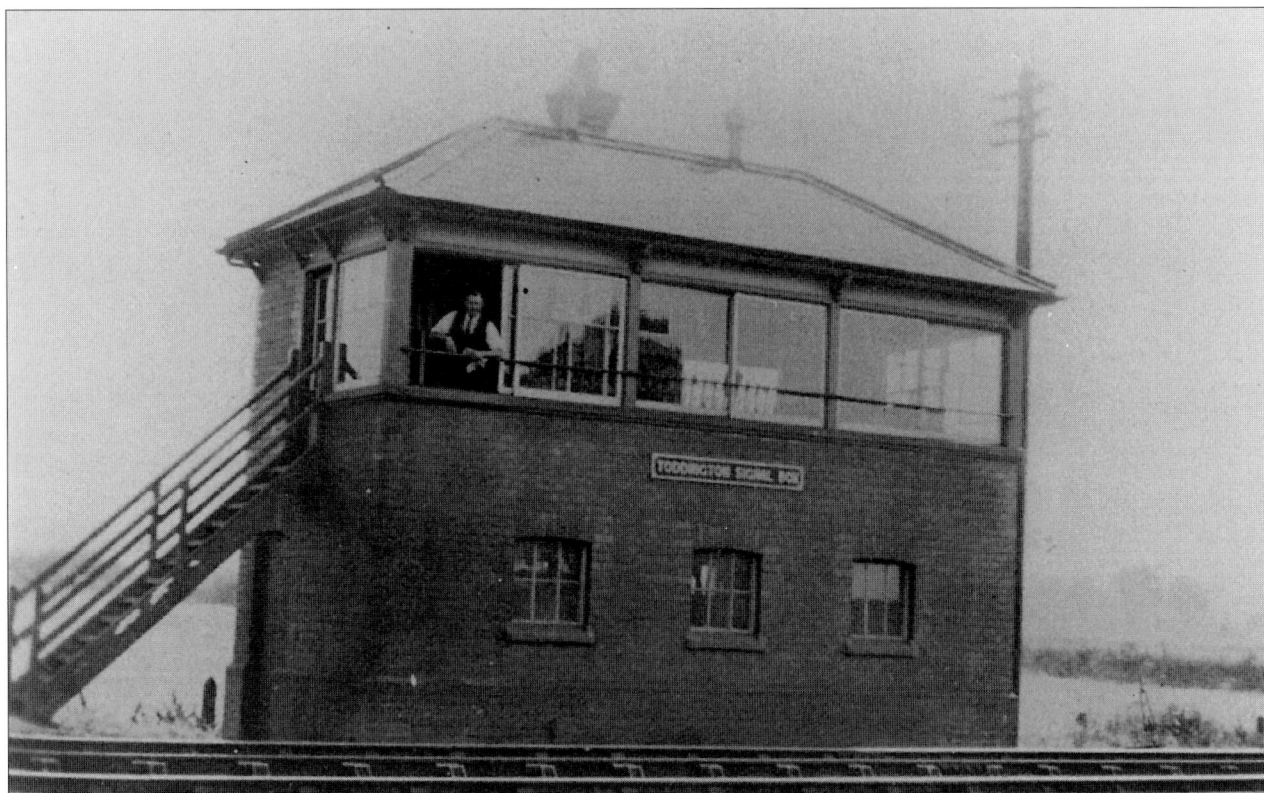

Signalman Slatter poses at the window of Toddington Signal Box, c. 1935.   *Photo: T W H Lane*

uously manned. The site of the derailment at 11 miles 60 chains became fit for use again on 10th September with a speed restriction of 10 mph, on this date the signalman gave 7 5 5 (box closed) for the last time and from that date the box was not required to 'switch in' under special instruction. The test trains from Honeybourne West Loop that had been using the line finished their special braking tests and the box was last manned on 22nd October 1976. The last train over the line, on 14th August 1977, was an engineers train, it does not appear in the Toddington train register yet in the Honeybourne West Loop Box register it shows as '•Z45' passing on the Down line at that place at 07.50 am and returning at 5.00 pm.

Toddington closed to passengers as from the 7th March 1960 and finally closed to goods on 2nd January 1967. Although all the sidings were taken out of use, one remained as a siding alongside the goods shed for the use of engineers trains etc. also the south crossover was retained for crossing purposes. The north cross-over was disconnected in May 1964 but still remained in situ. The track was dismantled in 1979/80.

A firemans view taken from the tender of 2-8-0 No. 2807 at Toddington looking south in June 1956. The train has been backed into the Up siding.   *Photo: L C Jacks*

7.18   Hayles Abbey Halt

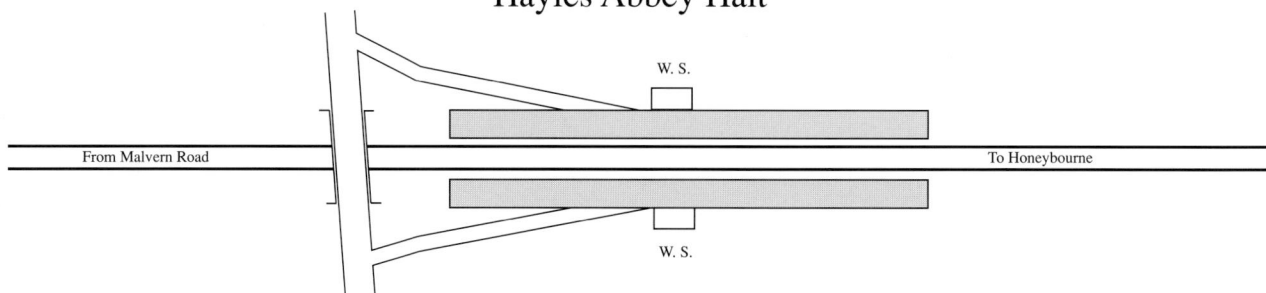

On the 24th September 1928 a new halt was opened at Hayles Abbey 10 miles 38 chains from Honeybourne East Loop. This was in conjunction with the opening of a museum amongst the ruins of the old Abbey. The Abbey having been founded in 1246 by Richard of Cornwall second son of King John. This was apparently carried out because of a vow Richard made when in dire peril at sea. The monastery was of the Cistercian order.

The halt with its two platforms constructed of sleepers came under the jurisdiction of the Toddington Station Master. Two corrugated huts were provided, being of the later rounded roof type. Lamp hooks were also provided and footpaths led from each platform to the adjacent road. The halt closed on 7th March 1960.

HAYLES ABBEY HALT	
TRAINS WILL LEAVE THIS HALT AT:—	
To CHELTENHAM WEEK-DAYS ONLY SECOND CLASS ONLY	To HONEYBOURNE WEEK-DAYS ONLY SECOND CLASS ONLY
7.53 10.22	8.5 11.58
1.43 2.59	2.9 3.0 5.12
6.31 8.42	6.24 10.50

One of the last timetables.   *Photo: A Baker*

Hayles Abbey Halt on 27th February 1960 looking north. Toddington's Up distant signal can just be seen to the left of the telegraph pole. This was replaced by a colour light some 308 yards to the south on 12th May 1969.   *Photo: D Bath*

Hayles Abbey Halt

W. S.

From Malvern Road   To Honeybourne

W. S.

7.19

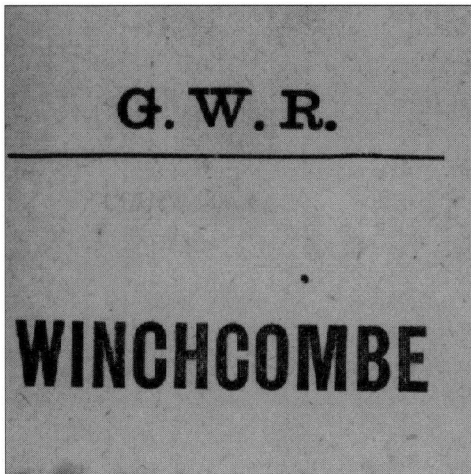

'Windy' Winchcombe was at last reached by the Great Western Railway on 1st February 1905. Its station at 12 miles exactly from Honeybourne East Loop was set on a curve. The area originally had been a deep wooded dingle with a stream running through it and lay very close to the small village of Greet, with Winchcombe a good 3/4 mile away. The main building was situated on the Down platform and like the building at Broadway, it had a verandah canopy extending to the footbridge from the natural pitch of the roof. The usual waiting room and gentlemens lavatory were situated on the Up platform. The platforms were the standard 400 ft in length. The Down platform was reached by the driveway at the top of which lay the Station Masters house and two adjacent sets of semi detached houses that helped with the accommodation of the staff. Immediately past the station lay the goods yard, including a weighbridge of 15 ton capacity that lasted in use until 1958, although it remains in situ. Behind this was the acetylene hut. Within the yard there were three mileage sidings that were serviced by a crane of 6 ton capacity, having a 18 ft radius. The 100 ft long goods shed had a 30 cwt crane having a 12 ft radius and two loading doors unlike the others along the route, for it was the largest. A small raised platform was added to the rear of the office beside the west door the milk at one time being loaded here. A cattle dock existed at the eastern end of the Down platform, having a siding that also acted as a head shunt.

On the opening of the line from Toddington only the Down platform was brought into use, the Up line being used by the contractor to gain access to the eastern face of the Greet Tunnel. The returning Up services were therefore crossed over onto the Up line soon after leaving the station. The distance between the two crossovers was 194 yards, which would only allow

Winchcombe

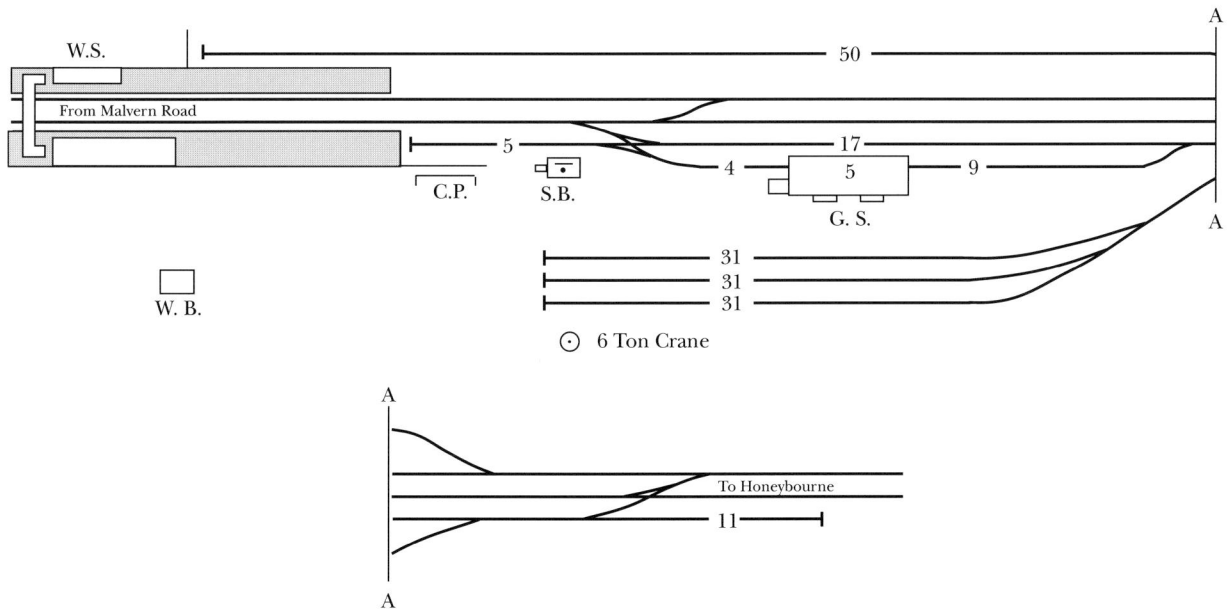

A view which did not last very long with Winchcombe being the terminus from February 1905 to June 1906. During this time the Down platform (left) became the arrival and departure platform, hence the starting signal which was subsequently dispensed with at the end of this period. Photo: T Petchey

A general view showing all the fixtures and fittings in the yard at Winchcombe, late one evening c. 1963. Photo: T Petchey

a train of 25 wagons plus brake van in the clear for running round.

The footbridge at the time of opening was still under construction and the station was not finished, painters being very much in evidence. Two catch points were installed to protect the passenger trains from movement of contractors trains.

On the Down line the points were 23 yards on the Cheltenham side of the Down platform and were worked by a lever in an adjacent ground frame, locked by an annetts key that was kept in the signal box when not in use. With the opening of the line to Bishops Cleeve this arrangement was done away with, together with another catch point situated on the Up main line, 6 yards on the Cheltenham side of the crossover at the west end of the goods yard and worked directly from the signal box.

The brick built signal box which cost £267 2s 2d to construct contained 31 levers and 6 of them were spare. The box was a Class 5 duty at first but by 1934 had become a Class 4.

The box saw two generations of signalmen from the same family, for in 1906, J S Marshall was transferred from Symonds Yat. His son, S Marshall subsequently joined the railway staff here in 1928, and later he became relief signalman for the line retiring in 1969. Thus two generations gave 63 years service on the line.

Winchcombe's first Station Master (Class 4) was Mr W J Edwards who reigned until January 1912 where upon he was succeeded by Mr E H Kirk. By 1906 the staff numbered as follows;

1	Station Master
1	Clerk
2	Signalmen
3	Porters
1	Porter (supernumerary)
1	Railmotor Conductor

The latter post was soon done away with due to the line opening to Bishops Cleeve (1st June 1906). By March 1934 the staff establishment stood at;

1	Station Master
1	Clerk (Goods)
2	Signalmen
1	Porter
1	Junior Porter
1	Goods Checker

After 1931, Gotherington came under the wing of the Station Master, adding 1 Signalman/Porter to the above tally. When Gretton Halt opened it also came under the supervision of Winchcombe. The figure of 8 staff was maintained until the early 1950s when it was increased to 12, a level maintained throughout that decade.

A small trolley way existed in the early years leading out of the yard down to the sewerage works that were under construction c. 1910. This line belonged to Johnson Bros. of Tamworth and it was on this trolley

Workforce:– Contractors men pose on the opening day at Winchcombe, 1st February 1905. Photo: T Petchey

The first auction held by the Winchcombe Co-Operative on 15th February 1905. Photo: T Petchey

way that most of the materials used in the construction of the sewerage works were delivered to the site.

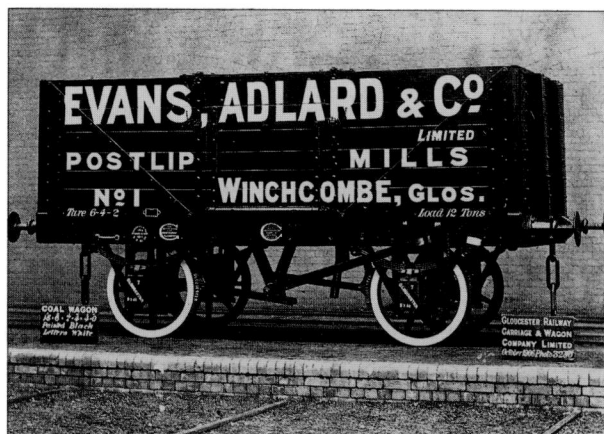

One of Evans, Adlard & Co private wagons, October 1906.
Photo: T Petchey

To help with the milk traffic at Winchcombe authorization was given for a direct road access to the Up refuge in April 1915 at a cost of £142. The ground here is very wet at the best of times and when the job came to be done the steam roller soon buried itself into the clay, with subsequent extrication proving very difficult.

Besides the race traffic trains stabled here, Winchcombe soon became the destination for excursion traffic in its own right. As early as August 1906 a Birmingham to Winchcombe excursion was run on a 'Monday and Saturday only' basis. It was later run through to Bishops Cleeve.

Total receipts for 1913 came to £5,837 and the total tonnage was 11,828 tons. By 1933 these figures read £4,261 and 8,320 tons respectively. However traffic did peak during World War II and in 1943 coaching receipts stood at a mere £2,980 but the tonnage was 17,045 tons. Agricultural machinery, fertilizers and foodstuffs made up the bulk of the inwards traffic but one of Winchcombe's local industries (Evans Adlard of Postlip Mills, a firm that had its own private wagons) received rags, which were made into top quality filter paper (industrial) and blotting paper for Lloyds Banks. All was sent out via the station.

The permanent way gang had a large section here that took in the tunnel to the west which also marked the summit of the line being 297 ft above sea level. Often other gangs would assist the local gangs when intensive work was required. It was on the 29th March 1928 that such a team of 40 men were

working at the eastern end of the tunnel, resleepering in and around that area. A goods train had

A 0-4-2T 14xx with a Down local service passes Winchcombe Goods Shed, c. 1955.
Photo: K Hopkins

started away from the station causing much smoke to lie in the cutting. Upon its passing the men set about their task where upon the 11.18 am motor ex-Cheltenham struck 5 men, killing 3 of them. Flag men had naturally been employed and the subsequent inquest returned a verdict of accidental death.

In the early days when the pace of life was not so hectic, the crews of the Gloucester to Honeybourne and Honeybourne to Gloucester local pick up goods either changed crews at Toddington or here. Apparently it was not uncommon for the crews to adjourn to the 'local' presumably the station master turned a blind eye as long as they were quick. The station closed to passengers on 7th March 1960 and goods ceased from 2nd November 1964. The Up refuge siding had been done away with in October 1963. The Up station waiting rooms and footbridge were soon razed to the ground after closure. The Main Station building lasted a little longer disappearing c. 1964. The Signal box was closed on 24th February 1965 when all the Down yard was taken out of use. It was not until c. July/August that the yard was cleared of remaining wagons by No. 7829 *Ramsbury Manor* (then allocated to Gloucester Horton Road). Not long after the last working the Signal box was demolished.

On the 25th August 1976 the 06.35 am Toton to Severn Tunnel Junction freight became derailed at a point east of the main road bridge running from Toddington to Winchcombe. It was a miracle that the train continued running for some distance until the curve became too much and it crashed blocking both lines at a point near the entrance of the old Down yard.

Winchcombe looking in the Up direction, the curve on which the station was set can clearly be seen in this scene taken on 27th February 1960. Note the offset station nameboard.   *Photo: D Bath*

The Down Sunday 'Cornishman' express coasts through Winchcombe behind class 47 No. 1672 Colossus *having been diverted from the Lickey route to allow for vital engineering work to be carried out. c. 1968.*   *Photo: G H Tilt*

7.20 Gretton Halt

The villagers of Gretton asked the Great Western Railway if they could have a siding to serve the needs of local farmers. This went before the GWR Traffic Committee on 28th February 1906 but was refused. However the construction of a halt was granted at an estimated cost of £310. Gretton Halt was opened along with the section from Winchcombe to Bishops Cleeve on 1st June 1906. At 13 miles 36 chains from Honeybourne East Loop it served the village of its namesake and Stanley Pontlarge. The 100 ft platforms had 'Pagoda' shelters on both sides. A 50 ft extension to these platforms was authorized in November 1906 costing £30. This halt came under the jurisdiction of the Station Master at Winchcombe. The halt lasted to the end of local services ie 7th March 1960 thus outlasting its larger neighbour at Gotherington.

Gretton Halt awaits its last week of local services. Looking east, this view was taken on 27th February 1960.   *Photo: D Bath*

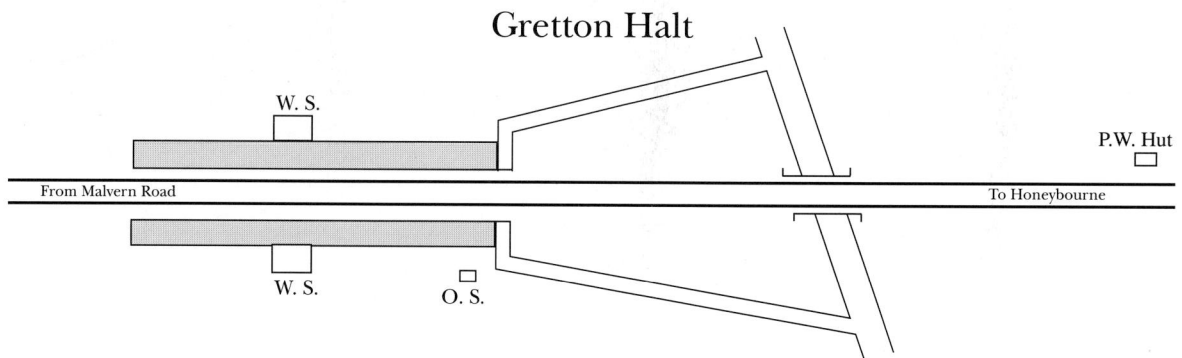

Gretton Halt

W. S.

P.W. Hut

From Malvern Road

To Honeybourne

W. S.   O. S.

7.21

G. W. R.

Gotherington

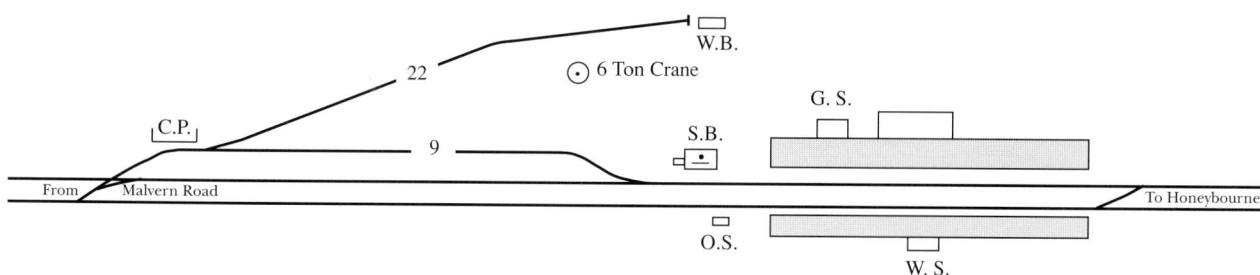

houses and the Station Master's house. The first Station Master from May 1906 until September 1907 was Mr G Swanatt. By March 1908 the authorized staff was:–

1 Station Master Class 3 and 1 Porter/Signalman.

By March 1934 only 1 Porter/Signalman was assigned to the station. From c. 1923 the station was supervised from elsewhere, coming initially under the Station Master at Bishops Cleeve and (from 1931) the staff came under the control of Winchcombe.

Commencing from 25th February 1911 any local goods train in either direction that had work to perform, was to be shunted onto the opposite line if being followed by a local or through passenger service. If the box was not open then it had to be shunted at Bishops Cleeve or Winchcombe yet if Gotherington Signal Box was open and to save time and any delay, if the train was short enough then the siding was to be used.

Before World War I (1913) receipts were in the region of £900 per year with total tonnage being 1,457 tons. By 1933 this had dropped off to £122 and 314 tons respectively. In its last full year (1940) the tonnage figure dropped to 206 tons. Cattle and pigs were taken to Gloucester Market on Monday mornings but this traffic was not extensive. As traffic became increasingly sparse the station was demoted to the status of halt from 1st January 1941.

The Great Western must have had great expectations for developing traffic here for a large signal box was provided with 33 levers only 20 of which were in use. The traffic never alas materialized. The box throughout its life was 'open as required' but the timetable for January 1921 shows that it was open to traffic on a regular basis in midweek from 10.00 am

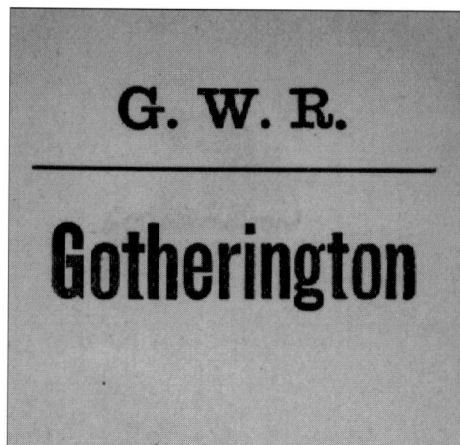

Gotherington at 15 miles 33 chains from Honeybourne East Loop was opened to the public on 1st June 1906. It had the usual facilities, the buildings here (like those at Bishops Cleeve) built of local Cleeve Hill stone. No footbridge was provided and so the usual barrow crossing crossed the lines at the Cheltenham end of the 400 ft platforms. A small gable goods shed was situated on the Up platform along with the main building. The goods facilities were further complimented by a 6 ton crane in the yard. Later in July 1909 provision for livestock was authorized at a cost of £192. The usual 15 ton weighbridge was provided and lasted until being scrapped in May 1949.

November 1906
When signal box is switched out, the Down distant signal lamp must be left burning at night.

The station was on the edge of the village and on the same drive were situated a pair of semi detached

Gotherington

to 12.30 pm. Probably it was open on summer Saturdays in the 1930s but no evidence exists, it was however opened when out of gauge trains were about, on Sundays in particular.

The signal box, sidings and connections were taken out of use on 3rd April 1949, and removed on 11th September 1949. Finally the halt closed to passengers on 13th June 1955.

This Station today is a private house, the owner having restored the platforms and buildings to their former glory.

Opening day at Gotherington, 1st June 1906 showing the main building on the Up platform. *Photo: P Abbott*

The closed halt of Gotherington stands forlorn, a shadow of its former self. It closed in June 1955 and this photo was taken on 27th February 1960.
Photo: D Bath

7.22

G. W. R.

Bishops Cleeve

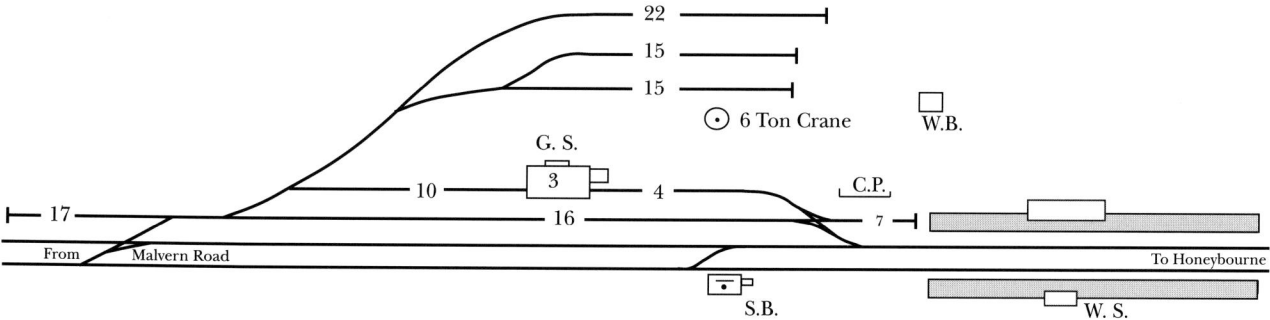

The signal box locking frame was installed as early as 12th February 1906 but when brought into use on the opening only 14 levers were in use with 17 still spare, showing yet again a very temporary initial layout as had been the case at Broadway, Toddington and Winchcombe. When inspected in July for the opening to Cheltenham the BoT Inspector noted alterations to the interlocking with 22 levers in use and 9 spare. With the opening of the line to Malvern Road East on 1st August 1906 a block switch was provided in the signal box.

The yard contained all the usual facilities, the goods shed having a 30 cwt crane. A loading dock was situated to the south end of the Up platform. Some stone traffic and cattle traffic was generated from here and by the start of World War I the total goods tonnage was 4,199 tons yielding receipts of £1,557. Twenty years later it was beginning a downward slide at 3,387 tons with total receipts being no better than £1,843.

From c. 1923 Gotherington came under the wing of the Station Master at Bishops Cleeve, all staff coming under his jurisdiction, but by 1931 this had been transferred to the Winchcombe Station Master.

Although staff patterns are a little unclear the GWR Traffic Committee had authorized that by March 1908 there should be:–

1	Station Master
2	Signalmen
1	Porter
1	Lad Porter

Bishops Cleeve station at 16 miles 76 chains from Honeybourne East Loop opened to passengers on 1st June 1906 when the line was brought into use from Winchcombe. The omnibus service that had served the station from Winchcombe since February 1905 now ran only from Bishops Cleeve to Cheltenham.

The platforms were of the standard 400 ft with waiting room and a mens lavatory on the Down side and the main station on the Up platform. All the buildings here were constructed of the local Cleeve Hill stone. There was no footbridge provided here so the barrow crossing had to be used by passengers and staff alike. This was the scene of one of the most tragic accidents in the lines history whereby two sisters returning from the cloak room were cut down by an express in August 1928. They mistook an express for their stopping train and ran in front of it on the barrow crossing. A verdict of accidental death was recorded.

Bishops Cleeve

112

Note the use of local stone for the buildings taken in this view of Bishops Cleeve, c. 1910, with a steam railmotor on a Down local service to Cheltenham.
Photo: Gloucestershire Record Office

GWR No. 7820 Dinmore Manor *awaiting the road outside Bishops Cleeve Signal Box. June 1959*
Photo: L C Jacks

The ex 2.34 pm (Saturdays only) Honeybourne to Cheltenham passes Bishops Cleeve Signal Box behind No. 9727. Taken on 27th February 1960.

Photo: D Bath

By March 1934 it was:–

1	Station Master Class 5
3	Signalmen Class 4
1	Porter

Total wages – £765

Like all the other stations along the line, Bishops Cleeve also had staff houses, being one pair of semi detached and the Station Master's house.

A weighbridge was provided here being of a 15 ton capacity and was withdrawn in early 1964.

Several race trains were stored and serviced here in the early days but nothing on the scale of Toddington further up the line. Sometimes on these specials the Queen's coach would be added and it was here that Her Majesty would detrain.

From the 1st September 1950 the booking office closed, by this time the staff numbered 4 and the station came under the supervision of Cheltenham.

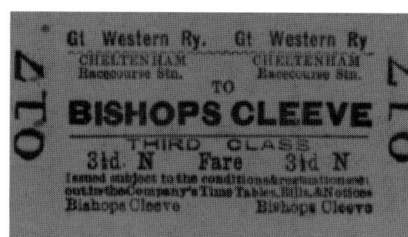

This style of ticket was issued between 1937 and 1940. However this single from Cheltenham Race Course Station to Bishops Cleeve is dated as late as 14th October 1959.

Courtesy: T David

Freight and passenger traffic declined, although the station closed on 7th March 1960 the goods yard remained open until 1st July 1963. The box lasted until 11th August 1965, its closure making the block section one from Toddington to Malvern Road East.

7.23 Cheltenham Race Course Station

Race Course Station at 18 miles 63 chains from Honeybourne East Loop was opened on 12th March 1912. It consisted of two platforms each of 700 ft in length, being 15 ft wide and 3 ft high. Later the Down platform was extended to 960 ft at the South end. Lavatories were situated on both platforms. The waiting room/booking office was situated on the Down side near the road bridge, which was the only means of crossing from one platform to another. The footpaths led from each platform and were on a gradient of 1 in 14 with barriers at the entrance to slow down surging crowds and help the ticket collectors in the task of identifying 'fare dodgers'.

Two official sources show that a wooden signal box was proposed here, situated on the Down side at the South end of the platform. However photographic evidence suggests that a box had always been at the North end on the Up side. This 6 lever box was manned only on race days and in general by Cheltenham district relief signalmen. These relief signalmen cannot have been considered country lads for on the top of the train register for the meeting held 15th April 1914 reads :–

cuckoo heard on the racecourse 3.43 pm!.

It was often the practice in the early days to stop the Up afternoon railmotor during a race. The last race meeting during World War I, was held 15th April 1915, there being no races during 1916 to 1918, the first meeting after hostilities being the meeting 8th/9th May 1919. The signal box had not been open during this time to help with shortening the section.

With the onset of the 1920s came the start of the prestigious 'Blue Riband' event, the Cheltenham Gold Cup. It was first run in 1924 and held in the March of each year during the 3 day meeting. The GWR soon attracted many people to the event, laying on special passenger traffic, running up to 8 in 1924 and 10 trains in 1930.

The Cheltenham Race Course booking office at the top of the station approach on the Down side.   *Photo: A Baker*

The March Festival of 1935 saw the signal box open all week for the first time. This was the first occasion of which the horses were unloaded/loaded here, on the platforms at the Race Course Station. Until then they had been taken through to Bishops Cleeve whence they had been transported by road to the course or ridden by their grooms!

During 1936 the box was manned from July through to September on Saturdays between 11 am and 6 pm to assist with traffic, this becoming the usual arrangement in succeeding years.

Most of the local passenger trains would continue to stop at the station on race days as well as the specials

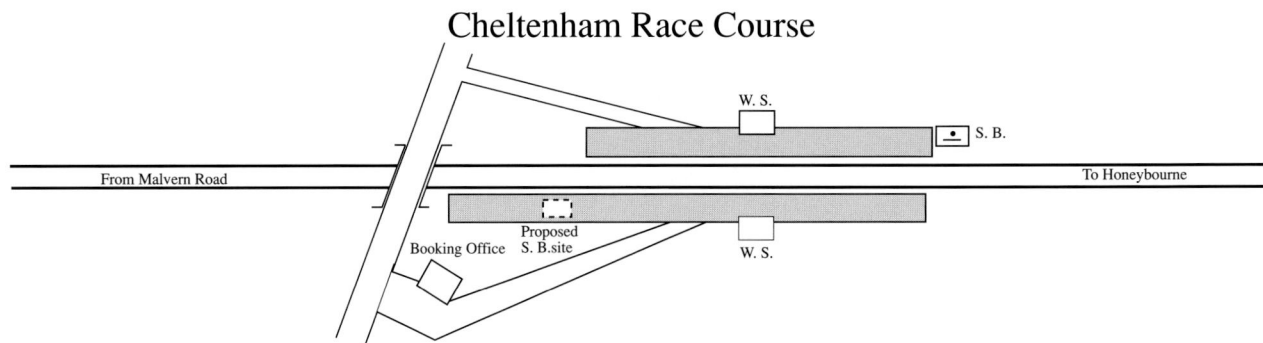

Cheltenham Race Course

The Stephenson Locomotive Society ran a farewell trip on the line on the last day of through services. It is seen here as members take photographs at Cheltenham Race Course on 23rd March 1968.   *Photo: G H Tilt*

laid on. Some of the through expresses made additional stops. The GWR also ran specials to here on normal race days.

Race traffic was very important to the GWR. Not only did the Company have Cheltenham to serve but also other famous courses were dotted about its system and later Stratford Racecourse was also given a Station.

With the opening of the Cheltenham Race Course Station the GWR soon set up a pattern of traffic that was to last to the end of the line viz six trains arriving via the Cheltenham direction and several from the north. While all this was going on all the other normal services would run but the freight traffic would be held back until the race traffic was out of the way.

To accommodate these trains the sidings at certain stations along the route had to be emptied in advance. In the early days the Cardiff and Bristol (Bedminster)

trains were stored at Bishops Cleeve with the engines running to Gloucester to be turned. Later from the 1930s onwards these services were handled at Winchcombe with the engines going to Honeybourne to turn and take water at Toddington on their return. At Winchcombe the coaches from the Bristol were put in the Up refuge and the Cardiff in the Down goods siding. When both engines returned the Cardiff engine pulled the Bristol rake out, allowing the Bristol engine to go to the Cheltenham end of the coaches which it then pulled back into the Up refuge to await its allotted departure. The Cardiff engine then went to its own stock.

At Toddington 3 or 4 trains could be stored and serviced, the London 1st Class, London Mixed and Tote were the regulars. The trains were stored on the packing shed line, middle road and Up refuge being crossed over via the southern crossover and setting back. One of these workings went back to Paddington via Kingham during the early 1920s instead of the normal route via the Stroud Valley line. The engines were again run light engine up to Honeybourne and turned.

At Broadway the Hereford train would be cleaned, again with the engine going up to Honeybourne, the train being stored in the Down refuge by the goods shed.

In the other direction stock would be worked through to Malvern Road and engines would be serviced at the shed. The order in which the south bound trains would return was normally:–

1 London 1st Class
2 London Mixed
3 Bristol (Bedminster)
4 Cardiff
5 Hereford
6 Tote

Returning in the opposite direction were:–

Leamington

Wolverhampton

Worcester (Henwick)

The London 1st Class contained the saloon carriage of Miss Dorothy Paget who frequented the races a lot and had been introduced to racing by her cousin Mr J H Whitney, the owner of Easter Hero who won the Gold Cup in 1929 and 1930. She then proceeded to be the owner of the most successful horse of the day, 'Golden Miller'. 'The Miller' ran to victory in the race from 1932 to 1936 (a feat that has never been surpassed) and in 1934 went on to win the Grand National, the only horse to win both in the one season. Miss Paget's

The last steam hauled race special from Paddington is seen at Cheltenham Race Course on 14th March 1963 behind Castle No. 7029 Clun Castle.
Photo: W Potter

Returning race special to Paddington run behind Western D1028 Western Hussar *seen at Honeybourne West Loop. The stock and the locomotive having come from servicing at Worcester. This was to be the last day of working these specials via the line, being dated 18th March 1976.* Photo: A Baker

reputation was fearsome but she was very generous to all the railway staff, tipping all concerned very generously.

The first mention of a diesel car running along the line shows up in the box register when the meeting of 2nd November 1934 took place, being offered under the bellcode of '4' from Malvern Road East at 10.33 am and returning at 4.39 pm from the Bishops Cleeve direction later that day. Diesel rail cars had been introduced earlier that summer to the route, commencing on 9th July running between Birmingham Snow Hill and Cardiff.

The World War II saw racecourse traffic take on the same pattern as World War I. The course was closed after the March meeting of 1942 and reopened for the March meeting of 1945.

Traffic began to decline throughout the 1950s, due to competition from coach companies and more people owning their own cars, and so the station was closed on 25th March 1968. The signal box with its sliding window shutters, used to protect the windows when not in use, had closed on 9th February 1964.

British Rail decided to reopen the station for the meeting of 18th March 1971, and it was used for subsequent meetings. The Queen detrained here on 7th April on her way to Cheltenham. Latterly empty stock was worked through to Worcester or Gloucester for servicing although on occasion multiple units were stored at Honeybourne. The 3 day festival meeting on 16/17/18th March 1976 saw the last of these workings, for after the accident at Winchcombe on 25th August 1976 the line was effectively closed. This however did not prevent race specials running, being run via Lansdown Station where the passengers were omnibussed out to the racecourse, a practice that is continued to this day.

7.24 Cheltenham (High Street Halt)

High Street Halt at 20 miles 35 chains from Honeybourne East Loop was opened 1st October 1908 and consisted of two platforms each of 155 ft in length, 8 ft wide and 3 ft high. It was situated to the south of the High Street. Each platform had a small waiting room and office. These platforms were connected by an arched subway and were reached from the High Street by means of a footpath and steps. The engineers bill for its construction went before the GWR Traffic Committee in March 1908 and was estimated to cost £1,246. The cost of construction came to £1,248. The difference of £2 being accounted for by additional signalling work! This halt was supervised from the outset by St. James Station, but how long this can have lasted is unclear for tickets could easily be obtained from the guard on the railmotors. Due to wartime economies the halt closed 30th April 1917, and never reopened.

A steam railmotor arriving at High Street Halt Cheltenham with an ex Honeybourne service. Of special note are the two Pagodas which are constructed from Universal Roof Covering supplied by Messrs S Taylor & Co Birmingham. It was this company that supplied the roofing materials for the booking office at Cheltenham Racecourse (see page 114) and the verandah and footbridge roof at Malvern Road.
Photo: T Sims

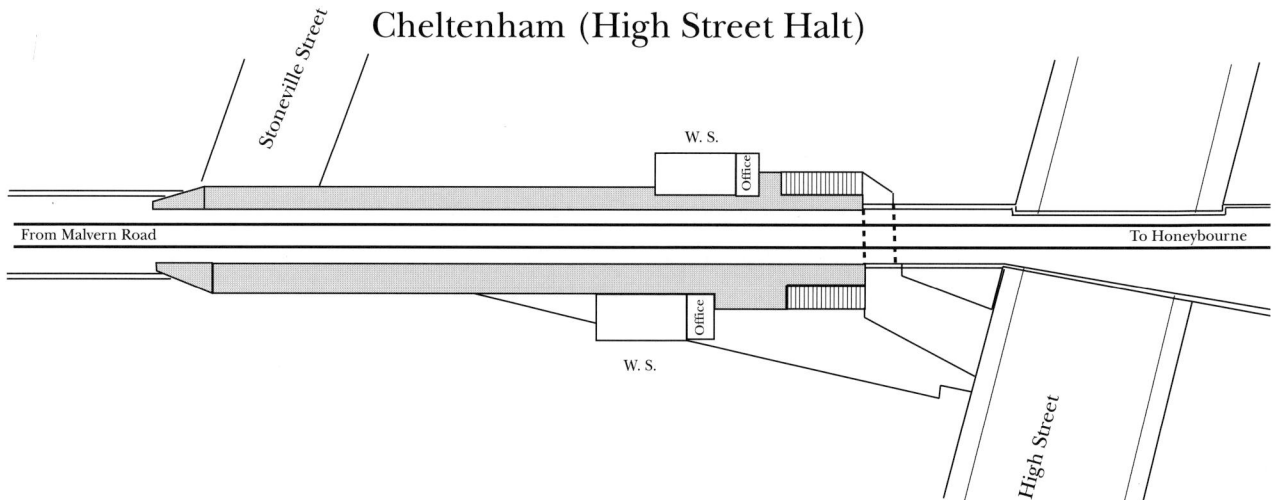

Cheltenham (High Street Halt)

Stoneville Street

W. S.

Office

From Malvern Road

To Honeybourne

Office

W. S.

High Street

7.25

Malvern Road Station lay to the south of the junction with the line from Stratford and that of the one from Cheltenham St. James. The name was derived from the road immediately to the north and from which it was approached by a long driveway. The station was 21 miles 3 chains from Honeybourne East Loop and 29 miles 1 chains from Stratford on Avon. It was opened on 30th March 1908, with a central island platform serving both main running lines and a bay at the north end. It was where in this bay that the local

branch trains to and from Honeybourne reversed before going back into the terminus station at St. James. Before the construction of the large station all branch trains stopped short of Malvern Road Station at Malvern Road East Signal Box (20 miles 62 chains) and reversed from there into the terminus. When Sunday services commenced in 1909, they used this old procedure and did not run to Malvern Road Station. St. James was much nearer to the centre of the town.

All through expresses stopped at the station from 1st July 1908 but did not reverse to St. James to which a connecting service was run by either using the local services to and from Honeybourne or the services to Gloucester and Kingham. The curved island platform was reached via a footbridge from the booking office situated at the end of the driveway on the Down side. The Up platform facing measured 860 ft long, the Down 702 ft long.

To the west of the station lay several loop sidings and locomotive facilities, access to these was controlled by two signal boxes, one at either end of the layout. To the north was Malvern Road East, opened 15th July 1906 having 49 levers of which 5 levers were spare. This box replaced the Bayshill Signal Box that had controlled the access to the old loco shed which had stood in the line of the route of the new line to Honeybourne. To

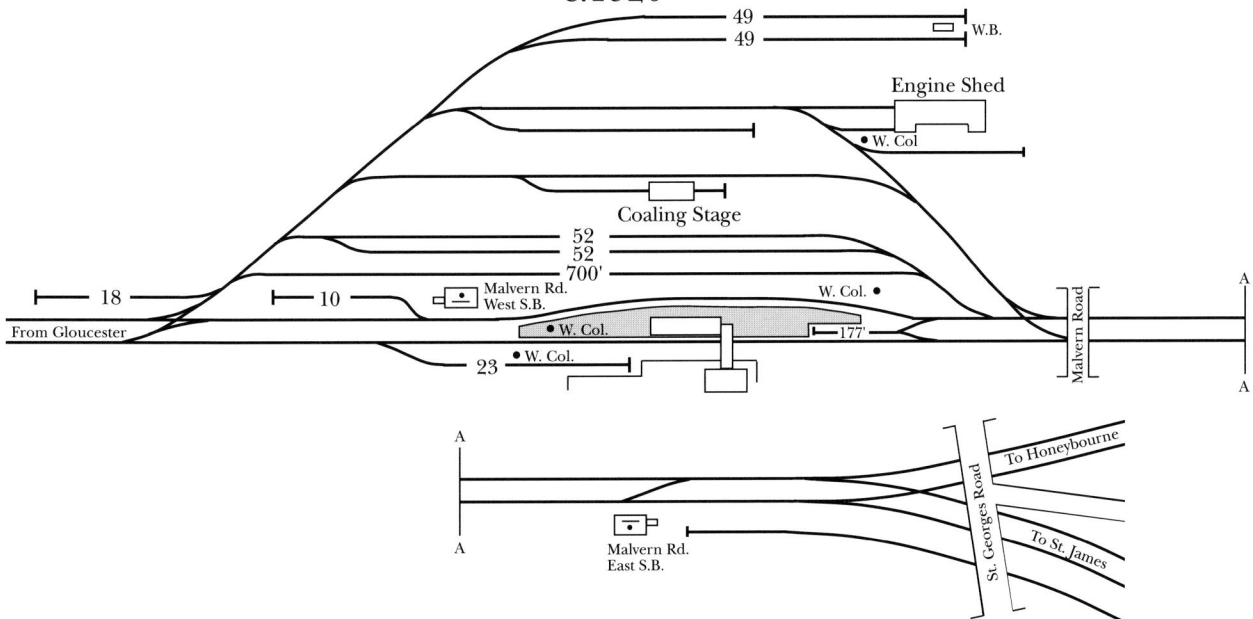

Taken from St. Georges Road bridge of the junction controlled by Malvern Road East signal box. The line in the foreground on the left leads into St. James while the one on the right leads to Stratford. Late 1965.   *Photo: G H Tilt*

Cheltenham Malvern Road shed on 8th June 1963. No. 8491 and No. 8743 stand outside the shed, which closed in March 1964.

Photo: J Wood

With rising gradients of 1 in 108 and 1 in 200 (between Malvern Road and Bishops Cleeve), instructions were issued to the effect that any freight trains could be banked as far as Bishops Cleeve. The assisting loco attached to the guards van and upon reaching there detached.

Staffing figures are unclear for they were included with St. James which took general responsibility for the station along with High Street Halt and Race Course Station.

Britannia No. 70045 Lord Rowallan *stands opposite Cheltenham Spa Malvern Road West Signal Box on a Wolverhampton to Ilfracombe and Minehead train on 7th August 1965.*
Photo: W Potter

the south was Malvern Road West which was open by June 1908 having 37 levers, it replaced a temporary box that dated from 8th August 1906. Long distance services were suspended for a period towards the end of World War I, this included closure of certain stations on the Great Western Railway system. Malvern Road was one of these, opening again on 7th July 1919.

The weighbridge in the yard was of 15 ton capacity (replaced in 1930 by a 20 ton version) but very little in the way of goods were handled here and no crane was provided. Most freight traffic was dealt with at the St. James Station.

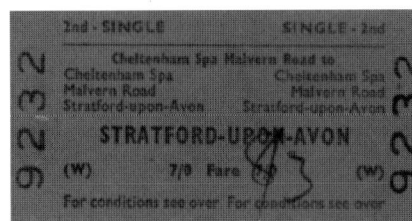

The very last ticket issued from Cheltenham Spa Malvern Road to Stratford Upon Avon, 1st January 1966.
Courtesy: T David

The station closed to traffic on 3rd January 1966. Malvern Road West Signal Box closed on 5th June 1966, the Malvern Road East Signal Box lasted until 3rd November 1970.

In the bay platform at Malvern Road the ex 2.30 pm St. James waits to depart (2.36 pm) behind No. 8488. Having arrived behind No. 4116 with 8488 in tow, 4116 would be detached. This was taken on the last day of local services, 5th March 1960.
Photo: D Bath

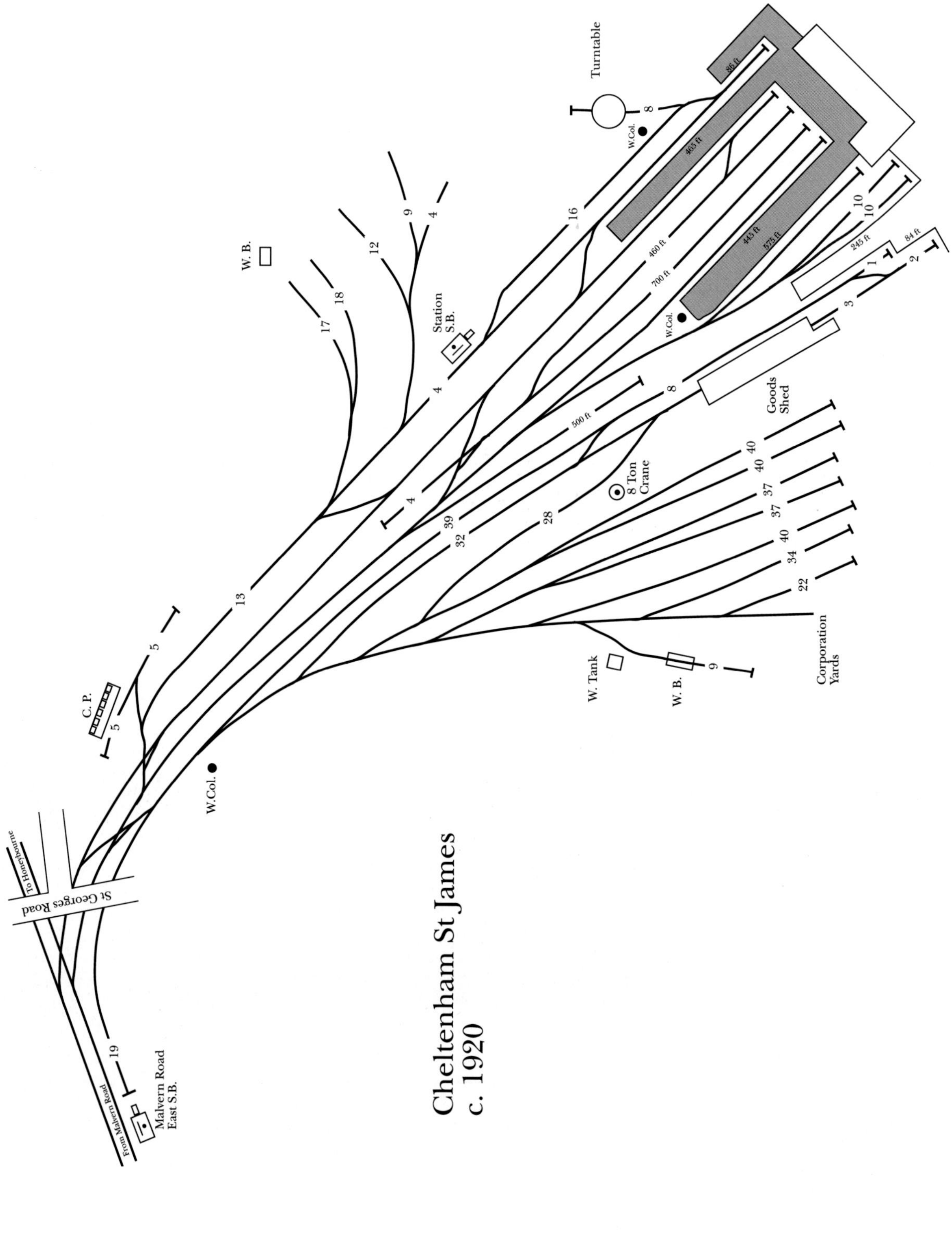

122

Cheltenham St James
c. 1920

Turntable

W.Col. ●

8

465 ft

16

460 ft

W.Col. ●

700 ft

445 ft

575 ft

10

10

245 ft

3

1

84 ft

2

Goods
Shed

8

W. B.

9

4

500 ft

Station
S.B.

12

9

4

17

18

4

39

32

28

8 Ton
Crane

40

40

37

37

40

34

22

Corporation
Yards

W. Tank

W. B.

9

13

5

C. P.

5

W.Col. ●

To Honeybourne

St Georges Road

Malvern Road
East S.B.

19

From Malvern Road

Malvern Road

7.26

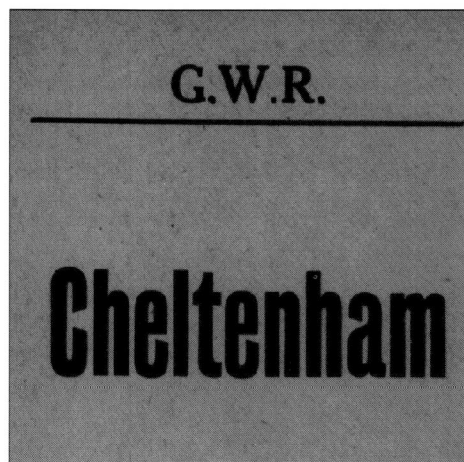

Cheltenham Station (later known as St. James) opened to traffic on the 23rd October 1847 and acted as the terminus for Gloucester trains and those from London. Originally it was laid to the broad gauge but this was replaced by the standard gauge in May 1872. The station probably had an all over roof and even in those early days had an extensive yard, which was later added to and greatly expanded as traffic increased. Some form of signalling existed in the early days but at present very little is known.

By 1893 this layout was controlled by two signal boxes; Bayshill Signal Box and Cheltenham Station Signal Box both of which are believed to have opened in 1893. The former which took its name from the neighbouring district had a 33 lever frame that controlled the throat of the station yard, and lasted until 15th July 1906, when it was replaced by Malvern Road East Signal Box being a little further to the south. The Cheltenham Station Signal Box was of the same construc-

General view of the layout at St. James in late 1965, looking towards the station.   *Photo: G H Tilt*

The grand exterior of St. James station shows well in this view taken on 27th February 1960. *Photo: D Bath*

tion as the Bayshill Box having a brick base and timber top. At first a 45 lever frame was installed but this was replaced in 1920 by a 53 lever frame at a cost of £910. The box lasted until 15th June 1966.

Large quantities of goods were handled in the yard here, which was provided with a 205 ft goods shed containing 4 cranes within of 30 cwt capacity, plus a yard crane of 8 ton capacity.

Prior to the new engine shed at Malvern Road being built in 1907, engines were maintained at a shed of broad gauge origins, which was positioned opposite to where the Malvern Road East Signal Box eventually stood. The broad gauge shed was converted for narrow gauge locomotives on the abolition of the wider gauge and the turntable that had been in use had been taken away by 1895. The shed was done away with in 1906 because the alignment of the new line from Honeybourne required to go through its immediate area. The new shed at Malvern Road was intended to get a turntable but one was never installed because one was

available at the St. James Station, which enabled the turning of engines to be carried out. Malvern Road shed was doubled in size during World War II, but still no turntable was provided and any large engines requiring turning either went to Gloucester or turned on the triangle between Hatherley Junction, Lansdown Junction and Gloucester Loop Junction signal boxes. The shed had large coaling facilities and water cranes and was finally closed on 2nd March 1964.

From the 11th May 1908 the station became known as Cheltenham St. James, being finally given the title Cheltenham Spa (St. James) from the 1st February 1925. It was from this station that the Great Western ran its famous crack train 'The Cheltenham Flyer', inaugurated on 9th July 1923. Although it did not achieve much distinction on the early part of the run up as far as Swindon, it made up for that on the downhill run thence to London over which it was timed to be the 'fastest train in the world' at that time.

With the withdrawal of services from Kingham in October 1962 and the loss the previous year of services from the former Midland and South Western system in September 1961 the station finally closed on 3rd January 1966. The station also closed to goods from that date although the coal yard remained open until 31st October 1966, this being worked as a long siding from Malvern Road East Signal Box after the closure in the June of that year of the Station Signal Box.

Arriving with an afternoon train from Gloucester is Mogul 2-6-0 No. 6349. Seen here at Platform 3 on 7th August 1964. Note the GW on the tender. Photo: J Wood

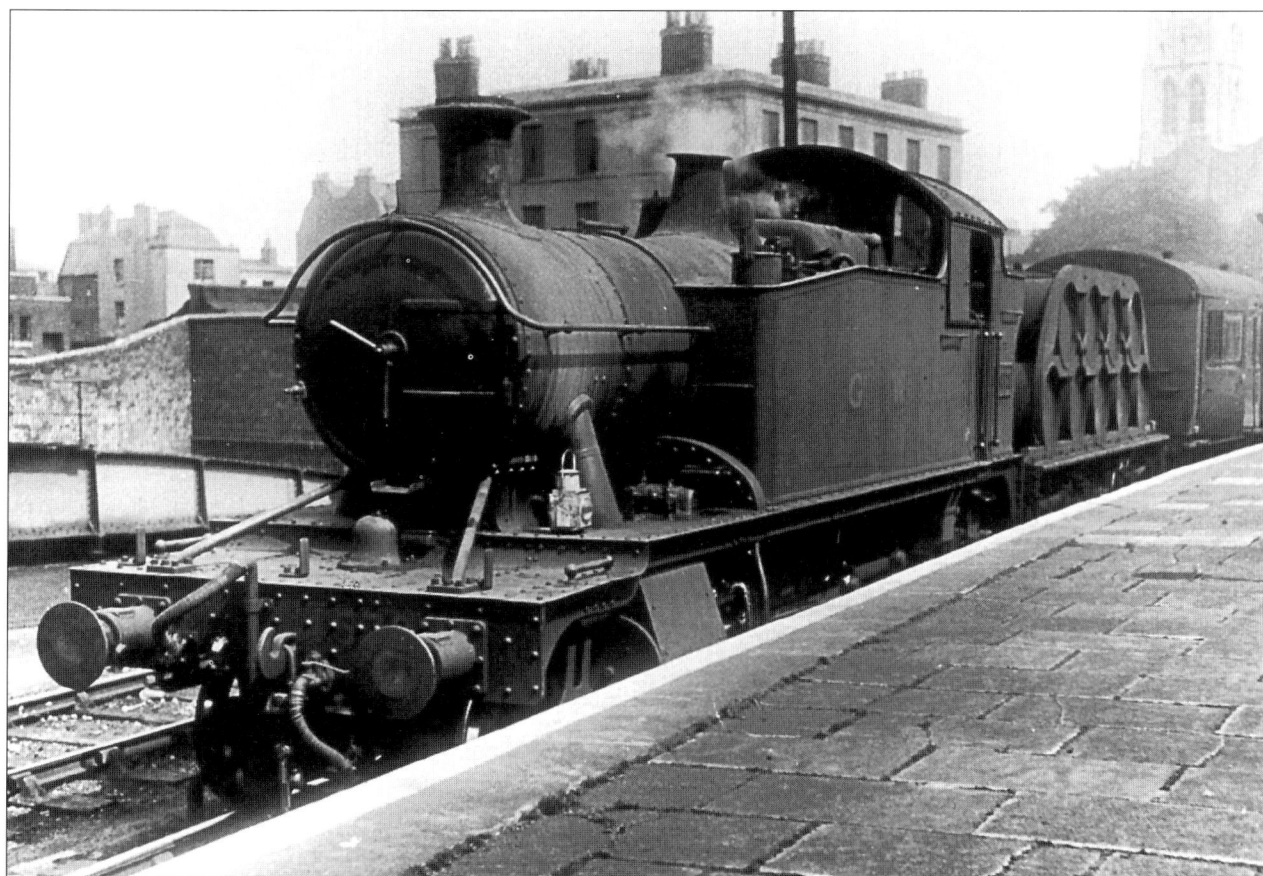

The last ticket collected dated 1st January 1966.

Prairie 2-6-2 No. 4578 stands at St. James with a 'Cordon' and auto coach on 9th August 1948. Photo: Evesham Almonry

Two views of the blanketing at Winchcombe in the Autumn/Winter of 1949. Note the empty wagons in the distance which when required were let down the incline to the working area by gravity.   *Photo: Authors Collection*

Looking towards the roadbridge, excavation on the Down road in progress Autumn/Winter 1949.   *Photo: Authors Collection*

8

Blanketing

Throughout the history of the line the problem of poor drainage had always raised its ugly head, in fact it was a constant headache to the permanent way gangs. Renewal of trackbed on certain sections of the line became necessary due to the clay sub soil clogging the ballast, rainfall having caused the clay to soften and form a slurry that in turn clogged the ballast and blocked the drainage system. This mainly occurred in the cuttings where the clay was forced to the surface. Finally after many problems enough money was set aside after World War II for proper remedial work to be carried out.

Occupation of long lengths of line became necessary, one track being renewed at a time with traffic working

The scene at Norton Junction on 23rd April 1957. On the left No. 2870 has been shunted onto the Up road. This has been carried out to allow No. 7026 Tenby Castle *(centre) with the 09.00 am Wolverhampton to Penzance express to pass the freight train. The Down 'Cornishman' has been diverted due to blanketing work on the Honeybourne to Cheltenham section of the line. On the right Worcester Shed have sent out No. 6947* Helmingham Hall *which will back onto the train and take it over the ex Midland route where it will rejoin the Western line again at Cheltenham. No. 7026* Tenby Castle *would then go to Worcester to await the return working.*   Photo: *Courtesy of the National Railway Museum, York (T E Williams Collection)*

on the other line enabling materials to be removed by mechanical excavating plant. The excavation was carried to a depth of 2–5 feet depending on the extent of the damage. Having disposed of this material a layer (blanket) of stonedust was laid forming a membrane on which a layer of graded ballast was added. Top ballast was then added to which the track was laid.

This would then be repeated on the other line. The occupation of the remaining line would be given up at night to allow trains to run at reduced speed. Traffic was worked on the single line by electric train token.

The first blanketing was carried out in October and November 1949 at Winchcombe, on the section from the station through to the tunnel (a distance of 24 chains). Possession of the line was taken on 15 weekends with services replaced from Cheltenham to Honeybourne by Bristol Blue Buses. The Down line was done first and the Up then followed. All the waste materials were conveyed to the spoil tip at Stoke Gifford. So heavy were these trains of waste that they needed banking assistance from the station up through the tunnel. The Up refuge at this time was occupied by ballast wagons with the new materials for the work. Simultaneously similar work was carried out in Dixton Cutting between Gretton Halt and Gotherington with single line working being carried out between Bishops Cleeve and Winchcombe. Some blanketing was also carried out at Bishops Cleeve in the summer of 1950 (50 chains). Some further work was also carried out to the south of Cheltenham Racecourse around the 1955–7 period.

This was followed in 1957 by more major work in Stanton Cutting. The contract was awarded to R M Douglas and was by far the biggest such work to be undertaken along the line, with the work commencing in the March of 1957. All drainage between 7 miles 22 chains and 8 miles 35 chains was affected on both lines. The slopes of the cuttings being trimmed and regraded, yielding 6,669 cubic yards of materials. The actual blanketing took place between 7 miles 37 chains to 7 miles 58 chains and 8 miles 13 chains to 8 miles 32 chains on the Down side and between 7 miles 34½ chains to 8 miles 32 chains on the Up line. A total of 14,827 cubic yards was excavated for the new formation. The spoil was tipped between 8 miles 34 chains and 8 miles 66 chains. The R M Douglas workforce were conveyed by coach every day from Cheltenham departing at 6.15 am and returned from the site departing at 6.45 pm. This work lasted until September/October of that year. For the duration of the work

a temporary signal box with 5 levers was brought into use. It was located on the Up side just to the south of Laverton Halt, and was named Stanton Cutting Signal Box. The work was carried out during the day by the contractor. At nights the line was open to freight traffic, utilizing the line that had not been lifted. The electric train token worked the section from the temporary signal box to Toddington Signal Box. Access to the work site on this section could be gained from both ends. The work lasted for 3 months on the Up road and for 3 months on the Down. The Stanton Cutting Signal Box was manned for 24 hours a day on two 12 hour turns, worked by relief signalmen S Marshall and H Burrows. When the work was completed 11,000 sq yards of the embankments were sown with grass seed supplied by Sutton Seeds.

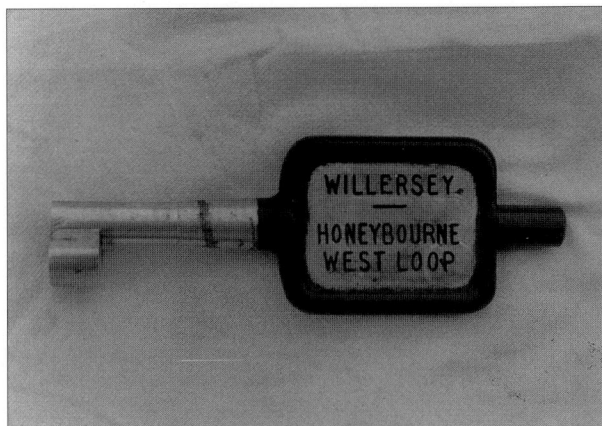

One of the temporary aluminium tokens used in conjunction with blanketing.   *Photo: A Baker*

The following year saw the signal box relocated at Willersey, just to the north of the halt and again on the Up side. This split the Honeybourne West Loop to Broadway section. Work was carried out in both of these new block sections between 2nd February 1958 to 6th April 1958. On the section from Willersey to Broadway access to the work site could only be gained from the Willersey end and as at Stanton Cutting all 5 levers in the temporary Willersey Signal Box were in use. On the section to West Loop access could be gained from either end, work in this section was carried out at Weston Sub Edge. To eliminate any alterations to the pointwork at these temporary sites when changing over from working on the Down line to working on the Up, the running line was slewed which created a 'S' in the track at some stage of the work. The waste spoil from these jobs went to the tip siding 'B' at Honeybourne.

With the opening of the new signal box at Evesham in March 1957 and the connection between the two systems (ex GWR/LMS) through running direct to Ashchurch soon took place. Through GW/WR trains such as 'The Cornishman' were diverted at Honeybourne and run to Norton Junction (Worcester) and there met by a locomotive which took over and went on Down to Bristol via the LMS route. The same procedure occurred in the other direction.

The local services terminated at either end of the sections being worked on, and passengers were bused between these points.

The Down Sunday 'Cornishman' (headboard reversed) passes the Honeybourne West Loop Junction with Castle No. 4077 Chepstow Castle on 23rd August 1959. Lying in the sixfoot and cess are evidence of much signalling engineers activity. This was in preparation for the new Honeybourne West Loop. The old West Loop Signal Box can just be seen under the Worcester to Oxford railway bridge, by the rear of the train. The bracket signal on the Up side (left) had recently replaced the original tall all wooden bracket that stood in the same spot for over fifty years.   *Photo: G England*

At the time this picture was taken (6th July 1933) this 4-4-0 County was the last in service. No. 3834 County of Somerset *heads a south bound train. She was withdrawn in November 1933. Seen here at Stratford on Avon station just to the north of the Alcester Road bridge.*

Photo: L T Parker

Railcar No. 3, one of the original 'Flying Bananas' and one of the first to be seen at Stratford. Seen here in the Up refuge by Shottery Lane footpath c. 1934.

Photo: A T Locke

9

Rise and fall

The pattern of passenger traffic was virtually unaltered throughout the history of the line. Local services were run via Honeybourne. The express traffic between the industrial Midlands and Devon and Cornwall resorts was intermingled by a few South Wales trains. Although the through services did not become popular until after World War I, they soon became more extensively used by the Birmingham populace. All the trains started from either Wolverhampton or Birmingham Snow Hill and it was soon realised that seats were readily available on these trains. The trains on the Midland Railway at New Street, who had come from afar were often overcrowded.

From the outset of through workings (upon the opening of the North Warwick line on 1st July 1908) a service was run from Wolverhampton (10.00 am) to Penzance and return. There then followed several short lived long distance services. On the above date a Cardiff to Yarmouth train was introduced running for the summer only and again in 1909. It was not revived for the 1910 season. In 1909 a service was run between Birkenhead and Bristol (this train was named the 'Shakespeare Express' for the 1910 season only) but it soon ceased with the outbreak of World War I. Towards the end of the War through services were suspended.

With the introduction of the 1928 summer timetable, 14 through services were running along the route in midweek and on Friday nights and Saturdays, 31 such trains used the line. Such destinations as Cardiff, Gloucester, Ilfracombe, Penzance (2), Swansea, Taunton, Truro, Weston Super Mare (7) and Weymouth, could all be reached by trains from Birmingham Snow Hill. The pattern did not alter greatly in the 1938 timetable except for a few less Saturday Only trains, midweek services now ran to Cardiff from Birmingham Snow Hill using diesel railcars. Through services were again suspended during the World War II from 25th September 1939 to 1st October 1945 due to an alternative route (the Lickey) being available. Yet the timetable for May 1944 does show one 'A' head-code working from Birmingham Snow Hill to Cardiff and return. After the War traffic built up again as it had done after World War 1. This peaked again in the 1950s and by 1959 services to and from Birmingham

Snow Hill were run to Fishguard Harbour, Ilfracombe, Kingswear, Minehead, Newquay, Paignton, Pembroke Dock, Penzance, Swansea and Weston super Mare on summer Saturdays.

The route proved a valuable link in the GWR network and it also proved an invaluable diversionary route throughout its lifetime.

While the LMS was doing the major reconstruction programme which included the demolition of Cofton Tunnel (1926–1929) on the Lickey route, the line saw the running of LMS engines and stock. Towards the end of the line's life diversions came off the LMR line, occurring in March 1969, July 1971 and January 1972.

A most notable diversion over the line occurred on 15th January 1936, when all traffic between Paddington and South Wales was diverted through Gloucester, Cheltenham, Stratford, Hatton, Leamington, Oxford and Didcot after a night sleeper train ran into a goods van and trucks, at Shrivenham near Swindon (the locomotive involved was 'King' Class No. 6007 *King William* III, which due to the crash had to be rebuilt). Locomotives seen that day at Stratford included:–

2906 *Lady of Lyon*	4099 *Kilgerran Castle*
2928 *Saint Sebastian*	4952 *Peplow Hall*
2971 *Albion*	4960 *Pyle Hall*
3410 *Columbia*	4978 *Westwood Hall*
3417 *Lord Milday of Flete*	4993 *Dalton Hall*
4038 *Queen Berengaria*	5009 *Shrewsbury Castle*
4057 *Princess Elizabeth*	5027 *Farleigh Castle*
4080 *Powderham Castle*	5036 *Lyonshall Castle*
4091 *Dudley Castle*	5038 *Morlais Castle*
4092 *Dunraven Castle*	5927 *Guild Hall*
4096 *Highclere Castle*	

The line also became a means of conveying 'out of gauge' traffic from Birmingham to the docks, including many items for overseas. Most of this traffic had to be moved at very low speeds and was usually worked when it did not cause too much disruption to normal services. If clearances were close then the track would be temporarily slewed, just for the passing of these loads.

The Bordesley to Swindon goods soon became the turn for getting 'dead' or 'condemned' locomotives

132

Star No. 4017 Knight of Liège *heads a north bound Torquay to Birmingham express. Seen here at the north end of Stratford on Avon station 13th July 1935.*   Photo: L T Parker

Castle No. 5001 Llandovery Castle *with 8 wheeled tender stands just beyond the Alcester Road bridge awaiting departure on a south bound train. This tender was experimental being built in 1931 of 4,000 gallon capacity.*   Photo: A T Locke

Wartime (i) American Austerity S160 No. 2407 seen heading a northbound freight near the SMJ junction, Stratford on 18th September 1943.
Photo: A T Locke

Wartime (ii) LMS 2-8-0 No. 8414 pulls away from Stratford near to the Junction with branch into the Birmingham Road (Goods) on a northbound freight. Taken on 10th April 1944.
Photo: A T Locke

back to the 'Shrine'. For many loco's this was to be the last trip, and ex Cambrian Railway's engines were seen on this trip together with many older GWR types. One of the more unusual sights to be seen down the line, occurred when No. 9 of the Vale of Rheidol's 1 ft 11½ in gauge locomotive travelled on a well wagon next to 2–8–0 No. 3844 on the 9.10 am Bordesley to Swindon on 15th December 1959. This locomotive was on its way to Swindon works for overhaul.

Classes 60xx and 47xx locomotives (although the latter were allowed before World War II to work from Tyseley to Honeybourne via the North Warwick line) were the only engines barred from the line and most of the remaining classes saw service along it. But before 1927 a weight restriction imposed between Standish Junction and Yate on the Midland route meant that axle loading was restricted and newer more powerful engines of the GWR could not traverse the Stonehouse Viaduct. Until then 'Atabara' and 'Flower' classes and later 38xx 4–4–0 'Counties' had the main share of expresses. These were superseded in succession by 29xx 4–6–0 'Saints', 49xx 'Halls' and then 'Castles'. The first known working of a 'Hall' on the line occurred 15th June 1929, when No. 4930 *Hagley Hall* worked a Birmingham to Chepstow race special. Although 'Castles' had appeared at Stratford on many occasions on the London excursions via Hatton it was not until 6th March 1933 that the class began to work Wolverhampton to Penzance expresses. The first sightings of this class on through workings along the route had taken place on 30th November 1931, when No. 5009 *Shrewsbury Castle* was in charge of the Up 5.45 pm Swansea to Birmingham express.

With nationalization in 1948 the GWR disappeared 'on paper' overnight and gradually different types of locomotives could be seen, LMS types became more common and SR types were not so rare. When the Racecourse Junction was opened at Stratford, BR standard types became common, the bulk of which were mainly 92xxx 2–10–0's.

Although the passenger traffic was not of an intense nature it could still prove to be very busy with many services being run in several parts according to demand. So although the tables shown are for scheduled traffic they do not reflect the extras that were put on.

Railcars were used on the line being introduced on 9th July 1934. The first diesel railcars were of the express buffet type (Nos. 2–4) and worked between Cardiff and Birmingham Snow Hill. They had separate cabs at each end and could seat 44 passengers. They were eventually replaced by the last railcars to be built (Nos. 35–38 in 1941–2) having a cab at one end only and run as two pairs of twin units being provided with a corridor connection. An additional coach was sandwiched between the units and they proved very popular with the demand outstripping capacity they soon had to be replaced by locomotive hauled train formations. The first sighting of a diesel multiple unit at Stratford was on 16th September 1956 on a working from Llandudno. The following year (17th June) saw the introduction of Intercity DMU's between Birmingham Snow Hill to Cardiff and Swansea. The following year (9th June) saw improvement still further, there being 1 service to Carmarthen, 1 to Swansea and 3 to Cardiff using Cross Country DMU sets.

A returning southbound theatre special to Poole is seen here departing from Stratford behind No. 34044 Woolacombe *on 14th April 1964 with No. 2210 in the Up refuge siding.*
Photo: G England

GWR No. 6932 Burwarton Hall *on the 3.45 pm Birmingham Snow Hill to Cardiff express passing Mogul GWR No. 7322 working the 1.50 pm Bordesley Jctn to Stoke Gifford at Winchcombe. May 1960.* Photo: L C Jacks

Castle No. 7026 Tenby Castle *heads a Sunday Penzance to Wolverhampton express having burst out of Greet (Winchcombe) Tunnel on 26th August 1962.* Photo: G England

Britannia No. 70053 (formerly Moray Firth*) near Toddington with Driver E G Bowe on 31st July 1965.* Photo: G England

British Railways allocated names to many trains in the 1950s to try to bring pride back into the railways, a Wolverhampton to Penzance express received the nameboard 'The Cornishman', commencing on 30th June 1952. In its first year (only) it carried a slip coach for Taunton that was later worked back by a parcels train. The first working of the Down 'Cornishman' was hauled by 'Castle' Class engine No. 4092 *Dunraven Castle*. However the South Wales diesel multiple units and 'The Cornishman' were diverted to the Lickey route from the 10th September 1962, the last working of 'The Cornishman' on the GWR route occurring on the 7th September 1962 hauled by No. 7001 *Sir James Milne*. Although this working had been worked mainly by 'Castles', 'Halls' and 4–6–0 'Counties' could be seen on the service especially at the height of the season when the train was run in several parts.

Through services still survived on a regular basis despite the demise of 'The Cornishman' until No. 7029 *Clun Castle* hauled the last West of England steam working on 4th September 1965. Although steam officially disappeared from Western Region from the 31st December 1965, British Railways standard classes and ex LM types could still be seen along the line well into the August of 1966.

The route continued to be used for Summer 'Saturdays Only' trains but by the Summer of 1966 only 4 such workings were using the route to the south west. From the 3rd September 1966 these workings ceased.

Diesel locomotives were no strangers to the line with the bulk of the workings being undertaken by Brush & Peak diesel variants and many early Hydraulic classes could be seen.

Due to the route continuing to decline in traffic it was used for crew training purposes. These test trains would consist of a rake of carriages and the crews would come from Banbury, Bescot and Tyseley. During a period from 1965 through to 1967 many crews and locomotives were put through their paces along the line. Some would be terminated at Stratford upon Avon, others would go onto Honeybourne and if the weather was really good and the instructors patience had not been tried to the full, then it would be terminated at Toddington. Here they would await until a clear path could be found for the return working. They were stabled in the up siding between the goods shed and the Main line. During the Spring of 1967 it was not unusual to see D.8xx 'Warships' in the siding.

The last services over the entire line were worked by Single Diesel Multiple Units forming a connecting service between Leamington and Gloucester. These were strengthened to three car sets during busy Saturdays. This service ceased from 23rd March 1968.

Having closed the intermediate stations of Milcote and Long Marston on 3rd January 1966 the Northern section from Honeybourne to Stratford upon Avon still saw Worcester to Birmingham services, these finishing on 5th May 1969.

Plans had been drawn up for some time to make economies. One of these was to single the line (February 1967) from Stratford to Honeybourne this being in conjunction with the rationalization of the Oxford to Worcester route at the same time. This latter line did in fact become singled in parts in September 1971. The Branch line from Honeybourne to Stratford was to be worked by Tokenless Block and controlled by Norton Junction Signal Box near Worcester. BR then decided to return the line in full, keeping it for diversionary purposes and concentrated its freight traffic upon the Lickey Incline route. It was soon found that operational difficulties still existed over the Lickey due to the complex (slow) working of loose coupled freight trains. Therefore most of that traffic was worked over the Stratford upon Avon to Cheltenham line from May 1970 until it's closure. At first all the remaining Signal Boxes were 24 hour manned worked with extensive diversions at weekends, enabling other routes to be upgraded. Sadly this last only briefly, afternoon shifts being dispensed with in October 1973.

There had been a manning problem at Milcote Signal Box during the 1972/3 period. It had been proposed under the 1967 scheme to single line that the level crossings at Milcote and Long Marston should become Automatic Half Barriers (AHB). So in June 1972 AHB were again proposed for Milcote coming under the supervision of the Long Marston Signal Box. At the end of June the British Rail Board decided that the line would close within a year, so the provision for AHB being the cheapest means of demanning were shelved. The decision to close the line must have been reversed yet again because by May 1975 the AHB scheme was again proposed for Milcote and Long Marston. With it came the clarification that the 'through route' was

The last steam hauled (Saturdays only) ex 12.30 pm Penzance to Wolverhampton at Malvern Road. Castle No. 7029 Clun Castle *was specially requested for this last scheduled working. 4th September 1965.*

Photo: W Potter

safe even to the extent that the line speed would be restored to 75 mph from 50 mph (then in force) during the 1976-78 period. The installation of the AHB would have been carried out at Milcote during the first half of 1977 at a cost of £25,000, with Long Marston again being proposed as its supervisory box. The accident at Winchcombe (25th August 1976) stopped all these plans from coming to fruition.

The line made an ideal route for the movement of preserved locomotives during the early 1970's. One of the first being No. 70000 Britannia which was towed to the Severn Valley Railway from Redhill via Tyseley on 27th March 1971 travelling via Honeybourne West Loop (reversing) and Worcester. With the 150th celebrations of the Stockton and Darlington Railway held in 1975 the line was again used but this time the locomotives were allowed to be under their own power. No. 75029 *The Green Knight* ran up the line light engine, on 27th July and returned after the celebrations with 2 carriages on 1st September. This was immediately followed by the double headed working of No. 46201 *Princess Elizabeth* and No. 35028 *Clan Line* hauling 4 carriages. It was a majestic sight, one which the author will never forget and indeed it only served to kindle the hope that one day the line would be saved.......

The tables show how the traffic built up on the through route (Stratford to Cheltenham):–

Date Passenger	Midweek	FO + Saturdays	Sundays
7/1908	4	4	NIL
7/1911	8	21	1
7-9/1928	14	31	NIL
7-9/1938	9+4 DRC	20	4
5/1944	1	–	–
6/1947	6	18	2
6-9/1959	6+9 DMU	27+4 DMU	2+4 DMU
1966	4 DMU	8+4 DMU	NIL

DRC = Diesel Railcars   DMU = Diesel Multiple Units

Date FGT	Midweek	FO + Saturdays	Sundays
1/1908	8	N/A	3
7/1911	11	11	5
1-4/1917	22	21	7
7-9/1928	28	24	6
7-9/1938	43	34	7
10/1944	43	40	16
6/1947	32	31	16
6-9/1959	28	19	6
7/1972	17		

FGT = Freight Goods Trains

The last northbound 'Cornishman' at Stratford, piloted by Grange No. 6861 Crynant Grange *and Castle No. 7001* Sir James Milne *on Friday 7th September 1962.*

Photo: G England

10

A New Dawn

Again proposals to close the line were put forward by British Rail in early 1976 because the traffic did not justify the operating expenses. It was at this stage that four individuals sought to save the line, they were not the first to think about it for there had been several attempts before when the line had come under threat in the late 1960s.

This time however from humble beginnings an embryo Society was formed, with the intention of retaining the route (which proved too late and too expensive an objective in the event especially after the severing of the track due to an accident at Winchcombe in August). But the die was cast and support grew rapidly in the local district, many were the meetings that followed both public and with officials. Public meetings became PR exercises backed by films etc., and official meetings became concentrated on getting councils to get them to take a 'No Claim' stance when the land became available from BR, so that the Society could go ahead and save the trackbed. By the time BR decided that it would sell, all the track had been lifted and sold for scrap. But a lease was taken on the yard at Toddington (March 1981) and immediately a Company (The Gloucestershire Warwickshire Railway) was formed to raise capital for the purchase. Since that successful floatation of the new GWR the line has taken on a new future and the 'Navvy' volunteers have set about in earnest creating a railway that caters for the tourist industry bringing much happiness to all who come in contact with it.

On the 2nd April 1984 at Toddington *Cadbury* No. 1 (an 0–4–0 tank built by Avonside) ran a test train to see if the rebuilt line was suitable for public operation. Reopening was sanctioned by the Department of the Environment and public services commenced over a short section of track on the 22nd April.

After arriving late on the scene (in preservation terms) the Company already owns the trackbed from the Cheltenham Borough boundary to a point just north of Broadway at a bridge known as Springfield Lane. At present (1994) the remainder of the trackbed northwards is under negotiation. Services operate between Toddington and Winchcombe (opened 2nd August 1987). With extensions being added in a southerly direction (1994 to Far Stanley), the company unlike other projects has not got itself into heavy debt. There are never enough volunteers to help with the hundreds of tasks. Some assistance has come from Gloucestershire County Council as a Manpower Services Community Project based at Winchcombe. This enabled many mundane tasks to be undertaken, while introducing unemployed persons to many skills.

The line into Cheltenham from the Borough boundary will probably never materialize as a railway again. At the northern end the trackbed from the Evesham Road level crossing area to the old SMJ bridge has become a roadway. Warwickshire County Council has purchased the rest of the trackbed from there on down to Long Marston level crossing, half of which is used by cyclists the other half being retained for use by the GWR at a future date. The remaining land between Long Marston and Honeybourne main line overbridge is owned by BR and the old branch line still exists from Honeybourne Station to serve the MOD camp and scrapyard, albeit at the time of writing mothballed pending a decision on its future. The scrapyard owner brought the redundant 7 acre Long Marston site in 1988, through which it is hoped that a corridor of land can be retained so that the line might one day reach Stratford again.

Had the line stayed open then newer types of locomotives would have been seen, indeed at Stratford a Class 58 has been seen. In 1988 a new HST 125 service ran for the summer only from Paddington to Stratford (under the title 'The Stratford Pullman'). This rekindled many memories of the old Shakespeare expresses and excursions from London. Today Stratford still has steam workings from the capital, even the old GWR flagship No. 6000 *King George* V doing a turn, thus Stratford is seeing engines it never was intended to. So having come full circle the route from Stratford to Cheltenham is again in the making and for all concerned is undoubtably a 'Labour of Love'.

The Gloucestershire Warwickshire's 1990 Extravaganza, with GWR No. 3440 City of Truro *leaving Toddington with the 11.00 am train for Gretton.*
                                                                    Photo: Dick Blenkinsop

Driver/Instructor Colin Jacks acknowledges the photographer as GWR 2-8-0 No. 2857 departs Winchcombe on Saturday 11th April 1992 with the ex 1200 from Toddington
                                                                    Photo: P W Durham

Appendix A

Coffeepot Demise

The withdrawal of services on the Honeybourne to Cheltenham section of the line on 7th March 1960 brought to an end the long standing use of 1 carriage plus 1 engine services, known locally as 'The Coffeepot'. The 0–4–2T 14xx engines performed on these services, being driven from either engine, or from the far end of the coach, saving time in running round at either end of its journey and on reversal at Malvern Road. Well into the 1920s steam railmotors were used and then the '517' class, the forerunner of the 14xx class plied their trade with one carriage along the route. The latter soon ousted the older '517' class and maintained the services right up to the end.

During its last week of steam hauled services on the southern section (Honeybourne to Cheltenham) Nos. 1424, 4116, 8487, 8488, 8731 and 9727 were seen on the local services. The last train was hauled by No. 8731 on the 10.25 pm (Saturdays only) St. James to Broadway and 11.25 pm return. This took place on the 5th March, there being no Sunday service.

'The Coffeepot' demise. No. 8488 stands at Honeybourne, having arrived with the ex 2.30 pm from St. James Cheltenham on 5th March 1960.

Photo: D Bath

The last timetable March 1960 (NO SUNDAY SERVICES)

Down Services			SO	SO	6.52 Ex Moreton			SO
Honeybourne	7.25	9.45	1.17	2.34	6.5	7.20	8.15	
Weston Sub Edge	7.31	9.51	1.23	—	6.11	N	8.21	
Willersey	7.34	9.54	1.26	—	6.14	N	8.25	
Broadway	7.40	9.59	1.30	2.45	6.18	7.30	8.29	11.25
Laverton	7.45	10.4	1.35	2.50	6.23	—	8.34	—
Toddington	7.50	10.9	1.40	2.55	6.28	7.38	8.40	—
Hayles Abbey	7.53	10.12	1.43	2.59	6.31	—	8.43	—
Winchcombe	7.58	10.17	1.47	3.5	6.35	7.44	8.49	—
Gretton	8.2	10.21	1.51	3.10	6.39	7.48	8.53	—
Bishops Cleeve	8.9	10.28	1.57	3.18	6.47	7.54	8.59	—
Malvern Road	8.20	10.40	2.8	3.30	6.58	8.5	9.10	11.53
St James	8.22	10.42	2.10	3.32	7.0	8.7	9.12	11.55

N = Calls at Stations upon request to the guard

Up Services				SO	SO	To Moreton			SO	
St James	6.18		7.30	11.20	1.0	2.30	4.33	5.55	10.25	
Malvern Road	6.24	x	7.37	11.26	1.6	2.36	4.39	6.1	10.28	x
Bishops Cleeve	—		7.45	11.34	1.14	2.44	4.47	6.9	10.37	
Gretton	—		7.52	11.41	1.22	2.52	4.55	6.16	10.46	
Winchcombe	6.38		7.56	11.45	1.26	2.56	4.59	6.20	10.50	
Hayles Abbey	—		8.0	11.49	1.29	3.0	5.3	6.24	10.55	
Toddington	—		8.3	11.52	1.33	3.4	5.6	6.27	10.59	
Laverton	6.48		8.8	11.57	1.38	3.9	5.11	6.32	11.5	
Broadway	6.53		8.14	12.2	1.42	3.16	5.16	6.37	11.9	
Willersey	6.57		8.18	12.6	—	3.20	5.20	6.41	xx	
Weston Sub Edge	7.1		8.21	12.9	—	3.23	5.23	6.44		
Honeybourne	7.7		8.27	12.15	1.53	3.30	5.29	6.49		

x = Malvern Road East   SO = Saturdays Only

xx = Crossover at Honeybourne West Loop at 11.17/9 due to no crossing facilities at Broadway

Pannier No. 8743 is about to pass under the Swindon Lane Bridge Cheltenham with the ex 11.20 Cheltenham St. James to Honeybourne local service on 9th January 1960. This being two months before local services ceased on the southern portion of the line.
Photo: G England

Appendix B

Gradient Profile

Gradient Profile Malvern Road Junction to Stratford upon Avon (Jan 1953)

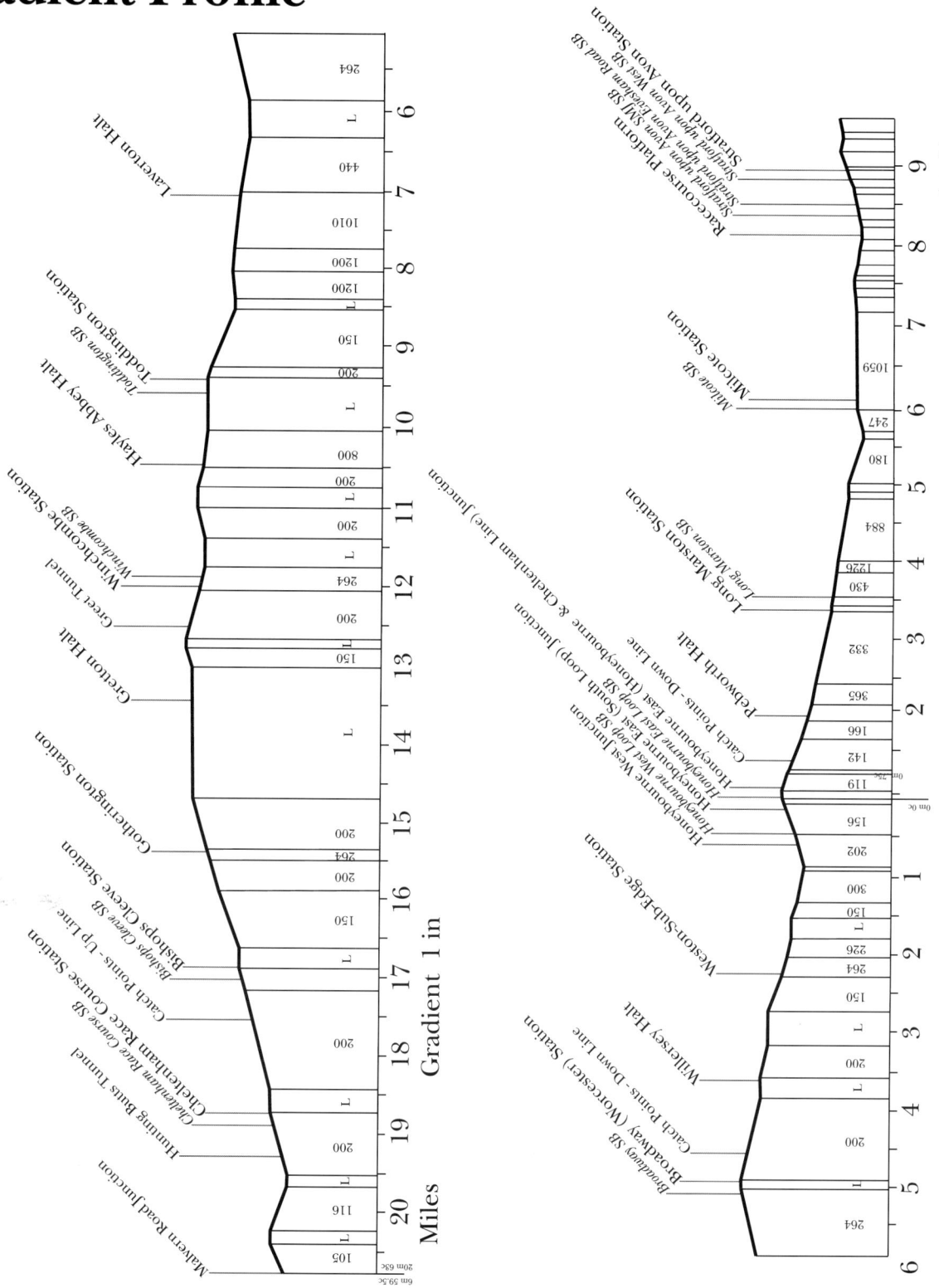

Gradient 1 in

Miles

Peter Abbott

A rare photographic combination heads a north bound freight train at Stratford on Avon station on 20th May 1948 of 2-8-0 No. 2882 and 2-8-0 No. 3040.   *Photo: L T Parker*

2721 Class No. 2760 was built in August 1899. It was superheated in January 1916 and Pannier Tanks were fitted in March 1916. It was withdrawn in October 1950 having run 959,362 miles. The photograph was taken at Cheltenham St. James c. 1906.   *Photo: T Guest*

Appendix C

Signal Box Register

Signal Box Register (as per Signalling Record Society)

Name & Prefix		Opened	Closed	Locking Frame Type	Ctrs	Size	Date	Block Switch	Remarks
Stratford on Avon	1	by 1890	C. 1891					NB	
Goods Jctn	2	OD 1891	1908			17			
	3	1908	13.8.1933	HT 3 BAR		29		✓	
Stratford on Avon	1	1908	13.8.1933	3 BAR		35		✗	Ex Leamington Engine Shed
East	2	13.8.1933		VT 5 BAR	4	55		✓	'upon' from 18.6.1951 Ex Acton West
Stratford on Avon	1		1891					✗	
Station						21			Renamed 'West' 1908
	2	1891	18.5.1969	HT 3 BAR	5$^{1}/_{4}$	29	13.2.1911	✓	'upon' from 18.6.1951
Shottery Footpath		C. 9.1899	C. 5.1902			14		✗	Z
Evesham Road	1		C. 1891						
Crossing	2	C. 1891	12.6.1960		5$^{1}/_{4}$	13			
	3	12.6.1960	22.9.1976	VT 5 BAR	4	50		✗	
East & West Jctn						15		p	Later 'S & M Junction'
			12.6.1960	Stud	5$^{1}/_{4}$	18	1908		& 'LMS Junction'
Milcote									G.F.29.6.1973
		1891	22.9.76	Stud	5$^{1}/_{4}$	21	C. 1907	✗	
Long Marston	1	by 1872	1892						G.F.24.3.1980
	2	1892				25			
			16.11.1981	VT 3 BAR	4	32	9.1936	✗	2nd Frame 2nd Hand
Weston Sub Edge		1.8.1904	8.10.1950			27		✓	'Bretforton & W.S.E.' to 1907
Willersey		2.2.1958	6.4.1958	Stud		5			Z ex Stanton Cutting
Broadway	1	1.8.1904	1.12.1904			13		✗	Z to Berwig
	2	1.12.1904	10.10.1960	Stud	5$^{1}/_{4}$	37		✓	
Stanton Cutting		C. 3.1957	C. 9.1957	Stud		5			Z to Willersey
Toddington		1.12.1904	22.10.1976	Stud	5$^{1}/_{4}$	29		✓	
Winchcombe		1.2.1905	24.2.1965	Stud	5$^{1}/_{4}$	31		✓	
Gotherington		1.6.1906	3.4.1949	Stud	5$^{1}/_{4}$	33		✓	
Bishop's Cleeve		1.6.1906	11.8.1965	Stud	5$^{1}/_{4}$	31		✓	
Cheltenham Race Course		12.3.1912	9.2.1964	Stud	5$^{1}/_{4}$	6		✓	
Cheltenham Spa Malvern Road East		15.7.1906	3.11.1970	HT	5$^{1}/_{4}$	49		✓	E-52
Cheltenham Spa Malvern Road West	1	8.8.1906	6.1908						Z
	2	6.1908	5.6.1966	HT	5$^{1}/_{4}$	37		✓	

		OD							
Lansdown Jctn	1	1881	10.5.1914						
	2	10.5.1914	26.7.1942	HT 3 BAR	4	35		✖	Named 'Lansdown Jctn Main'
	3								block post on Honeybourne
	LJ	26.7.1942	12.11.1977	VT 5 BAR	4	102		✖	line only from 23.11.1968
Bayshill		by 1893	15.7.1906			33			
Cheltenham Station		by 1893	15.6.1966			53			
Honeybourne South Loop		1.7.1907	13.10.1965	Stud	$5^{1}/4$	23		✓	
Honeybourne North Loop		1.8.1904	3.1933			31		✓	
Honeybourne Station South		C. 3.1909	7.3.1983	HT 3 BAR	$5^{1}/4$	57		✓	G.F. 20.9.1971 S=21
Honeybourne East Loop		1.8.1904	3.11.1970	Stud	$5^{1}/4$	25		P	
Honeybourne	1	1.8.1904	24.4.1960	Stud	$5^{1}/4$	25		✓	
West Loop	2	24.4.1960	24.3.1980	VT 5 BAR	4	50		✓	
Honeybourne	1		C. 1883						
	2	C. 1883	C. 3.1909			31		✓	
Honeybourne Station North		C. 2.1909	4.4.1965	HT 3 BAR	$5^{1}/4$	61		✓	E-66 New Frame 18.5.1942
Sheenhill		3.1944	17.7.1951	VT 5 BAR	4	30		✓	

Key
VT	Vertical twist frame		G.F.	Ground frame	
HT	Horizontal twist frame		Z	Temporary box	
Stud	GWR Stud Locking		✓	Denotes switch (including switch lever)	
OD	Box order date			provided from opening	
E	Extended		✖	Denotes switch not provided	
S	Shortened		P	Denotes switch added	

The old and the new at Evesham Road Crossing, Stratford c. March 1960. Note the new signals with crosses, awaiting commissioning and the coal bunker for the new box on the right.
Photo: A T Locke

Appendix D

Train Loads

Maximum Loads of Goods Trains.

Engines of 2–6–0 Type March 1907

	Coal	Goods	Empties
Stratford on Avon to Honeybourne East	42	60	60
Honeybourne East to Honeybourne West	60	60	60
Honeybourne West to Toddington	48	60	60
Toddington to Winchcombe	55	60	60
Winchcombe to Bishops Cleeve	60	60	60
Bishops Cleeve to Cheltenham	34	51	60
Cheltenham to Bishops Cleeve	36	54	60
Bishops Cleeve to Gotherington	46	60	60
Gotherington to Toddington	55	60	60
Toddington to Broadway	60	60	60
Broadway to Honeybourne West	48	60	60
Honeybourne West to Honeybourne East	55	60	60
Honeybourne East to Stratford on Avon	30	45	60

No. of wagons exclusive of brake van.

Maximum Weight of trains for 1963 (in tons)

	1	2	3	4	5	6
Birmingham to Stratford	455	420	420	392	364	350
Stratford to Cheltenham	455	420	420	364	336	322
Cheltenham to Stratford	455	420	420	364	336	322
Stratford to Birmingham x	420	392	364	308	280	266
Stratford to Birmingham o	364	336	308	252	224	210

x = Running through Stratford

o = Stopping at Stratford

Group Classifications for 1963

1. 10xx, 4037, 4073 Castles, BR Class 7 (70xxx)

2. Halls, Granges, BR Class 5 (73xxx)

3. Manor, Moguls, 41xx, 51xx, 61xx, 81xx, 56xx, 66xx, BR Class 4, 75xxx, 76xxx

4. 45xx, 55xx 36xx, 37xx, 46xx 57xx, 77xx, 87xx, 96xx, 97xx 34xx, 84xx, 94xx, BR Class 3, 77xxx, 82xxx

5. 22xx, 32xx BR Class 2 78xxx, 84xxx

6. 0-6-0T 'A' Group.

BR Standard 9F 2-10-0 No. 92152 passes Bishops Cleeve goods shed with a North bound load on 27th July 1963. At this time the sidings were still in place despite the goods facilities having been withdrawn at the beginning of the month. The view is taken looking towards Cheltenham from the Signal Box which still had another two years to go before closing in August 1965

Photo: W Potter

Appendix E

Fare Structure

The fares structure for Winchcombe;

	Date		Single	Return
Stratford	24/8/1906		1s 9½d	3s 7d
Evesham Road Halt	1/8/1906		1s 9d	3s 6d
Chambers Cx Halt	1/8/1906		1s 7d	3s 2d
Milcote	24/8/1906		1s 6½d	3s 1d
Long Marston	24/8/1906		1s 4d	2s 8d
Broad Marston Halt	1/8/1906		1s 2½d	2s 5d
Honeybourne	1/8/1906		1s ½d	2s 1d
	30/5/1905	Horses	5s	10s
		Carriages		
		4 & 2 Wheel	7s 6d	15s
Bretforton & WSE	1/8/1906		10d	1s 8d
Willersey Halt	1/8/1906		8½d	1s 5d
Broadway	1/8/1906		7d	1s 2d
	30/3/1905	Horses	5s	10s
		Carriages		
		4 & 2 wheel	7s 6d	15s
Laverton	1/8/1906		5d	10d
Toddington	1/8/1906		2½d	5d
Gretton Halt	1/6/1906		1½d	3d
Gotherington	1/6/1906		3½d	7d
Bishops Cleeve	1/6/1906		5d	10d
Cheltenham	1/8/1906		9d	1s 6d

All fares shown are 3rd Class only, being via steam rail cars.

View from the new East Box looking south towards the station, Stratford on Avon old East Box can clearly be seen to the left of the picture.

Photo: A T Locke

Bulldog No. 3353 Pershore Plum *(formerly* Plymouth*) coasts into Stratford on 29th June 1935.*

Photo: L T Parker

Appendix F

Station Reference Numbers

Station Reference Numbers For Internal Mail — January 1911.

5168	Stratford Goods Junction	5187	Gotherington
5169	Stratford Goods	5188	Bishops Cleeve
5170	Stratford East	5189	Cheltenham High Street – later 5190
5171	Stratford Engine Shed	5191	Cheltenham Engine Shed Sidings Junction
5172	Stratford	2607	Lansdown Junction
5173	Stratford West	2608	Malvern Road West
5174	Evesham Road Crossing	2609	Malvern Road
5175	East & West Junction	2610	Malvern Road East
5176	Chambers Crossing	2611	Cheltenham Engine Shed
5177	Milcote	2612	St. James
5178	Long Marston	2613	Cheltenham Goods Yard
5179	Broad Marston	6016	Honeybourne South Loop
5180	Weston Sub Edge	6017	Honeybourne North Loop
5181	Willersey	6018	Honeybourne Station South
5182	Broadway	6019	Honeybourne East Loop
5183	Laverton	6020	Honeybourne West Loop
5184	Toddington	6021	Honeybourne
5185	Winchcombe	6022	Honeybourne Station North
5186	Gretton	6023	Honeybourne Engine Shed

By Mid 1917 Cheltenham Race Course was 5189

2-8-0 No. 2807 stands outside Stratford engine shed in July 1960.   *Photo: L C Jacks*

Two spotters look on as 2-8-0 No. 3865 heads a northbound goods past the racecourse platforms Stratford on Sunday 30th January 1960.
Photo: G England

Duke No. 3269 Dartmoor *heads a northbound train out of Stratford c. 1935. The locomotive was withdrawn in March 1937.*
Photo: Authors Collection

Appendix G

Whistle Codes and Routeing Bells

Whistle Codes (in addition to text)

Down Direction

Evesham Road Crossing by 1960 train for Cheltenham via Evesham		1 short 1 crow
Milcote	for Honeybourne South Loop and Oxford	1 long 1 short
	for Honeybourne Station	1 long 2 short
	for Honeybourne West Loop sidings by August 1963	1 long 1 crow
Moreton in Marsh	for Stratford	3
Bishops Cleeve	for Cheltenham Loop at Gloucester	2
	by 1960	1 crow 2 short
	for Gloucester Central by August 1963	1 long 2 short

N.B. Upon the closure of Bishops Cleeve & Winchcombe signal boxes these whistles given at Toddington.

Malvern Road West,   for Kingham 1 long 1 short.

Up Direction

Toddington	for Honeybourne Station by 1917	2
	for Honeybourne Station by August 1963	1 long 1 short
	for Honeybourne West Loop sidings by August 1963	1 long 1 crow
	for the Fenny Compton line by August 1963	1 long 2 short
Honeybourne West Loop	for Fenny Compton line by 1960	1 long 2 short
Evesham South	for Stratford	2
	for Cheltenham	3

Routeing Bells (at 18/2/1961)

Down Line	Normal Code +	
At Milcote	1-5	For Honeybourne Station
	3-4	Via South loop for Oxford
At East Loop	1-5	Honeybourne West Loop Sidings (Terminating)

Up Line sent as 'Train Entering Section' (rare at that time on the Western Region)

At Toddington	2	For Stratford
	2-4-3	For Honeybourne West Loop Sidings
	2-5-1	For Fenny Compton Via Racecourse Jctn
	2-1-5	For Honeybourne Station
At West Loop	Bells reverted back to normal; 'is line clear' +	
	5-1	For Fenny Compton
	2-3-4	Light engine assisting from sidings

8.00 am Down Bordesley – Swindon goods shows Aberdare No. 2633 pulling dead Barnum No. 3225 on 17th April 1935. The Aberdare was condemned in September that year and the Barnum during the month of April. Taken in the Down loop at Stratford.

Photo: L T Parker

Grange No. 6855 Saighton Grange, *bereft of name and number plate speeds through the cutting north of Toddington on the ex 0655 am SO Wolverhampton Low Level to Penzance train on 31st July 1965.*

Photo: G England

Appendix H

Glossary of Terms and Bibliography

GLOSSARY OF TERMS

Absolute Block

Under this only one train is allowed into a block section at one time, except in a few cases where special exemption has been granted at certain junctions and large stations for connecting purposes.

Switch

A signal box capable of being switched 'in' or 'out' of circuit means that 'out' of circuit the signalman leaves all signals off and by doing this bypasses all bell and block indicator signals so that they come out at the next box along the line in either direction. Thus when 'in' circuit the section was shortened and bell and block indicators were worked by the signalman.

Tokenless Block

Sections of line divided by track circuits that indicate the position of a train to a signalman. It does not allow other trains into that same section that are already occupied.

BIBLIOGRAPHY

E T MacDermot History of GWR Vol 1 and 2

R A Cookes Track Layout Diagrams of the GWR and BR WR

K M Beck The West Midland Lines of the GWR

RCTS The Locomotives of the GWR

Various GWR Magazines and RCTS Journals, The Evesham Journal, Stratford on Avon Herald and the Cheltenham Chronicle & Examiner

Earl 4-4-0 No. 3207 Earl of St Germans *shunts at the Birmingham Road Stratford on 29th December 1936. Built in the same month she was withdrawn in July 1948*

Photo: L T Parker

Saint No. 2981 Ivanhoe *waits with a southbound troop train, outside Stratford on Avon West Signal Box c. 1934. Dating from 1905 this beautiful ex Atlantic (4-4-2) was withdrawn in 1951.* Photo: A T Locke

Evesham Road Crossing, beware men at work! Taking a well earned break while renewing and adjusting the decking on the crossing during a Sunday occupation. c. 1935. Photo: A T Locke